# UNIVERSITY UNITED METHODIST CHURCH

## Kansas City
## Kansas

## RECORDS

## 1919–2009

*• Members • Baptisms • Marriages •*
*• Deaths • Ministers •*

Compiled by
*Lavone Johnson Anglen*

HERITAGE BOOKS
2009

# HERITAGE BOOKS
### *AN IMPRINT OF HERITAGE BOOKS, INC.*

**Books, CDs, and more—Worldwide**

For our listing of thousands of titles see our website
at
www.HeritageBooks.com

Published 2009 by
HERITAGE BOOKS, INC.
Publishing Division
100 Railroad Ave. #104
Westminster, Maryland 21157

International Standard Book Numbers
Paperbound: 978-0-7884-5020-4
Clothbound: 978-0-7884-8249-6

# DEDICATION

This book is dedicated to the many families who have supported University United Brethren Church, University Evangelical United Brethren Church, and University United Methodist Church. Since 1919, the families of University Church have ministered to their community through denominational mergers, a changing neighborhood, and the inevitable losses from death and relocation.

Lavone Johnson Anglen

# TABLE OF CONTENTS

University Evangelical United Brethren Church - 32nd and Parrallel Ave. - Kansas City, Kan.

# ACKNOWLEDGEMENTS

This publication of the history of the University United Methodist Church, located at 32nd and Parallel in Kansas City, Kansas, was prepared for the 90th anniversary of its founding in 1919. Information in this book is drawn directly from handwritten records of baptisms, marriages, deaths, membership, and ministers, from 1919 through 2009. Information relating to the history of Kansas City University and University Church was extracted primarily from the "History, University United Methodist Church" which was published in 1994 in the program for the *75th Anniversary Celebration of University United Methodist Church.*

Compiling this book has been a labor of love. As a lifetime member of University Church and its historian for the past 12 years, I believe we should preserve our records to honor University's faithful members and ministers. I could not have produced this book without the help of Evelyn Maddox, a former member, who provided technical assistance in preparing the manuscript for publication. I am also grateful for the encouragement and assistance of my good friend Beverly Thompson Griffith who helped edit this book.

Lavone Johnson Anglen

# HIGHLIGHTS OF 90 YEARS

The University United Methodist Church in Kansas City, Kansas, began as University United Brethren Church. It was first organized in the Kansas City University Chapel in 1919 by Dean W. S. Reece. University Church's early years were intertwined with Kansas City University although each institution has gone through a series of changes over the past 90 years.

Kansas City University was established in Kansas City, Kansas, in 1896, by the General Conference of the Methodist-Protestant Church of Pittsburgh, Pennsylvania. In 1914 it was consolidated with Campbell College, which was a United Brethren college in Holton, Kansas. After that, Kansas City University was jointly operated by the Methodist-Protestant and United Brethren denominations.

In 1919, Dean W. S. Reese organized a United Brethren church in Union Hall on the campus of Kansas City Kansas City University and served as its pastor. There were 22 charter members.

In 1920, Dr. C. R. Fralick was assigned as pastor to the "University United Brethren Church," and with this name the new church was officially admitted to the Kansas Conference. Land on the northeast corner of 32nd and Parallel was purchased that year. Membership rose to 120.

The next year, 1921, Dr. Frank May became pastor. When Dr. May was made Chancellor of Kansas City University, he was replaced at University Church by the conference superintendent, Dr. Testerman, until a permanent minister could be found. The church's cornerstone was laid in 1922 and the . same church has been in use at the same location since then. On the first Sunday in July, 1923, the congregation marched from Wilson Hall to the new church building where they worshipped in the basement--since this was the only completed portion of the building.

Dr. Stanley B. Williams became pastor in 1923. With a gift of $5,000 from the United Brethren Erection Society, members were able to sufficiently finish the building so that the 1924 Commencement Services could be held in the church.

In September, 1924, the building was finished and the furniture installed for the Dedication Service. The beautiful windows in the sanctuary are works of art and are considered to be among the finest in the Kansas City area. All art windows are memorial windows to various members of the church. Two of the finest are *Christ in Gethsemane* by Heinrich Hofmann (copy) and *Christ Blessing the Children* by Bernard Plackhorst. They were completed by Kansas City Stained Glass Works whose address was 512-514 Wyandotte in Kansas City, Missouri. The business was in operation from about 1880 to at least 1886--when the business had 15 to 20 skilled assistants. By 1940 there was no listing for Stained Glass Works because Interstate 70 had displaced the building.

In 1930, a parsonage was constructed on the north side of the church. Dr. Stanley Williams and his family were its first occupants.

The Kansas City University campus was closed in the fall of 1931. The Depression had caused declining enrollment and the university moved to York College in York, Nebraska in 1933. The mortgage on the Kansas City campus, which included three buildings and 12 acres, was foreclosed on April 1, 1932 by the Mercantile Commerce Company of St. Louis, Missouri. The loss of the college, its students, and faculty, helped University Church become a church with a more active presence in the community.

On January 13, 1935, the former Kansas City University campus and buildings were acquired by the Order of Augustinian Recollects, a Catholic monastic order, and renamed the Monastery of St. Augustine. Eventually, the university was purchased by the Seventh Day Adventists who are the current owners in 2009.

In 1935, W. R. Holt was appointed pastor of University UB Church and he served in this capacity for 33 years. His wife, Freda Clay Holt, was a charter member of the church and a graduate of Kansas City University.

In 1945, University United Brethren church merged with the Evangelical Church and became known as University Evangelical United Brethren Church. In 1958, the Fellowship Hall and Education Wing were dedicated under the leadership of Dr. Holt. Dr. Holt brought many members into the church during his pastorship. In 1968, the church merged with the Methodists and it became the University United Methodist Church. Dr. Holt retired from the church shortly afterward.

Reverends LeRoy Rayson, Jerrald Harnden, Ira DeSpain, Ed Stephenson, and Roy West successively served the congregation after Dr. Holt's retirement. In 1988, Reverend Marie Gasau became the first less-than-fulltime minister as well as the first woman pastor. Since then, all ministers have been .less-than-fulltime: Reverends Rob Harper, Lynn Lamberty, Cynthia Smart, Seong Lee, Gary Roellchen, Marlene Miller, and Sharon Albert.

By the 1990's the neighborhood had significantly changed from all-white to a majority of African-Americans who did not embrace University UM Church. In the late 1990's the church began working to overcome the neighborhood's perception of the "white church on the hill." Rev. Lamberty instituted *Next Generation,* which was to be a dynamic ministry designed for urban Kansas City, Kansas. University UM Church and its members was committed to being a life-changing presence in our community. We were called to model diversity and to welcome persons from all backgrounds.

Rev. Cynthia Smart, our first African-American minister, was called to serve with Rev. Lynn Lamberty in 2002-2004. Her leadership attracted neighborhood youth to serve as acolytes and to affiliate with University in a variety of programs for youth and women. Following Rev. Smart's departure, Pastor Michael Thomas, an African-American, came to University; Pastor Thomas served as Minister of Evangelism alongside Rev. Lynn Lamberty until both were called to other churches.

In 2008, Rev. Lamberty was awarded the 2008 Harry Denman Evangelism Award at the Kansas East Conference of the United Methodist Churches, where he received a standing ovation for his 11 years of service to University United Methodist Church. Rev. Seong Lee, of Korean ancestry, who followed Rev. Lamberty, left in 2009. Thanks to the work of many dedicated ministers and members, University is now truly diverse in membership and ministry.

At the present time, visiting clergy fill the pulpit on Sundays and members oversee church programs. Our membership has been declining since the 1990's but members are convinced that University United Methodist Church is called to do more than wait for death. University United Methodist Church and its faithful members have been working for 90 years, and are still working, to make a difference.

*Christit in Gethsemane,* by Heinrich Hofmann

*Christic Blessing the Children* , **by Bernard Plackhorst**

**Kansas City University, Mather Hall**

# RECORDS
# 1919 - 2009

## MEMBERS, BAPTISMS, MARRIAGES, DEATHS, MINISTERS

# RECORD OF MEMBERS

## 1919 - 2009

**Record of Members**

| Name | Date Received | Birth | By Whom | How | Status | Remarks |
|---|---|---|---|---|---|---|
| Adams, Faye (Mr.) | Mar. 28, 1937 | | W. R. Holt | Conf. of Faith | Oct. 21, 1968 Death | |
| Adams, Faye (Mrs.) | Mar. 28, 1937 | | W. R. Holt | | Death Jun. 03, 1963 | |
| Adamson, Larry (Mrs.) E. | Jan. 22, 1964 | | | Trans. Donnely | 1967 Removed | |
| Addison, Marsha (Shelly) | Sept. 27, 1964 | | W. R. Holt | From "S" List | RCC Dec. 1978 | Harnden |
| Alexander, Marion (Murphy) | | | | | Jan. 13,1958 Removed | |
| Alexander, Martha (Mrs.) Tucker | Sept. 27, 1964 | | W. R. Holt | Conf. of Faith | Nov. 15, 1986 Withdrawal | R. West |
| Alleman, M. E. (Mr.) | Jun. 15, 1924 | | S. B. Williams | Transfer | Feb. 28, 1981 Death | DeSpain |
| Alleman, M. E. (Mrs.) | Jun. 15, 1924 | | S. B. Williams | Transfer | Death Jan. 12, 1966 | |
| Alleman, Paul | Apr. 12. 1925 | | | | Jan. 13, 1958 Removed | |
| Alleman, Stanley | | | | | Ltr. Granted 4/30/1950 | |
| Alleman, Vera May | | | | | Removed Without Cert. | |
| Allen, Nettie | Oct. 23, 1932 | | | | Death (Reinstate) | |
| Allen, W. A. (Mrs.) | | | | | Nov. or Dec. 1954 Death | |
| Allison, Melvin E. | Jan. 06, 1957 | 9/3/1928 | W. R. Holt | Conf. of Faith | Jan. 22, 1978 Transfer | |
| Allison, Sandra Sue (C. Zimmer) | Jan. 06, 1957 | 5/15/52 | W. R. Holt | | to Z married C.Zimmer | |
| Allison, Dora Mae (Mrs. M. E. ) | Jan. 06, 1957 | 2/4/27 | W. R. Holt | Ltr. London Hts. | Jan. 22, 1978 transfer | |
| Amstutz, Joyce Picknick | | | | Transfer from "P" | married Picknick | |

2 - MEMBERS

**Record of Members**

| Name | Date Received | Birth | By Whom | How | Status | Remarks |
|---|---|---|---|---|---|---|
| Anderson, Helen (Carlson) | | | W. R. Holt | Transfer from "C" | RCC 12/03/1981 | DeSpain |
| Anderson, Ola (Mrs. C. O.) | Dec. 10, 1961 | | W. R. Holt | Ltr. from Methodist | Jul. 18. 1980 Death | |
| Anglen, Lavone Marie (Johnson/Hedge) | | | | | Mar.09/18/1990 | Gasau |
| Anglen, Paul Gene | Apr. 28, 1991 | | M. Gasau | Trans. Baptist | | Gasau |
| Armstutz, Joyce (Picknick) | | | | Tran From "P" | Transfer Picknick | |
| Arterburn, Homer S. | Apr. 17, 1960 | | W. R. Holt | Tran. Oliver Mem. | Jan. 1986 Death | Stevenson |
| Arterburn, John Dennis | Apr. 02, 1972 | | R. L. Rayson | Conf. of Faith | RCC Nov. 11, 1996 | Lamberty |
| Arterburn, Ruth (Mrs. H. S.) | Apr. 17, 1960 | | W. R. Holt | Tran. Oliver Mem. | Nov. 10, 1986 Withdrawl | R. West |
| Ashley, Carolyn | Easter, 1952 | | W. R. Holt | | Removed 4/5/1959 | |
| Atkins, Joanne (Mrs.) | Nov. 16, 1930 | | S. B. Williams | Conf. of Faith | 1961 Ltr. To Meth. Ch. | |
| Bailey, Carol (McKensie) | Mar. 26, 1967 | 2/16/1957 | W. R. Holt | Conf. of Faith | Transfer to McKensie. | |
| Bailey, Robert Charles | Mar. 06, 1960 | | W. R. Holt | Ltr. Central Meth. | | |
| Bailey, Robert Charles Jr. | Apr. 06, 1969 | 3/22/1959 | R. L. Rayson | Conf. of Faith | RCC Nov. 20, 1989 | Gasau |
| Bailey, Shirley (Mrs. R. C.) | Mar. 06, 1960 | 11/20/1929 | W. R. Holt | Conf. of Faith | | |
| Baker, JoAnne Marsh (Atkins) | | | | Transfer Atkins | | |
| Baker, Larry | Easter, 1952 | | W. R. Holt | Conf. of Faith | Removed 1967 | |
| Baker, Lois (Sweeney/Shirley) | | | | Mar. Sept. 12, 1953 | Div. Sweeney Sept. 1958 | |
| Barfield, Lee | | | W. R. Holt | Conf. of Faith | Apr. 29. 1960 Death | |

3 - MEMBERS

**Record of Members**

| Name | Date Received | Birth | By Whom | How | Status | Remarks |
|------|--------------|-------|---------|-----|--------|---------|
| Barfield, Rosalee (Mrs. ) | Mar. 27, 1932 | | S. B. Williams | Conf. of Faith | Apr. 16, 1994 Death | Gasau |
| Barfield, Rosemary (Moody) | Apr. 01, 1956 | | W. R. Holt | Conf. of Faith | Dec.1971 to Moody | |
| Barrett, Deloris (Mark) | Apr. 18, 1954 | | W. R. Holt | Conf. of Faith | Mar. Mark Aug. 07, 1954 | |
| Barton, Jacqueline K. | Apr. 27. 2003 | | Lamberty/ Smart | | | |
| Barton, Wayne Jr. | Apr. 27, 2003 | | Lamberty/Smart | Platte Woods UMC | | |
| Bassett, George (Mr.) | 1950 | | W. R. Holt | Conf. of Faith | May 18, 1960 Death | |
| Bassett, Marie (Mrs. George) | 1950 | | W. R. Holt | Woodson U. B | Apr. 15, 1997 Death | Harper |
| Bassett, Ruth Marie (Moody) | 1950 | | W. R. Holt | Conf. of Faith | to Moody Dec. 1970 | |
| Bauer, Dorothy June | Dec. 11, 1960 | 8/7/1932 | W. R. Holt | Conf. of Faith | April 1972 Transfer | |
| Baumgart, Jan Clair (Stott Mrs.Dan) | Apr. 21, 1967 | | W. R. Holt | C of F, TSF. From S | Death 1989 Gasau | Gasau |
| Bayne, Herbert E. | Dec. 29, 1957 | | W. R. Holt | Conf. of Faith | RCC 12/1978 | Harnden |
| Bayne, Marie (Mrs. H. E.) | Dec. 29, 1957 | | W. R. Holt | Conf. of Faith | RCC 12/1978 | Harnden |
| Bays, Ruth (Mrs.) | Nov. 14, 1926 | | S. B. Williams | Letter | Feb. 16, 1972 Death | |
| Beach, Mae (Mrs.) | Aug. 31, 1924 | | S. B. Williams | | Apr. 30, 1953, Death | |
| Becker, Edna (Mrs. Vincent) | May. 12, 1959 | 12/6/1910 | W. R. Holt | Letter | TSF July 1970 | |
| Becker, Vincent | May. 12, 1959 | 6/6/1910 | W. R. Holt | Letter | Transfer July 1970 | |
| Bengston, A. B. | | | | | 1951 Death | |
| Bengston, G. C. | | | | | Apr. 19, 1953 Letter | |

4 - MEMBERS

**Record of Members**

| Name | Date Received | Birth | By Whom | How | Status | Remarks |
|---|---|---|---|---|---|---|
| Bengston, G. C. (Mrs.) | | | | | Apr. 19, 1953 Letter | |
| Bengston, Glenn Walter | May. 08, 1949 | | W. R. Holt | | Apr. 19, 1953 Letter | |
| Bengston, Woodyne (Mann) | | | | | Apr. 19, 1953 Letter | |
| Bennet, Edna (Mrs.) Decker | May. 12, 1959 | | W. R. Holt | Letter | Error as Becker | |
| Bernard, Ann (Werth) | | | | m. Jun. 06, 1954 | Apr. 05, 1959 Removed | |
| Bernard, Debby | Apr. 02, 1961 | | W. R. Holt | Conf. of Faith | Withdrew | |
| Bernard, Eugene | Apr. 02, 1961 | | W. R. Holt | Conf. of Faith | Withdrew | |
| Bernard, Norma Jean (Mrs. E.) | Apr. 02, 1961 | | W. R. Holt | Conf. of Faith | Withdrew | |
| Berry, Cleo (Mr.) | Apr. 21, 1957 | | W. R. Holt | Ltr. | Withdrawal Jan. 30, 1980 | |
| Berry, Dwight Allan | Apr. 14, 1963 | 2/7/1953 | W. R. Holt | Conf. of Faith | Withdrawal Jan. 30, 1980 | |
| Berry, Irene (Mrs. Cleo) | Apr. 21, 1957 | | W. R. Holt | Ltr. Queens Garden | Transfer Mar. 18, 1979 | Harnden |
| Berry, Michael | Apr. 02, 1961 | 12/2/1950 | W. R. Holt | Conf. of Faith | Withdrawal Jan. 30, 1980 | |
| Berry, Patricia Ann (Hoyt) | Apr. 21, 1960 | 8/4/1946 | W. R. Holt | Conf. of Faith | M. Jun. 10, 1967 Hoyt | |
| Berve, Beatrice (Mrs. ) | Apr. 24, 1960 | | W. R. Holt | Conf. of Faith | Death Dec. 21, 1990 | Gasau |
| Berve, John David | Apr. 24, 1960 | | W. R. Holt | Conf. of Faith | | |
| Berve, Margaret (Mrs. J. D. ) | Apr. 24, 1960 | | W. R. Holt | Conf. of Faith | | |
| Bible, Kittie (Mrs.) | | | | | 1952 Death | |
| Biggs, Myrna (Mrs. Emmit) | Jul. 10, 1960 | | W. R. Holt | Conf. of Faith | C. T. Victory Hills -1976 | |

**Record of Members**

| Name | Date Received | Birth | By Whom | How | Status | Remarks |
|------|------|------|------|------|------|------|
| Bitatoe, Marilyn (Ensley) | Jan. 22, 1964 | | | Trans. From Ensley | 1967 Removed | |
| Blackburn, JoDonna (Mrs. R, N, Hartig) | | | | Tran. Hartig | Nov. 21, 1963 Transfer | |
| Blanchard, Joe | Oct. 25, 1925 | | S. B. Williams | | Apr. 25, 1956 Im. Baptist | |
| Blanchard, Joe Jr. | Oct. 25, 1925 | | S. B. Williams | | Jan. 13, 1958 Removed | |
| Blanchard, William | | | | | Feb. 10, 1953 Letter | |
| Blanchard, William (Mrs.) | | | | | Feb. 10, 1953 Letter | |
| Blevin, Elizabeth (Mrs.) (Riley/Spatz) | Apr. 23, 1944 | | W. R. Holt | Conf. of Faith | Riley, Feb. 1973 Spatz | |
| Blevin, Richard Elton | Mar. 29, 1970 | 12/4/1959 | R. L. Rayson | Conf. of Faith | Death Dec. 01, 1964 | |
| Blood, Pamela (Mrs. Walter) | Sept. 17, 1972 | | R. L. Rayson | Tran. Rosedale UM | | |
| Blood, Walter | Sept. 17, 1972 | | R. L. Rayson | Tran. Rosedale UM | | |
| Boerstler, Bessie (Mrs.) | Jan. 05, 1964 | | W. R. Holt | Ltr. Baptist | Feb.14, 1966 Death | |
| Bogart, William E. (Mrs.) | Nov. 1943 | | W. R. Holt | | Nov. 29, 1954 Withdrawl | |
| Boggio, Jo Ann | Oct. 17, 1954 | | W. R. Holt | | Apr. 05, 1959 Removed. | |
| Boggio, Nola (Mrs. Thomas) | Oct. 17, 1954 | | W. R. Holt | Tran. Telescope | | R. West |
| Boggio, Thomas | Oct. 17, 1954 | | W. R. Holt | Tran. Telescope | Death May 05, 1987 | |
| Boggio, Thomas Lee Jr. | Sept. 27, 1964 | | W. R. Holt | Conf. of Faith | CT or W 1987 | Gasau |
| Bohndof, Jeff | Sept. 22, 1974 | | J. R. Harnden | C. T. | Bashor UMC 1976 | Harnden |
| Bohndof, Virgina | Sept. 22, 1974 | | J. R. Harnden | CT | Bashor UMC 1976 | Harnden |

6 - MEMBERS

**Record of Members**

| Name | Date Received | Birth | By Whom | How | Status | Remarks |
|------|--------------|-------|---------|-----|--------|---------|
| Bolton, Diana Lynn (Ehbauer) | Jun. 03, 1973 | 8/1/1955 | R. L. Rayson | Conf. of Faith | Rcc Nov. 20, 1989 | Gasau |
| Bolton, George Hewitt | Jun.03, 1973 | | R. L. Rayson | TSF Faith Meth. | Withdrawal Nov. 1983 | DeSpain |
| Bolton, Jeffrey George | Jun. 03, 1973 | 2/21/1961 | R. L. Rayson | Conf. of Faith | Withdrawal Nov. 1983 | DeSpain |
| Bolton, Rose Marie (Mrs. George) | Jun. 03, 1973 | | R. L. Rayson | TSF Faith Meth. | Withdrawal Nov. 1983 | DeSpain |
| Bond, Patricia | Jun. 03, 1979 | | J. R. Harnden | C.T. West. H. U. P. | TSF 7/20/1983 | DeSpain |
| Boylan, Ruth Jacobs (Mrs. Leo) | | | S. B. Williams | Conf. of Faith | | |
| Bradford, Elnora (Mrs. V. J. ) | 1950 | | W. R. Holt | | TSF Apr. 05, 1959 | |
| Bradford, V. J. (Mr.) | 1950 | | W. R. Holt | | 1951 Death | |
| Bradley, Gayle (Stott) | | | | | C. T. 1976 Stott | |
| Bradley, James | | | | | C. T. 1976 | |
| Bradley, Kristen | | | | | C. T. 1976 | |
| Bradley, Kyle | | | | | C. T. 1976 | |
| Bradley, Paul R. | Aug. 21, 1966 | | W. R. Holt | Ltr. Immanuel Bap. | | |
| Bradley, Vivian (Mrs. P. R.) | Aug. 21, 1966 | | W. R. Holt | Ltr. W. Highlands | | |
| Brewer, Raymond | | | | | Oct. 18, 1953 Letter | |
| Brinkemeyer, Sharon (Taylor) | | | | Trans. From "T" | Apr. 05, 1959 Removed | |
| Brockman, Margaret (Taylor) | Dec. 27, 1949 | | W. R. Holt | Conf. of Faith | Death Sept. 10, 1991 | Gasau |
| Bromfield, Ari (Mrs.) | | | | | Feb. 29, 1956 Death | |

7 - MEMBERS

# Record of Members

| Name | Date Received | Birth | By Whom | How | Status | Remarks |
|------|---------------|-------|---------|-----|--------|---------|
| Brooks, Mary Ann | Apr. 25, 1954 | | W. R. Holt | Conf. of Faith | Trans. To "S" Married | |
| Brotherton, Charles Duane | Dec. 24, 1989 | | M. Gasau | Conf. of Faith | | |
| Brotherton, Mary Elizabeth | Dec. 24, 1989 | | M. Gasau | Conf. of Faith | | |
| Brown, Forence (Mrs.) (Foley) | | | S. B. Williams | Conf. of Faith | Death Dec. 30, 2000 | Lamberty |
| Brown, Rose (Mrs. Roy) | Sept. 18, 1927 | | S. B. Williams | Tran. Oliver Mem. | Death May 03, 1989 | DeSpain |
| Brown, Roy | Sept. 18, 1927 | | S. B. Williams | Tran. Oliver Mem. | Death Oct. 24, 1970 | |
| Brown, Roy (Mrs.) | Sept. 18, 1927 | | S. B. Williams | | | |
| Browne, Ruby | Jun. 24, 2007 | | L. Lamberty | Other Denom. | | |
| Browne, Serena | Jun. 24, 2007 | | L. Lamberty | Conf. of Faith | | |
| Brucker, Ann (Mrs. E) | Feb. 11, 1968 | 7/22/1941 | W. R. Holt | Tran. EUB, PA. | TSF Jan. 1973 | |
| Brucker, Edward | Feb. 11, 1968 | 10/24/1940 | W. R. Holt | Tran. EUB, PA. | TSF Jan. 1973 | |
| Brunker, Edith (Halverhaut) | Apr. 09, 1944 | | W. R. Holt | | Sept. 06, 1957 Removed | |
| Bryant, Barbara Gail (Mrs. E. Holcomb) | | | W. R. Holt | Married | Eugene Holcomb | |
| Bryant, Donald (Donnie) | 1953 | | W. R. Holt | Conf. of Faith | Restored membership | |
| Bryant, Janie (Mrs. Lyle) | Apr. 09, 1944 | | W. R. Holt | Ltr. Christian | TSF Sept. 06, 1988-Colo. | Gasau |
| Bryant, Lola (Mrs.) | Jan. 05, 1964 | | W. R. Holt | Ltr. Bethel Presby | TSF Jun. 04, 1967 Ltr. | |
| Bryant, Lyle | Apr. 09, 1944 | | W. R. Holt | Ltr. Christian | Death Apr. 1981 | DeSpain |
| Buckhard, Jim | Jun. 03, 1979 | | J. R. Harnden | C. T | Rcc-Nov. 21, 1988 | Gasau |

8 - MEMBERS

**Record of Members**

| Name | Date Received | Birth | By Whom | How | Status | Remarks |
|------|------|------|------|------|------|------|
| Buckhard, Linda | Jun. 03, 1979 | | J. R. Harnden | C. T. | Rcc-Nov. 21, 1988 | Gasau |
| Bucklinger, W. D. (Mr.) | | | | | Apr. 05, 1959 Removed | |
| Bucklinger, W. D. (Mrs.) | | | | | Apr. 05, 1959 Removed | |
| Bukaty, Eleanor Frances (Mrs.) (Pigg) | Dec. 10, 1961 | 3/28/1947 | W. R. Holt | Conf. of Faith | TSF CA. June 1978 | Harnden |
| Bumgartner, Harold V. (Mr.) | | | | | Oct. 11, 1958 Death | |
| Bumgartner, Hulda (Mrs.) | 1940 | | W. R. Holt | Tran. Lutheran | Death Jan. 18, 1969 | |
| Burnam, Harry | Jul. 15, 1956 | | W. R. Holt | Conf. of Faith | C. T. 1974 | |
| Burnam, Oletha (Mrs. Henry) | Jul. 15, 1956 | | W. R. Holt | Conf. of Faith | C. T. 1974 | |
| Burnett, Julie Hollander | Apr. 14, 1968 | | W. R. Holt | Conf. of Faith | | |
| Burns, Niccole Renee (Neal) | Oct. 13, 1991 | | Gasau | TSF Jan. 15, 1998 | See Niccole Neal | Lamberty |
| Burris, John | Sept. 08, 2002 | | Lamberty/Smart | Reaff.of Faith | | |
| Burtner, Charles | Aug. 05, 1956 | 5/21/1943 | W. R. Holt | Conf. of Faith | 1963 Removed | |
| Burtner, Dale | Aug. 05, 1956 | 10/15/1941 | W. R. Holt | Conf. of Faith | 1963 Removed | |
| Bushnell, Duane Jay | May. 26, 1968 | 1/25/1957 | W. R. Holt | Conf. of Faith | Rcc -Nov. 20, 1989 | Gasau |
| Bushnell, Elsie (Mrs. W. E.) | 1940 | | W. R. Holt | Conf. of Faith | TSF Ark.Apr. 02, 1991 | Gasau |
| Bushnell, Naomi | | | W. R. Holt | | Transfer to Slater | |
| Bushnell, Ruth | | | W. R. Holt | | Transfer to Jones | |
| Bushnell, Warren Eugene | May. 26, 1968 | 4/18/1955 | W. R. Holt | Conf. of Faith | TSF Apr. 10, 1985 | Stevenson |

## Record of Members

| Name | Date Received | Birth | By Whom | How | Status | Remarks |
|------|---------------|-------|---------|-----|--------|---------|
| Bushnell, Wilford E. | 1940 | | W. R. Holt | Conf. of Faith | Death Jan. 1985 | Stevenson |
| Byrd, Nancy Jane (Mrs. R. E.) | Jun. 10, 1962 | 1949 | W. R. Holt | Conf. of Faith | Rcc Dec. 03, 1981 | DeSpain |
| Byrd, Ronald Eugene | Dec. 03, 1967 | 1949 | W. R. Holt | Conf. of Faith | W 1975 | |
| Cain, Alana | Apr. 18, 1954 | | W. R. Holt | Conf. of Faith | 1963 Removed | |
| Cain, Gary Bryant | Apr. 18, 1954 | | W. R. Holt | Conf. of Faith | 1963 Removed | |
| Cain, Sheryl Dee | Apr. 18, 1954 | | W. R. Holt | Conf. of Faith | 1963 Removed | |
| Callahan, Mark | Apr. 22, 1973 | 11/29/1960 | R. L. Rayson | Conf. of Faith | Rcc Dec. 1978 | |
| Calvin, Grover | Jan. 31, 1932 | | S. B. Williams | Ltr. | TSF Dec. 1956 | |
| Calvin, Grover (Mrs.) | Jan. 31, 1932 | | S. B. Williams | Ltr. | TSF Dec. 1956 | |
| Canfield, Gayle Ann (Mrs. M.) Dowd | Apr. 21, 1957 | 6/22/1945 | W. R. Holt | TSF Dowd | TSF 11/27/1973 | |
| Canfield, Michael | Oct. 11, 1964 | | W. R. Holt | Conf. of Faith | TSF 11/27/1973 | |
| Cannady, Dennis | 1952 | | W. R. Holt | | 1957 Ltr. Presby. Church | |
| Cannady, Earl | 1952 | | W. R. Holt | | 1957 Ltr. Presby. Church | |
| Cannady, Earl (Mrs.) | 1952 | | W. R. Holt | | 1957 Ltr. Presby. Church | |
| Cannady, Judith Fay | 1952 | | W. R. Holt | | 1957 Ltr. Presby. Church | |
| Carlson, Dorothy (Van Dyke) | Mar. 28, 1937 | | W. R. Holt | Conf. of Faith | Apr. 05, 1959 Removed | |
| Carlson, F. R. | | | | Conf. of Faith | 1956 Removed | |
| Carlson, F. R. (Mrs.) | | | | | TSF 9/27/1958 to A | |

10 - MEMBERS

# Record of Members

| Name | Date Received | Birth | By Whom | How | Status | Remarks |
|------|------|------|------|------|------|------|
| Carlson, Herbert | | | | | 1967 Removed | |
| Carlson, John | Apr. 09, 1939 | | W. R. Holt | | 1967 Removed | |
| Carmitchel, Charles A. | | | W. R. Holt | Ltr. United Presby. | Death Apr. 10, 1991 | Gasau |
| Carmitchel, Charles Jr. | | | | | | |
| Carmitchel, Irma (Mrs. Charles) | | | W. R. Holt | Ltr. United Presby | Death May. 30, 1975 | |
| Carmitchel, Ramona (Mrs. C.) (Odneal) | | | | | TSF Bashor Meth. 1965 | |
| Carter, Cathie (Sevedge) | 1953 | | W. R. Holt | | Transferred to "S" | |
| Carter, Thomas | 1953 | | W. R. Holt | Ltr. | 1966 Ltr. To 1st Christian | |
| Carter, Thomas (Mrs.) | 1953 | | W. R. Holt | Ltr | 1966 Ltr. To 1st Christian | |
| Cass, George (Mrs.) | | 11/14/1926 | S. B. Williams | Ltr. | Transfer to Ruth Bays | |
| Cates, James Paul | Apr. 02, 1961 | 2/11/1948 | W. R. Holt | Conf. of Faith | TSF -Salina, Reinstate | Gasau |
| Cates, Linda Mae (Sterrett) | Apr. 22, 1962 | 11/9/1941 | W. R. Holt | Conf. of Faith | Transfer to S. | |
| Cathell, Golda (Mrs.) | Apr. 09, 1944 | | W. R. Holt | Ltr. Congregational | | |
| Cathell, Janet (Stugis) | Apr. 09, 1944 | | W. R. Holt | Conf. of Faith | M. Donald Sturgis, Died | |
| Cathell, Joyce (Rich) | Apr. 09, 1944 | | W. R. Holt | Conf. of Faith | M. Rich Aug. 20, 1955 | |
| Catron, J. Lee | 1952-1953 | | W. R. Holt | | Aprl. 05, 1959 Removed | |
| Catron, J. Lee (Mrs.) | 1952-1953 | | W. R. Holt | | Apr. 05, 1959 Removed | |
| Chalender, Robert | 1951-1952 | | W. R. Holt | Conf. of Faith | Apr. 05, 1959 Removed | |

11 - MEMBERS

**Record of Members**

| Name | Date Received | Birth | By Whom | How | Status | Remarks |
|------|---------------|-------|---------|-----|--------|---------|
| Charles, Bertha (Mrs.R.) (Edm.McClean) | 1936 | | W. R. Holt | Conf. of Faith | Death Aug. 1979 | |
| Charles, Buford | Apr. 06, 1958 | | W. R. Holt | Conf. of Faith | Withdrew | |
| Charles, Eldon | Mar. 28, 1937 | | W. R. Holt | Conf. of Faith | 1967 Removed | |
| Charles, Louise (Geo. Miller) | Apr.06, 1958 | 9/24/1929 | W. R. Holt | Tran. From Bap. | Married Geo. Miller | |
| Charles, Martha Ann (Mrs. Buford) | Apr. 06, 1958 | 12/8/1936 | W. R. Holt | Conf. of Faith | Withdrew | |
| Charles, Maxine (Mrs. Eldon) | Apr. 18, 1954 | | W. R. Holt | Conf. of Faith | Nov. 21, 1956 Death | |
| Charles, Ray | | | | | Sept. 22, 1965 Death | |
| Charles, Raymond George | Apr. 17, 1938 | | W. R. Holt | Conf. of Faith | 1967 Removed | |
| Charlson, Crystal (Mrs.) (Day) | Mar. 1943 | | W. R. Holt | Conf. of Faith | Rem. Death May 1995 | Lamberty |
| Charlson, Linda (Mrs. R.) | Apr. 17, 1960 | 10/3/1946 | W. R. Holt | TSF Endsley | Nov. 27, 1973 Removed | |
| Charlson, Reggie | Feb. 10, 1957 | 10/3/1946 | W. R. Holt | Conf. of Faith | Nov. 27, 1973 Removed | |
| Charlson, Ronald (Ronnie) | Feb. 10, 1957 | 9/11/1943 | W. R. Holt | Conf. of Faith | Nov. 27, 1973 Removed | |
| Chisham, Billy | Apr. 17, 1938 | | W. R. Holt | Conf. of Faith | Removed 2/18/1964 | |
| Chisham, Grace (Mrs. Wm.) | Apr. 17, 1938 | | W. R. Holt | Ltr. | Death 1978 | Harnden |
| Chisham, Mary Ann | Apr. 17, 1938 | | W. R. Holt | | Feb. 18, 1964 Removed | |
| Chisham, Russell | Apr. 17, 1938 | | W. R. Holt | | Death Jul. 22, 1964 | |
| Chisham, William E. | Apr. 17, 1938 | | W. R. Holt | Ltr. | Death Jul.13, 1982 | DeSpain |
| Christy, Howard C. (Mrs. ) | 1950 | | W. R. Holt | | Nov. 01, 1963 Death | |

**Record of Members**

| Name | Date Received | Birth | By Whom | How | Status | Remarks |
|------|---------------|-------|---------|-----|--------|---------|
| Christy, Robert | 1950 | | W. R. Holt | | 1957 Removed | |
| Clark, Virginia (Mrs. Neves) | | | | | Jan. 10, 1954 Transfer | |
| Clay, Martha | | | | Ltr. | Mar. 31, 1961 Death | |
| Clemm, Katherine A. (Mrs. W. F. ) | May. 26, 1968 | 4/9/1925 | W. R. Holt | Ltr. Wesley Meth | Rcc Dec. 1978 | Harnden |
| Clemm, Sandra Gale | May. 26, 1968 | 6/30/1956 | W. R. Holt | Conf. of Faith | TSF WA. Dec. 1978 | DeSpain |
| Clemm, Walter F. | May. 26, 1968 | 10/6/1920 | W. R. Holt | Ltr. 1st Cong. | Removed Dec. 1978 | Harnden |
| Clevenger, David | Apr. 09, 1944 | | W. R. Holt | Conf. of Faith | Removed 4/5/1959 | |
| Clevenger, Jack | | | | | Jan. 13, 1958 Removed | |
| Clevenger, JoAnn (Marshall) | Apr. 09, 1944 | | W. R. Holt | Conf. of Faith | Married Marshall | |
| Clevenger, Lee (Mrs.) (1st) | Feb. 09, 1930 | | S. B. Williams | Conf. of Faith | Mar. 28, 1957 Death | |
| Clevenger, Lee (Mrs.) (2nd) | Jun. 22, 1969 | | R. L. Rayson | TSF. Wyan. | CT 1976 | |
| Clevenger, Lee Sr. | Feb. 09, 1930 | | S. B. Williams | Conf. of Faith | Apr. 05, 1959 Removed | |
| Clevenger, Lee Sr. | Jun. 22, 1969 | | R. L. Rayson | TSF. Wyan. | CT 1976 | |
| Clevenger, Pearl (Davidson) | | | | Conf. of Faith | Removed without cert. | |
| Cloughley, John R. | Dec. 10, 1933 | | S. B. Williams | Conf. of Faith | 1955 Death | |
| Cloughley, Julie Annette | 1952 | | W. R. Holt | COF Apr. 18, 1954 | 1958 Removed | |
| Cloughley, Margaret | Jan. 31, 1932 | | S. B. Williams | Conf. of Faith | Death Oct. 29, 1997 | Lamberty |
| Cloughley, Roy | | | | | Apr. 30, 1950 Catholic | |

13 - MEMBERS

# Record of Members

| Name | Date Received | Birth | By Whom | How | Status | Remarks |
|---|---|---|---|---|---|---|
| Cloughley, Susann Deweese | 1952 | | W. R. Holt | COF Apr. 18, 1954 | 1958 Removed | |
| Cloughley, William | Apr. 04, 1926 | | S. B. Williams | Conf. of Faith | 1958 Removed | |
| Cloughley, William (Mrs.) | | | | | 1958 Removed | |
| Clyde, Janet (Mrs. Jim Riley) | Mar. 29, 1959 | 3/28/1950 | W. R. Holt | From "R" List | Rcc Dec. 03, 1981 | DeSpain |
| Cobb, Betty (Mrs. Lloyd) | Dec. 11, 1960 | 5/19/1935 | W. R. Holt | Conf. of Faith | Rcc Dec. 1978 | Harnden |
| Cobb, Lloyd | Dec. 11, 1960 | 2/3/1934 | W. R. Holt | Conf. of Faith | Rcc Dec. 1978 | Harnden |
| Cobb, Matthew Steven | Apr. 10, 1966 | 3/8/1956 | W. R. Holt | Conf. of Faith | Rcc Dec. 1978 | Harnden |
| Coffman, Emma (Mrs.) | | | | | 1957 Death | |
| Collins, Wanda | Jun. 04, 1989 | | M. Gasau | CT. Indian Heights | | |
| Collins, Wanda (Mrs.) | Nov. 10, 1974 | | J. R. Harnden | C. T. Mason | TSF 3/01/1981 | DeSpain |
| Collins, Willa J. | Mar. 23, 1975 | | J. R. Harnden | Conf. of Faith | Withdrew 12/1988 | Gasau |
| Collins, William | Nov. 10, 1974 | 8/16/1922 | J. R. Harnden | C. T. Mason | D. Mar.18, 2006 Trinity | |
| Combs, Leon | | | W. R. Holt | Conf. of Faith | Death May 18, 1975 | |
| Conner, W. M. (Mrs.) | | | | | Death 1952 | |
| Converse, Patty Sue (Mrs. V) (Warnick) | | | | | Ltr. Oct. 25, 1953 | |
| Cordill, Charles | | | | | Reunited 1951 | |
| Cordill, Joyce (Mrs. Charles) (Hill) | Apr. 14, 1968 | 11/14/1942 | W.R. Holt | Conf. of Faith | See Married Hill | |
| Cordill, Russell (Mrs.) | | | | | Reunited 1951 | |

14 - MEMBERS

**Record of Members**

| Name | Date Received | Birth | By Whom | How | Status | Remarks |
|------|---------------|-------|---------|-----|--------|---------|
| Cramer, Robert | Oct. 01, 1972 | | R. L. Rayson | Tran. London Hgts. | TSF Clearview 12/11/1979 | Harnden |
| Cramer, Ruth (Mrs. Robert) | Oct. 01, 1972 | | R. L. Rayson | Tran. London Hgts. | TSF Clearview 12/11/1979 | Harnden |
| Cried, Lena (Mrs. ) | Apr. 01, 1956 | | W. R. Holt | Transfer | Feb. 03, 1958 Death | |
| Crockett, Arnett (Mrs. Davy) | Feb. 14, 1954 | | W. R. Holt | Ltr. Presbyterian | Death Oct. 20, 2000 | Lamberty |
| Crockett, Davy | Feb. 14, 1954 | | W. R. Holt | Ltr. Presbyterian | Death Apr. 23, 1982 | DeSpain |
| Crockett, Ginger | Feb. 14, 1954 | | W. R. Holt | Watch care | Catholic, Removed | |
| Crockett, Wanda (Mrs.) | Jun. 10, 1962 | | W. R. Holt | From "L" List | Rcc Nov. 01, 1998 | Lamberty |
| Crosier, Ruth (Mrs. Edwin) | | | | | Removed without cert. | |
| Crull, Roger Austin | | | | | Ltr. | |
| Cunningham, Joyce Dee (Newbanks) | Mar. 29, 1959 | 12/25/1949 | W. R. Holt | Conf. of Faith | To "N" List, Aug. 1969 | |
| Cunningham, Lawrence R. | Apr. 01, 1945 | 9/28/1907 | W. R. Holt | Ltr. | Death Oct. 10, 1996 | Lamberty |
| Cunningham, Linda (Mrs. Al Schmidt) | 1952 | 08/04.1940 | W. R. Holt | Child Care Roll | Joined in 1952 | |
| Cunningham, Maebelle (Mrs. L. R.) | Apr. 01, 1945 | 9/13/1910 | W. R. Holt | Ltr. | Death Aug. 21, 1999 | Lamberty |
| Cunningham, Marjorie (Mrs. John) | Apr. 17, 1927 | | S. B. Williams | Conf. of Faith | | |
| Cunningham, Vickie Sue (McKinzie) | Apr. 17, 1960 | 7/28/1951 | W. R. Holt | Conf. of Faith | TSF.Emporia 1994 | Lamberty |
| Daniels, Earl G. | 1950 | | W. R. Holt | Conf. of Faith | Death 3/24/1959? | |
| Daniels, Gertie (Mrs.) | | | W. R. Holt | Ltr. | Death 12/21/1969 | |
| Davenport, Lillie (Mrs.) | Dec. 12, 1920 | | Dr. May | Conf. of Faith | Jan. 16, 1961 Death | |

15 - MEMBERS

**Record of Members**

| Name | Date Received | Birth | By Whom | How | Status | Remarks |
|------|---------------|-------|---------|-----|--------|---------|
| Davidson, Naomi (Mrs. Ralph) (Slater) | May. 19, 1968 | | W. R. Holt | Conf. of Faith | R. 03/1983 or 8/2/86 | Spain/West |
| Davidson, Pearl (Mrs.) (Clevenger) | 1944 | | W. R. Holt | Conf. of Faith | Removed 1956 | |
| Davidson, Ralph Donald | May. 19, 1968 | 2/11/1929 | W. R. Holt | Conf. of Faith | Death Aug. 17, 1986 | R. West |
| Davis, Alreco | Jun. 24, 2007 | | L. Lamberty | | | |
| Davis, Julie | Jun. 24, 2007 | | L.Lamberty | Other Denom. | | |
| Dawdy, Timothy | Mar. 26, 1967 | 10/13/1956 | W. R. Holt | Conf. of Faith | TSF. Sept. 1, 1968 | |
| Dawson, Deborah Sue (Garnett) | | | | | Removed without cert. | |
| Dawson, Carol Mae | Apr. 30, 1944 | | W. R. Holt | Conf. of Faith | Apr. 05, 1959, Removed | |
| Dawson, James | | | | | | |
| Day, Carol (Tucker) | Mar. 26, 1967 | | W. R. Holt | Conf. of Faith | Removed Nov. 21, 1988 | Gasau |
| Day, Carolyn (Masters/Krummel) | Sept. 07, 1986 | | R. West | CT Prince of Peace | TSF 11/10/02 Tong. KS | Lamberty |
| Day, Douglas | Mar. 1943 | | W. R. Holt | W. C. of Church | Ltr.Village, 12/23/1966 | |
| Day, Irba R. | Feb. 1943 | | W. R. Holt | Conf. of Faith | Death Sept. 25, 1958 | |
| Day, John | Mar. 1943 | | W. R. Holt | W. C. of Church | Death Aug. 14, 1988 | Gasau |
| Day, Velma (Mrs. I. R.) | Feb. 1943 | | W. R. Holt | Ltr. | Death Sept. 23, 1985 | Stevenson |
| Deane/Doane, Sandra Gayle(Radotinsky) | | | | | TSF/ 9/26/1965 IA. | |
| Deaver, Evelyne Marie (Mrs.) | Jul. 22, 1962 | | W. R. Holt | Conf. of Faith | Death July 21, 1981 | DeSpain |
| Debus, Buddy | | | | | Removed 1967 | |

**Record of Members**

| Name | Date Received | Birth | By Whom | How | Status | Remarks |
|------|---------------|-------|---------|-----|--------|---------|
| Debus, Fred Wayne | Jun. 14, 1959 | | W. R. Holt | Conf. of Faith | TSF. Trinity 1968 | |
| Debus, Shirley | | | | | Removal 1/13/1958 | |
| Debus, Vernon | | | | | Death 1969 | |
| Debus, Vernon (Mrs.) | | | | | Removal 1967 | |
| Debus, Vernon Jr. | | | | | | |
| Decker, Edna (Mrs. Vincent) | May. 12, 1959 | 12/6/1910 | W. R. Holt | Ltr. | TSF. Jul. 1970 | |
| Decker, Vincent | May. 12, 1959 | 6/6/1910 | W. R. Holt | Ltr. | TSF. Jul. 1970 | |
| Delech, Mary Noel (Mrs. Henry) | Apr. 09, 1939 | | W. R. Holt | Conf. of Faith | Transfer to Baptist 1973 | |
| Delich, Barbara | | | | | Catholic member | |
| Delich, Carolyn Irene | 1950 | | W. R. Holt | | TSF Chicago 1961 | |
| Delich, Clifford Don | Sept. 27, 1964 | | W. R. Holt | Conf. of Faith | Removed Nov. 27, 1973 | |
| Delich, David | Apr. 02, 1961 | | W. R. Holt | Conf. of Faith | Removed Nov. 27, 1973 | |
| Delich, Hazel (Mrs. Michael) | | | W. R. Holt | Conf. of Faith | TSF Wolcott Mar.1972 | |
| Delich, Rosemary | Aug. 25, 1963 | 3/22/1943 | W. R. Holt | Conf. of Faith | TSF Norman, OK. 1966 | |
| DeSpain, Barbara E. | Jul. 06, 1980 | | I. DeSpain | CT. Valley View | CT Aldersgate 8/27/84 | Stevenson |
| Dillon, Murial (Mrs.) | | | | | Withdrawal 1952 | |
| Ditmars, Thomas E. | Apr. 19, 1925 | | S. B. Williams | Letter | Tran. EUB Calif. 1966 | |
| Ditmars, Thomas (Mrs.) | Apr. 19, 1925 | | S. B. Williams | Letter | Tran. EUB Calif. 1966 | |

17 - MEMBERS

# Record of Members

| Name | Date Received | Birth | By Whom | How | Status | Remarks |
|------|---------------|-------|---------|-----|--------|---------|
| Divilbiss, Roderick | | | | | Removed 1967 | |
| Divilbiss, Roderick Phillys (Mrs.) | Mar. 26, 1961 | | W. R. Holt | TSF Emmanuel | Removed 1967 | |
| Divilbiss, Roland Wilbur | Mar. 26, 1961 | | W. R. Holt | TSF Emmanuel | TSF. TN, Nov. 2, 1971 | |
| Divilbiss, Ronald | | | | | Tran. Emmanuel Bap. | |
| Divilbiss, Sondra (Mrs. R. W.) | Mar. 26, 1961 | | W. R. Holt | TSF Emmanuel | TSF. TN, Nov. 2, 1971 | |
| Divilbiss, Tommy | 1952 | | | | Child Watch Roll | |
| Divilbiss, William T. | | | | | Ltr. Presby. St. Louis | |
| Divilbiss, William T. (Mrs.) | | | | | Ltr. Presby. St. Louis | |
| Dixon, Chris | Sept. 08, 2002 | | Lamberty/Smart | RF | | |
| Dodd, Ineg (Mrs. Arthur M.) | Mar. 28, 1937 | | W. R. Holt | Conf. of Faith | CT Stoney Point 3/18/79 | Harnden |
| Dodd, James | Sept. 26, 1982 | | I. DeSpain | CT Asbury UMC | Withdrew Oct. 10, 1997 | Lamberty |
| Dodd, Linda | Sept. 26, 1982 | | I. DeSpain | CT Prairie Village | Withdrew Oct. 10, 1997 | Lamberty |
| Donahue, Frances (Mrs. R.) , (Warnick) | Jan. 24, 1932 | | S. B. Williams | From Warnick | Death 1990 (?) | Lamberty |
| Donley, Jackie D. Adamson/White) | | | | From Gladys White | TSF. Adamson | |
| Dotterrer, Irene (Miss) | Apr. 17, 1938 | | W. R. Holt | Conf. of Faith | Removed 4/5/1959 | |
| Dowd, Gayle Ann (Canfield) | Apr. 21, 1957 | 6/22/1945 | W. R. Holt | Conf. of Faith | Married Michael Canfield | |
| Dowd, Harry | | | W. R. Holt | Conf. of Faith | Death Feb. 17, 1971 | |
| Dowd, Larry Eugene | 1952 | | W. R. Holt | Conf. of Faith | TSF. Sept. 15, 1970 | |

18 - MEMBERS

**Record of Members**

| Name | Date Received | Birth | By Whom | How | Status | Remarks |
|------|---------------|-------|---------|-----|--------|---------|
| Dowd, Maxine (Mrs. Harry) | | | W. R. Holt | Conf. of Faith | | |
| Dowd, Nedra | Sept. 27 1964 | | W. R. Holt | Conf. of Faith | Withdrew Nov. 03, 1987 | West |
| Dragoo, Emmitt | Mar.28, 1937 | | W. R. Holt | | Removed 4/5/1959 | |
| Dragoo, Emmitt (Mrs.) | Mar. 28, 1937 | | W. R. Holt | | Removed 4/5/1959 | |
| Draney, Edward | | | | | Removed 1/13/1958 | |
| Draney, Gerald | Apr. 09, 1944 | | W. R. Holt | Conf. of Faith | Removed 1/3/1958 | |
| Drayden, Doris (Garrett) | | | | | Was Doris Garrett | |
| Drayden, John | 1997 | | R. Harper | | | |
| Dryer, Linda Sue (Mrs. Dan) (Zimmer) | Apr. 01, 1956 | 7/13/1944 | W. R. Holt | Conf. of Faith | TSF. Mar. 25, 1971 | |
| Dudley, Christy | Jun. 01, 1986 | | E. Stevenson | Conf. of Faith | TSF. 03/21/1988 | West |
| Dudley, Janet Ann (Mrs. J. E. ) | Mar. 14, 1965 | 111/13/1944 | W. R. Holt | TSF.McMaken | CT 03/21/88 Bonner Spr. | West |
| Dudley, John Edward | Mar. 14, 1965 | | W. R. Holt | Ltr. | Removed Nov. 07, 1999 | Lamberty |
| Dugan, June (Mrs. ) | Apr. 02, 1972 | | R. L. Rayson | Conf. of Faith | Reinstated Apr. 18. 1982 | DeSpain |
| Dunivan, Barbara (Mrs. C.) (Schmidt) | Aug. 9, 1959 | 7/27/1939 | W. R. Holt | Conf. of Faith | 10/13/1992 Reinstated | Harnden |
| Dunivan , Betty Jean (Hardsaw) | | | | TSF. Hardsaw | Removed 1967 | |
| Duvall, Mary (Mrs.) | Apr. 09, 1944 | | W. R. Holt | Conf. of Faith | Death 02/09/1968 | |
| Dysart, John (Mrs.) | Oct.     1955 | | W. R. Holt | Transfer | Ltr.Grandview Pr 1965 | |
| Dysart, Karen | | | | | Withdrew 1976 | |

19 - MEMBERS

# Record of Members

| Name | Date Received | Birth | By Whom | How | Status | Remarks |
|---|---|---|---|---|---|---|
| Dysart, Norman | Apr. 25, 1965 | | W. R. Holt | Ltr.Over. Park Bap. | Withdrew 1976 | |
| Dysart, Ruth | | | | | Withdrew 1976 | |
| Eagle, James N. | Jan. 08, 1967 | | W. R. Holt | Ltr. Wyan. Meth. | TSF Zion, KCK 8/12/82 | DeSpain |
| Eagle, Janie (Mrs. J. N.) | Jan. 08, 1967 | | W. R. Holt | Ltr. W. Highland P | TSF Zion, KCK 8/12/82 | DeSpain |
| Eagle, John E. Jr. | Apr. 12, 1959 | 3/15/1931 | W. R. Holt | Ltr. Presbyterian | Removed Dec. 1978 | Harnden |
| Eagle, Sue (Mrs. J. E.) | Apr. 12, 1959 | 2/20/1931 | W. R. Holt | Conf. of Faith | Removed Dec. 1978 | Harnden |
| Eagon, Orville | | | W. R. Holt | | Ltr. TSF.California | |
| Eagon, Orville (Mrs.) | | | W. R. Holt | | Ltr.TSF California | |
| Eaken, Wanda June | | | | | Removed 1/13/1958 | |
| Early, June Margaret (Mrs. Marvin) | Jun. 03, 1973 | | R. L. Rayson | Ref. London Hts. | Removed Dec. 03, 1981 | DeSpain |
| Early, Laura Elaine (Mrs. Marvin) (Riley) | Apr. 21, 1957 | 9/13/1946 | W. R. Holt | C of F., TSF Riley | TSF Olathe First 10/89 | Gasau |
| Early, Marvin M. Jr. | Jun. 03, 1973 | 6/11/1945 | R. L. Rayson | Conf. of Faith | TSF Olathe First 10/89 | Gasau |
| Early, Marvin M. Sr. | Jun. 03, 1973 | | R. L. Rayson | Ref. London Hts. | Death 1976 | |
| Eaton, Edward Anton | Jan. 03, 1965 | 9/19/1956 | W. R. Holt | Conf. of Faith | | |
| Eaton, John E. (Jack) Jr. | 1950 | 10/14/1917 | W. R. Holt | Conf. of Faith | Death Feb. 22, 2007 | Lamberty |
| Eaton, Joneen Elaine (Sigette) | Apr. 10, 1966 | 5/27/1954 | W. R. Holt | Conf. of Faith | | |
| Eaton, Virginia (Mrs. J. E. Jr. ) | 1950 | | W. R. Holt | Conf. of Faith | Death Jul. 08, 2003 | Lamberty |
| Edgar, Elvin D. | | | W. R. Holt | | Ltr.of Tran. 08/11/1953 | |

20 - MEMBERS

# Record of Members

| Name | Date Received | Birth | By Whom | How | Status | Remarks |
|---|---|---|---|---|---|---|
| Edgar, Elvin (Mrs.) | | | W. R. Holt | | Ltr. of Tran. 08/11/1953 | |
| Edwards, June (Mrs.) | Apr. 02, 1972 | | R. L. Rayson | Ltr. Covenant Bap. | TSF 1976 | |
| Ehbauer, Diane (Bolton) | | | | | | |
| Eidson, Terry William | Apr. 21, 1957 | 9/14/1945 | W. R. Holt | Conf. of Faith | TSF Trinity 06/29/1970 | |
| Ellington, Lynn (Neal) (Hollander) | Sept. 27, 1964 | | W. R. Holt | Conf. of Faith | | |
| Ellis, Earl D. | | | | | Removed 1/13/1958 | |
| Ellis, Earl D. (Mrs. ) | | | | | Removed 1/13/1958 | |
| Ellis, Eva Lou (Grauberger) | Nov. 13, 1938 | | W. R. Holt | Watch Care Child | TSF Ill. Apr. 1957 | |
| Ellis, Homer L. | Nov. 13, 1938 | | W. R. Holt | Ltr. Ohio | TSF Fla. Death 1987 | Rayson |
| Ellis, Mary (Mrs. Homer L.) | Nov. 13, 1938 | | W. R. Holt | Ltr. Ohio | TSF Fla. 12/27/94 Death | Rayson |
| Ellis, Nancy Lee | | | | | Removed 1/13/1958 | |
| Enders, Marguerite (Mrs. W.) | | | W. R. Holt | Transfer | TSF May 1975 Lenexa | |
| Enders, Wray (Dr.) | | | W. R. Holt | Transfer | TSF May 1975 Lenexa | |
| Endsley, Carolyn (Mattney) | | | | | Transfer to Mattney | |
| Endsley, Marilyn (Batatoe) | | | | | Transfer to Batatoe | |
| Endsley, Myron | | | W. R. Holt | | Removed Nov. 27, 1973 | |
| Endsley, Myron (Mrs.) | | | | | Death Dec.1969 | |
| Ensley, Linda (Charlson) | Apr. 17, 1960 | | W. R. Holt | Conf. of Faith | Transfer to Charlson | |

21 - MEMBERS

# Record of Members

| Name | Date Received | Birth | By Whom | How | Status | Remarks |
|---|---|---|---|---|---|---|
| Evans, Elizabeth (Hathaway/Riley) | | | | | Hathaway remar. Riley | |
| Everhart, Marjorie (Mrs. R. L.) | Mar. 26, 1967 | 1/23/1938 | W. R. Holt | TSF Trinity Meth. | TSF Dec. 15, 1971 | |
| Everhart, Richard L. | Mar. 26, 1967 | 8/15/1934 | W. R. Holt | TSF Trinity Meth. | TSF Dec. 15, 1971 | |
| Everhart, Roger Lynn | Apr. 11, 1971 | 4/1/1958 | R. L. Rayson | Conf. of Faith | TSF Dec. 15, 1971 | |
| Everly, Elmer D. | Oct. 17, 1954 | | W. R. Holt | Conf. of Faith | Removed 1967 | |
| Everly, Irene (Mrs. E.) | Oct. 17, 1954 | | W. R. Holt | Conf. of Faith | Removed 1967 | |
| Eversole, Homer | | | W. R. Holt | | Aug. 10, 1956 Death | |
| Eversole, Homer (Mrs.) | | | W. R. Holt | | | |
| Eversole, Judy | | | | Child watch care | | |
| Fairchild, Carol (Mrs. Don) | Dec. 18, 1960 | | W. R. Holt | Conf. of Faith | Withdrew 1976 | |
| Fairchild, Donaldson (Don) | Dec. 18, 1960 | | W. R. Holt | TSF Bap. Iola, KS | Withdrew 1976 | |
| Fath, Nellie M. (Mrs. ) | Jul. 10, 1960 | | W. R. Holt | Ltr. Wash. Ave. | Death Jan. 08, 1964 | |
| Fath, Nora | May. 22, 1938 | | W. R. Holt | Ltr. | Death 1973 | |
| Fath, William | May. 14, 1944 | | W. R. Holt | Conf. of Faith | Death Mar. 27, 1980 | Harnden |
| Faust, L. F. | Oct. 17, 1920 | | Dr. Fralick | Ltr. | Death 03/25/1955 | |
| Faust, Lillian (Capt.) (Johnson) | | | | Ltr. | LTR 1953, Mrs. Johnson | |
| Ferguson, Marie | | | | | Death Jan. 21, 1970 | |
| Fields, Cheryl | Aug. 31, 2003 | | Lamberty/Smart | | | |

22 - MEMBERS

**Record of Members**

| Name | Date Received | Birth | By Whom | How | Status | Remarks |
|---|---|---|---|---|---|---|
| Fields, Gladys | Apr. 01, 1945 | | W. R. Holt | Ltr. | Death Dec. 18, 2002 | Lamberty |
| Fields, John | Apr. 09, 1944 | | W. R. Holt | Conf. of Faith | Transfer to Christian | |
| Fields, Walter | Apr. 01, 1945 | | W. R. Holt | Ltr. | Death Aug. 08, 1986 | West |
| Finn, Berlin W. | Apr. 17, 1927 | | S. B. Williams | Ltr. | Death Nov.22, 1980 | DeSpain |
| Finn, Elizabeth | Apr. 17, 1927 | | S. B. Williams | Ltr. | Death July 16, 1994 | Harper |
| Flander, Mary Ann (Mrs.) (Syulshi) | Apr. 25, 1954 | | W. R. Holt | TSF Syulshi | Withdrew 1976 | |
| Foley, Victor | | | | | Removed 4/5/1959 | |
| Forbes, Dennis | Jan. 06, 1957 | 11/2/1946 | W. R. Holt | Conf. of Faith | | |
| Forbes, June | Jan. 06, 1957 | 2/19/1924 | W. R. Holt | Ltr. Baptist | Death Nov. 29, 2001 | Lamberty |
| Forbes, Kenneth | Jan. 06, 1957 | 3/29/1951 | W. R. Holt | Conf. of Faith | TSF.May 1978 Stoney Pt. | Harnden |
| Forbes, Michael | Sept. 27, 1964 | | W. R. Holt | Conf. of Faith | TSF.Mar. 1973 Stoney Pt. | |
| Forbes, Noel | Jan. 06, 1957 | 2/2/1924 | W. R. Holt | Ltr. Methodist | Feb. 11,1972 Death | |
| Forbes, Peggy (Mrs. Dennis) | Nov. 21, 1971 | 12/8/1947 | R. L. Rayson | Ltr. London Hts. | Death 06/26/2005 | Lamberty |
| Forrest, Rhonda | Oct. 01, 2006 | | L. Lamberty | Conf. of Faith | | |
| Foster, Georgia Bea | Apr. 29, 1962 | 10/31/1936 | W. R. Holt | Conf. of Faith | Removed Dec. 1978 | Harnden |
| Foster, Nancy (Simmons) | Mar. 23, 1975 | | J. R. Harnden | Conf. of Faith | Removed Nov. 21, 1988 | Gasau |
| Foster, Ronald Lee | Apr. 29, 1962 | 9/16/1935 | W. R. Holt | Conf. of Faith | Removed Dec. 1978 | Harnden |
| Fraikiowak, Virginia (Mrs.) (Neves) | | | | | TSF. To IL. 2/10/1958 | |

23 - MEMBERS

# Record of Members

| Name | Date Received | Birth | By Whom | How | Status | Remarks |
|------|---------------|-------|---------|-----|--------|---------|
| Fralick, Lorene | Dec. 30, 1978 | | J. R. Harnden | TSF St. Pauls | TSF St. P. 3/01/93 | Gasau |
| Fralick, Ona N. | 1920 | | Fralick/Williams | Ltr. | W. 1976 Death 8/28/78 | Harnden |
| Frazier, Kenya | Oct. 27, 2002 | | Lamberty/ Smart | | | |
| Frazier, Rickey Jr. | Feb. 25, 2006 | | L. Lamberty | | | |
| Frederick, Helen (Mrs.) | Jun.    1921 | | Dr. May | Ltr. | Removed 1/13/1958 | |
| Freidell, Carolyn (Mrs. ) | Mar. 29, 1970 | | R. L. Rayson | Ltr. Stoney Pt. Ch. | TSF Sunset Hills10/3/91 | Gasau |
| Freidell, Larry H. | Mar. 29, 1970 | 12/1/1950 | R. L. Rayson | Ltr. Stoney Pt. Ch. | Removed 11/7/1999 | Lamberty |
| Freidell, Linda M. (Hollander) | Mar. 29, 1970 | 2/6/1949 | R. L. Rayson | Ltr. Stoney Pt. Ch. | Married. Hollander | |
| Fry, Harold | 1964 | | W. R. Holt | TSF 1st Presby | TSF Presby 10/19/1966 | |
| Fry, Hazel (Mrs.) (Yoxall) | Sept. 18, 1927 | | S. B. Williams | Ltr. | Married John Yoxall | |
| Fry, James | Aug. 05, 1955 | | W. R. Holt | Conf. of Faith | Removed Oct. 1967 | |
| Fry, James (Mrs) (Sackman) | | | | TSF Sackman | Removed Oct. 1967 | |
| Fry, Maude (Mrs.) | Oct. 17, 1954 | | W. R. Holt | Conf. of Faith | Death 1965 | |
| Fry, Nancy Ann (Mrs. H.) (Hoagland) | 1964 | | W. R. Holt | TSF Hoagland | | |
| Fry, Rosemary (Plakus) | Apr. 18, 1954 | | W. R. Holt | Conf. of Faith | Married Chris Plakus | |
| Gable, Elsie (Mrs. Lee) | Oct. 01, 1972 | | R. L. Rayson | TSF. London Hgts. | Death Jan. 1977 | Harnden |
| Gallipeau, Connie Lee (Johnson) | Sept. 26, 1965 | | W. R. Holt | Ltr. Central | TSF. "J"/ Johnson | |
| Gallipeau, Jerry | Sept. 26, 1965 | | W. R. Holt | Conf. of Faith | Death Oct. 22/1987 | West |

24 - MEMBERS

**Record of Members**

| Name | Date Received | Birth | By Whom | How | Status | Remarks |
|------|--------------|-------|---------|-----|--------|---------|
| Gallipeau, Maxine (Mrs. Jerry) | Sept. 26, 1965 | 2/24/1925 | W. R. Holt | Ltr. Central | Death Aug. 24, 2006 | Lamberty |
| Gallipeau, Michael | Sept. 26, 1965 | | W. R. Holt | Ltr. Central | TSF. Stephens 9/22/97 | Lamberty |
| Garnett, Arthur Glenn | Nov. 10, 1963 | 3/24/1928 | W. R. Holt | Ltr. Elkhart, KS | TSF Lebanon 11/16/92, | Gasau |
| Garnett, Deborah Sue (Dawson) | Nov. 10, 1963 | 6/19/1958 | W. R. Holt | Conf. of Faith | Removed 11/20/89 | Gasau |
| Garnett, Elizabeth Ann | Nov. 10, 1963 | 7/20/1953 | W. R. Holt | Conf. of Faith | Withdrawal 11/4/86 | West |
| Garnett, Elma Pauline | Nov. 10, 1963 | 9/29/1928 | W. R. Holt | Ltr. Elkhart, KS. | TSF. Lebanon 11/16/92 | Gasau |
| Garnett, Jaqueline Elaine | Nov. 10, 1963 | 6/28/1956 | W. R. Holt | Conf. of Faith | Removed Nov. 20, 1989 | Gasau |
| Garnett, Jerry Lynn | Nov. 10, 1963 | 3/27/1951 | W. R. Holt | Conf. of Faith | Removed Nov. 20, 1989 | Gasau |
| Garrett, Doris (Drayden) | Apr. 28, 1991 | | Gasau | TSF OD Baptist | Married John Drayden | |
| Gasau, Aaron P. | Oct. 23, 1988 | | Gasau | TSF Aldersgate | 11/8/1995 CT Basalt, CO | Harper |
| Gasau, Jake F. (Jacob) | Oct. 23, 1988 | | Gasau | TSF Aldersgate | 11/8/1995 CT Basalt, CO | Harper |
| Gasau, Jerry F. (Jerald) | Oct. 23, 1988 | | Gasau | TSF Aldersgate | 11/8/1995 CT Basalt, CO | Harper |
| Gentry, Christine (Mathews) | | | | | Removed 4/5/1959 | |
| George, Jimmie | 1950 | | W. R. Holt | | | |
| Gerber, Barbara (Krueger) | 1952 | | W. R. Holt | TSF. Krueger | | |
| Gerster, Bonnie | Apr. 14, 1968 | 11/14/1955 | W. R. Holt | Conf. of Faith | TSF. Bristol 10/2/1972 | |
| Gerster, Robert | Apr. 14, 1968 | 5/12/1956 | W. R. Holt | Conf. of Faith | TSF. Bristol 10/2/1972 | |
| Gibbs, Ardith | Mar. 29, 1959 | | W. R. Holt | Conf. of Faith | | |

25 - MEMBERS

# Record of Members

| Name | Date Received | Birth | By Whom | How | Status | Remarks |
|---|---|---|---|---|---|---|
| Gibbs, Merideth | Mar. 29, 1959 | | W. R. Holt | Conf. of Faith | Death Feb. 1985 | Stevenson |
| Gibbs, Phillip Dean | Mar. 29, 1959 | 5/27/1943 | W. R. Holt | Conf. of Faith | TSF. 10.02.1969 Pres. | |
| Gicalone, Charlene (Mrs.) (Grubb) | | | W. R. Holt | Conf. of Faith | Mar. L. Grubb 10/04/1980 | |
| Gicalone, Edwin | Feb. 09, 1930 | | S. B. Williams | Conf. of Faith | Removed 4/5/1959 | |
| Gicalone, Edwin (Mrs.) | | | | | | |
| Gicalone, Frank Jr. | Feb. 09, 1930 | | S. B. Williams | Conf. of Faith | Removed 1967 | |
| Gicalone, Frank Jr. (Mrs.) | | | W. R. Holt | | Removed 1965 | |
| Gicalone, Frank Sr. | Apr. 09, 1939 | | W. R. Holt | Conf. of Faith | Removed 4/5/1959 | |
| Gicalone, Frank Sr. (Mrs.) | Apr. 09, 1939 | | W. R. Holt | Conf. of Faith | Removed 4/5/1959 | |
| Gicalone, Jill Sue (Hershberger) | Mar. 29, 1961 | | W. R. Holt | Conf. of Faith | Married Hershberger | |
| Gicalone, Julie (Mrs. Philip) | Apr. 02, 1972 | | R. L. Rayson | Ltr. Asbury UMC | TSF. Apr. 1974 Divorce | |
| Gicalone, Karen Ann (LeClaire) | | | W. R. Holt | | TSF Ralph LeClaire | |
| Gicalone, Leland | | | W. R. Holt | | Removed 1967 | |
| Gicalone, Nedra (Cackler) | Feb. 12, 1984 | | DeSpain | OD Tong. Christian | Removed 11/21/88 | Gasau |
| Gicalone, Philip Anthony | Apr. 02, 1961 | 10/26/1947 | W. R. Holt | Conf. of Faith | Withdrew 1980 | |
| Gicalone, Sharon | Dec. 21, 1975 | | J. R. Harnden | Conf. of Faith | | Harnden |
| Givler, Ann Elizabeth | Apr. 18, 1954 | 12/16/1961 | W. R. Holt | Transfer | TSF.Oct. 2, 1955 Calif. | |
| Givler, Edwin George | Apr. 18, 1954 | | W.R. Holt | Transfer | TSF. Oct. 2, 1955 Calif. | |

26 - MEMBERS

**Record of Members**

| Name | Date Received | Birth | By Whom | How | Status | Remarks |
|------|---------------|-------|---------|-----|--------|---------|
| Glenn, Gertrude Anna (Mrs.) | Apr. 01, 1923 | | Dr. May | | Removed 1967 | |
| Godfrey, Edmond | 1950 | | W. R. Holt | | Removed 1967 | |
| Godfrey, Edmond (Mrs.) | 1950 | | W. R. Holt | | Removed 1967 | |
| Goepfert, Delbert Lee | 1950 | | W. R. Holt | | Removed 4/5/1959 | |
| Goodrich, Paul (Mr.) | | | | | Ltr. Meth. 1967 | |
| Goodrich, Paul (Mrs.) | Apr. 09, 1939 | | W. R. Holt | Letter | Ltr. Meth. | |
| Gordon, David B. | Dec. 25, 1966 | 5/22/1910 | W. R. Holt | Conf. of Faith | Death 08/27/2005 | Gasau |
| Gordon, Hazel (Mrs. D. B. ) | Dec. 25, 1966 | | W. R. Holt | Ltr. Quindaro | Death Sept. 13, 1993 | Gasau |
| Gore, Frances (Mrs.) (McNervey) | | | | | Apr. 19, 1953 Ltr. | |
| Graham, Jackie (Mrs. ) | Apr. 09, 1939 | | W. R. Holt | Conf. of Faith | Removed 4/5/1959 | |
| Grant, Catherine Ellen | Mar. 23, 1975 | | J. R. Harnden | Conf. of Faith | Dec. 1975 TSF. St.Marks | |
| Grauberger , Albert Eugene Jr. | Mar. 29, 1959 | 2/11/1934 | W. R. Holt | TSF. D. Plaines, IL | TSF St. Pauls Epis 1961 | |
| Grauberger , Eva Lou (Ellis) | Mar. 29, 1959 | 3/1/1935 | W. R. Holt | Tran. Meth | TSF. St. Pauls Epis 1961 | |
| Graves, Clifford Elmer | May.05, 1957 | 9/10/1910 | W. R. Holt | Conf. of Faith | Removed 7/30/1958 | |
| Graves, Denise | Sept. 08, 2002 | | Lamberty/ Smart | | | |
| Graves, Dorothy Lucille | May.05, 1957 | 9/16/1911 | W. R. Holt | Conf. of Faith | Removed 7/30/1958 | |
| Grecian , Marian | Jun. 14, 1964 | | W. R. Holt | Ltr. Salina, KS. | TSF. Jul. 26, 1971 | |
| Grecian , Melvin | Jun. 14, 1964 | | W. R. Holt | Ltr. Salina, KS. | TSF. Jul. 26, 1971 | |

27 - MEMBERS

**Record of Members**

| Name | Date Received | Birth | By Whom | How | Status | Remarks |
|------|---------------|-------|---------|-----|--------|---------|
| Green, Arthur | Oct. 25, 1955 | | W. R. Holt | TSF. Baptist | To First Southern Baptist | |
| Green, Fred J. | | | | | Apr. 19, 1953 Ltr. | |
| Green, Fred J. (Mrs.) | | | | | Apr. 19, 1953 Ltr. | |
| Green, G. A. (Mrs.) | Nov. 27, 1932 | | S. B. Williams | Conf. of Faith | Death 11/26/1965 | |
| Green, Maurine Frances | Apr. 21, 1957 | 2/11/1945 | W. R. Holt | Conf. of Faith | Removed Bap. 1963 | |
| Green, Shanika | Apr. 23, 2006 | | L. Lamberty | Conf. of Faith | | |
| Green, Wanda (Mrs.) (Ogden) | Mar. 26, 1939 | | W. R. Holt | Ltr. | TSF. First Southern Bap. | |
| Greener, Anna Mae (Halverhout) | | | | TSF Halverhout | Joined Bap. 1955 | |
| Greenwood, Allen | Jan. 02, 1983 | | I. DeSpain | PF | | |
| Greenwood, Jane (Mrs. Al) | Feb. 22, 2002 | | L. Lamberty | Horton 2/03/002 | | |
| Greenwood, Patricia | Jan. 02, 1983 | | I. DeSpain | PF | Apr. 01, 2001 OK | Lamberty |
| Gregg, Charlene Fay (Mrs. V.) (Abney) | 1950 | | W. R. Holt | Was C.F. Abney | Death Nov. 01, 1994 | |
| Gregg, Vernon Carl | | | | | Removed 4/5/1959 | |
| Grove, Wilma (Mrs.) (Kmisley) | | | | | Removed without cert. | |
| Grubb, Charlene (Gicalone) | | | | Married L. Grubb | | |
| Grubb, Cory | Jun. 03, 2007 | | L. Lamberty | Conf. of Faith | | |
| Grubb, Helen Kensinger (Mrs. Norman) | | | | | Withdrew 1976 | |
| Grubb, Madeline (Mrs.) | Apr. 02, 1972 | | R. L. Rayson | Ltr. Bellvill, Ks UM | Death Nov. 01, 1994 | |

28 - MEMBERS

# Record of Members

| Name | Date Received | Birth | By Whom | How | Status | Remarks |
|------|--------------|-------|---------|-----|--------|---------|
| Guest, Arthur (Mrs.) | | | | | Death 1952 | |
| Gunz/Gung, Helen Lavon | Apr. 10, 1966 | 9/5/1954 | W. R. Holt | Conf. of Faith | Nov. 27, 1973 St. Peters | |
| Gunz/Gung, Pamela Ann | Apr. 10, 1966 | 10/22/1952 | W. R. Holt | Conf. of Faith | Nov. 27, 1973 St. Peters | |
| Gunz/Gung, Richard E. | Apr. 10, 1966 | 10/13/1928 | W. R. Holt | Conf. of Faith | Nov. 27, 1973 St. Peters | |
| Haglett, Jerry | Aug. 21, 1966 | 2/25/1940 | W. R. Holt | Cunningham, KS. | 09/01/1968 Concordia | |
| Haglett, Nancy (Mrs. Jerry) | Aug. 21, 1966 | 2/11/1937 | W. R. Holt | Camp Creek EUB | 09/01/1968 Concordia | |
| Hallier, Debra (Zimmer) | May. 08, 1966 | | W. R. Holt | | 7/22/1987 Shawnee | Gasau |
| Halverhout, Anna Mae ( J. Greiner) | Apr. 09,1944 | | W. R. Holt | Conf. of Faith | M. 5/21/1955 J. Greiner | |
| Halverhout, Edith (Wm. Brunker) | | | | | Married Wm. Brunker | |
| Halverhout, Edith (Mrs. A. W.) | | | W. R Holt | | Death Feb. 27, 1991 | Gasau |
| Handel, Oscar | Apr. 09, 1944 | | W. R. Holt | Conf. of Faith | Trans. Faith Bap. 1963 | |
| Handel, Oscar (Mrs.) | Apr. 09, 1944 | | W. R. Holt | Conf. of Faith | Trans. Faith Bap. 1963 | |
| Handel, Mary Ann | | | | | Trans. Faith Bap. 1963 | |
| Hanigan, Linda (Pigg) (Mrs. Leslie) | Dec. 10, 1961 | | W. R. Holt | Conf. of Faith | Transfer from Pigg | |
| Hanmon, Charles | Dec. 14, 1975 | | | | | |
| Hanmon, Delores Rae | Apr. 18, 1954 | | W. R. Holt | | | |
| Hansen, Beth (Mrs. Del) (Ditmers) | Feb.09, 1930 | | S. B. Williams | Conf. of Faith | TSF 1960 to Pres. Calif. | |
| Hanskins, William | Mar. 26, 1967 | 10/17/1951 | W. R. Holt | Conf. of Faith | | |

29 - MEMBERS

# Record of Members

| Name | Date Received | Birth | By Whom | How | Status | Remarks |
|---|---|---|---|---|---|---|
| Harbour, Eugene | | | W. R. Holt | Conf. of Faith | Death Mar. 1976 | Harnden |
| Harbour, Irene (Mrs. Eugene) | | | W. R. Holt | Conf. of Faith | Death Jan. 1976 | Stevenson |
| Harbour, Jack | Mar. 28, 1937 | | W. R. Holt | Conf. of Faith | Death Dec. 1956 | |
| Harbour, Laura (Mrs. R. E.) | | | W. R. Holt | Conf. of Faith | | |
| Harbour, Marvin R. | Jul.13, 1941 | | W. R Holt | Conf. of Faith | Rcc Dec. 03, 1981 | DeSpain |
| Harbour, Rheta Elizabeth (Slawson) | | | | TSF to Slawson | Married Donald Slawson | |
| Hardsaw, Betty Jean (Dunivan) | Apr. 05, 1942 | | W. R. Holt | Conf. of Faith | M.  Dunivan Dec.27, 1950 | |
| Hardsaw, David | | | W. R. Holt | Ltr. | Death Feb. 13, 1964 | |
| Hardsaw, Eloise (King) | | | | | Married to Larry King | |
| Hardsaw, Helen (Mrs. David) | | | W. R. Holt | Ltr. Methodist | Death 09/08/1992 | Gasau |
| Hardsaw, Jerry | Apr. 05, 1942 | | W. R. Holt | Ltr. Christian | Death Feb. 22, 1970 | |
| Hardsaw, Maurine (Mrs. Jerry) | Apr. 05, 1942 | | W. R. Holt | Ltr. Christian | TSF 11/18/1982 Stony Pt. | DeSpain |
| Hardsaw, Sherie Kay | Mar. 29, 1959 | 4/24/1947 | W. R. Holt | Conf. of Faith | | |
| Hargis , Charlotte | | | | | Withdrawal 8/1/1954 | |
| Harmon, Charles | Dec. 14, 1975 | | J. R. Harnden | Conf. of Faith | Rcc Dec. 03, 1981 | DeSpain |
| Harmon, Delores Rae (Mark) | Apr. 18, 1954 | | W. R. Holt | Conf. of Faith | CT 7/9/92 Bonner Sp. | Gasau |
| Harmon, Frank | 1950 | | W. R. Holt | | Removed 04/05/1959 | |
| Harmon, George | | | | | Removed 04/05/1959 | |

30 - MEMBERS

**Record of Members**

| Name | Date Received | Birth | By Whom | How | Status | Remarks |
|---|---|---|---|---|---|---|
| Harmon, Richard | | | | | TSF Welborn Church | |
| Harnden, Dee Ann | Jun. 16, 1974 | | J. R. Harnden | C. T. | TSF 9/7/1980 Ottawa, | DeSpain |
| Harnden, Marianne Christine | Apr. 06, 1980 | | J. R. Harnden | Conf. of Faith | TSF 09/7/80 Ottawa | DeSpain |
| Harris, James B. | | | | | Letter 1951 or 1952 | |
| Harris, James B. (Mrs.) | | | | | Letter 1951 or 1952 | |
| Hartig, Bertha (Mrs.Henry) | | | W. R. Holt | Conf. of Faith | Death 1997 | Lamberty |
| Hartig, JoDonna (Blackburn) | | | | | Mar. Robt.N. Blackburn | |
| Hartig, Ray | | | | | Removed no transfer | |
| Hass, Aileen Louise | Oct. 24, 1954 | | W. R. Holt | Conf.of Faith Luth. | Removal by request 1962 | |
| Hass, Milton Russell | Oct. 24, 1954 | | W. R. Holt | Conf.of Faith Luth. | Removal by request 1962 | |
| Hass, Russell | Oct. 24, 1954 | | W. R. Holt | Conf. of Faith | Removal by request 1962 | |
| Hataway, Cara Lee Jr. | Jan. 31, 1954 | | W. R. Holt | Conf. of Faith | W. 1988 | Gasau |
| Hataway, Deborah Lynn (Hocevar) | May. 08, 1966 | 9/23/1955 | W. R. Holt | Conf. of Faith | Removed Nov. 20, 1989 | Gasau |
| Hataway, Marilyn (Mrs.C. L.) Holt | Apr. 04, 1944 | 8/28/1935 | W. R. Holt | Conf. of Faith | W. 1988 Death 1989 | Gasau |
| Hataway, Shawn Ren'e (Laitner) | May. 08, 1966 | 11/4/1956 | W. R. Holt | Conf. of Faith | Removed Nov. 20, 1989 | Gasau |
| Hathaway, Henry A. | Apr. 23, 1944 | | W. R. Holt | Ltr. Presbyterian | Death Mar. 24, 1980 | Harnden |
| Hathaway, Lucille (Mrs. H.) | Apr. 23, 1944 | | W. R. Holt | Ltr. Presbyterian | Death Mar. 09, 1989 | Gasau |
| Hattaway, Judy (Tomecal) | | | | | TSF 7/12/1958 Baptist | |

31 - MEMBERS

## Record of Members

| Name | Date Received | Birth | By Whom | How | Status | Remarks |
|---|---|---|---|---|---|---|
| Hauskins, William | Mar. 26, 1967 | 10/17/1951 | W. R. Holt | Conf. of Faith | | |
| Havey, Mable (Mrs. Herbert) | Jan. 06, 1957 | 4/24/1916 | W. R. Holt | Conf. of Faith | | |
| Hayse, Billy | 1950 | | W. R. Holt | | TSF Topeka 05/17/1954 | |
| Heathman, G. L. (Mrs.) | Jun. 10, 1962 | | W. R. Holt | TSF Robinson EUB | TSF Lenexa Meth. | |
| Heathman, Gerald L. | Jun. 10, 1962 | | W. R. Holt | Tran. United Presb | Transfer to Lenexa Meth. | |
| Hedge, Lavone Marie (Johnson/Anglen) | Apr. 04, 1944 | 8/28/1934 | W. R. Holt | child watch 1935 | M. R. Hedge/P. Anglen | |
| Hedge, Ramon Hunter | Jul. 08, 1979 | 6/30/1934 | J. R. Hamden | TSF Platte Woods | Death Oct. 23, 1989 | Gasau |
| Heilman, Julie (Mrs. Michael) | Jun. 16, 1968 | 12/17/1943 | R. L. Rayson | Conf. of Faith | Removed Dec. 1978 | Hamden |
| Heilman, Michael G. | Jun. 16, 1968 | 1/12/1944 | R. L. Rayson | Conf. of Faith | Removed Dec. 1978 | Hamden |
| Heinzman, F. (Mrs.) | | | | | Death 11/27/1957 | |
| Henderson, Johnny | Mar. 23, 2008 | | L. Lamberty | Conf. of Faith | | |
| Hepner, Ruth (Miss) | Oct. 06, 1957 | | W. R. Holt | TSF Calvary | TSF London Heights Bap. | |
| Herod, Ruth (Mrs. Henry) | Oct. 13, 1968 | | R. L. Rayson | TSF Christian | Death Dec. 1975 | |
| Hershberger, Brian | Jun. 01, 1986 | | E. Stevenson | Conf. of Faith | | |
| Hershberger, Gina | | | Ira DeSpain | Conf. of Faith | | |
| Hershberger, Jill Sue (Mrs. L.) Gicalone | Mar. 29, 1961 | | W. R. Holt | TSF Gicalone | | |
| Hershberger, Larry | Jun. 03, 1984 | | I. DeSpain | PF | | |
| Hershberger, Scott | Jun. 03, 1984 | | I. DeSpain | PF | | |

32 - MEMBERS

# Record of Members

| Name | Date Received | Birth | By Whom | How | Status | Remarks |
|------|---------------|-------|---------|-----|--------|---------|
| Hicks, Ruth Pike (Kern) | Feb. 19, 1933 | | S. B. Williams | Conf. of Faith | Married Wm. Kern | |
| Hill, Hildred (Elliot) | | | | | | Harnden |
| Hill, Joyce Cordill (Mrs.) | Apr. 14, 1968 | 11/14/1942 | W. R. Holt | | Removed 1978 | |
| Hill, Louela Lee | | | | | | |
| Hill, Mary Virginia (Van Diver) | | | | | | |
| Hill, Mona (Mrs.) | | | | | Removed 4/5/1959 | |
| Hill, Sherman | | | | | TSF Baptist | |
| Hirt, Ethel (Mrs. Henry) | Sept.    1953 | | W. R. Holt | Conf. of Faith | Death Dec. 1976 | |
| Hirt, Henry | Aug. 20, 1978 | | J. R. Harnden | Conf. of Faith | Death Oct. 05, 1981 | DeSpain |
| Hoagland, Estelle (Mrs. Wm.) | | | W. R. Holt | Ltr. Congregational | TSF 1968 Pilgrim Cong. | |
| Hoagland, Janet (Nichols) | | | | | Married Charles Nichols | |
| Hoagland, L. Wm. | | | | | | |
| Hoagland, L. Wm. (Mrs.) | | | | | | |
| Hoagland, Nancy Ann (Fry) | | | | | Married Harold Fry | |
| Hoagland, Roy | | | | | Death Spring 1953 | |
| Hoagland, William | Apr. 09, 1939 | | W. R. Holt | Ltr. Congregational | TSF 1968 Pilgrims Cong. | |
| Hoatson, Viola Mae (Weinshank) | Oct. 13, 1991 | | W. R. Holt | Ltr. | Marr. Charles Weinshank | |
| Hobbs, Jamika Marini | | | Gasau | | | |

33 - MEMBERS

# Record of Members

| Name | Date Received | Birth | By Whom | How | Status | Remarks |
|------|---------------|-------|---------|-----|--------|---------|
| Hobbs, Marjorie Jean | Oct. 13, 1991 | | Gasau | | Death 1997 | Lamberty |
| Hoendorf, Bill | Easter, 1995 | 7/20/1919 | R. Harper | T. Brenner Hgts. | | |
| Hoendorf, Darlene (Johnson/Simmons) | 1935 | 7/27/1921 | S. B. Williams | | Married Hoendorf | |
| Hoffman, Robert | | | | | Removed 4/5/1959 | |
| Holcomb, Barbara (Bryant) | Apr. 09, 1944 | | W. R. Holt | | TSF 10/23/1968 Arv. CO. | |
| Holcomb, Eugene | | | W. R. Holt | | Removed 1967 | |
| Holesapple, Arlene (Mrs.) Smith | Apr. 13, 1941 | | W. R. Holt | Conf. of Faith | Letter granted 4/30/1950 | Lamberty |
| Hollander, Geneva (Mrs. Wm.) | 1950 | 5/4/1924 | W. R. Holt | Conf. of Faith | Death 08/01/2001 | |
| Hollander, Gregory Lee | Apr. 02, 1961 | | W. R. Holt | Conf. of Faith | TSF Nov. 1977 Atchison | Harnden |
| Hollander, Julia Ann (Burnett) | Apr. 14, 1968 | 2/27/1956 | W. R. Holt | Conf. of Faith | TSF Burnett | |
| Hollander, Linda (Mrs. Greg) | Mar. 29, 1970 | | R. L. Rayson | TSF St. Parrit | TSF Nov. 1977 Atchison | Harnden |
| Hollander, Lynn (Neal) | Sept. 27, 1964 | | W. R. Holt | Conf. of Faith | TSF Neal | |
| Hollander, William C. | 1950 | | W. R. Holt | Conf. of Faith | Death Apr.15, 2008 | S. Lee |
| Hollander, William Jr. | Apr. 14, 1968 | 9/13/1957 | W. R. Holt | Conf. of Faith | | |
| Holt, Freda (Mrs. W. R.) Clay | Oct. 06, 1935 | 06/09/1898 | W. R. Holt | Trans. UB | Death Apr. 29, 1970 | |
| Holt, Marilyn (Hataway) | Oct. 06, 1935 | 8/28/1935 | | W. C. of Church | Mar. 2/14/1954 Hataway | |
| Holt, W. R. (Dr.) | Oct. 06, 1935 | 04/09/1899 | W. R. Holt | Trans. UB | Death Feb. 1988 | West |
| Hoover, Dean Lee | May. 15, 1940 | | W. R. Holt | W. C. of Church | Withdrew 1975 | |

34 - MEMBERS

# Record of Members

| Name | Date Received | Birth | By Whom | How | Status | Remarks |
|------|------|------|------|------|------|------|
| Hoover, Edith (Mrs. Wm.) | | | W. R. Holt | Ltr. Meth. Rejoined | TSF 07-1973 Sun.AZ, | |
| Hoover, William | | | W. R. Holt | Ltr. Meth. Rejoined | TSF 07-1973 Sun.AZ, | |
| Hoover, William Carl Jr. | | | W. R. Holt | W. C. of Church | Withdrew 1975 | |
| Hoover, William Carl Jr. (Mrs.) | Apr. 21, 1957 | | W. R. Holt | Conf. of Faith | Withdrew 1975 | |
| Horseman, Louise (Mrs. George) | Jun. 14, 1964 | | W. R. Holt | Ltr. Methodist | Death Jun. 16, 1970 | |
| Hovey, Mabel | Jan. 06, 1957 | | W. R. Holt | Conf. of Faith | Death June 1978 | Harnden |
| Howard, Mary F. | | | | | Death | |
| Hoyt, Patricia Ann (Mrs. Lewis) (Berry) | Apr. 21, 1957 | 8/4/1946 | W. R. Holt | Conf. of Faith | Removed Dec. 1978 | |
| Hrzenak, Karen (Mrs. Dennis ) Wehrer | Apr. 21, 1957 | 10/7/1945 | W. R. Holt | Conf. of Faith | TSF Nov. 27, 1973 Cath. | |
| Hunt, Bryce E. | Apr. 09, 1944 | | W. R. Holt | Conf. of Faith | TSF Bashor 11/02/1968 | |
| Hunt, H. Bryce | Apr. 09, 1944 | | W. R. Holt | Transfer | Death Oct.02, 1958 | |
| Hunt, Martha (Mrs. B.) | Apr. 09, 1944 | | W. R. Holt | Ltr. Lutheran | Death June 1985 | |
| Hunter, Brian | Mar. 26 1967 | 8/5/1953 | W. R. Holt | Conf. of Faith | Withdrew 1980 | Harnden |
| Hunter, Karen (Willis) | Sept. 25, 1966 | 3/24/1951 | W. R. Holt | Ltr. Methodist | Withdrew 1988 Calif. | Gasau |
| Hunter, Robert | Mar. 26, 1967 | 1/5/1957 | W. R. Holt | Conf. of Faith | TSF 11/03/93 Tong. UMC | Gasau |
| Ice, Ann (Mrs. R. E. ) | Apr. 14, 1968 | 1/17/1930 | W. R. Holt | Ltr. Gretna Meth. | Removed Nov. 27, 1973 | |
| Ice, Rebecca | Apr. 14, 1968 | 12/30/1956 | W. R. Holt | Conf. of Faith | Removed Nov. 27, 1973 | |

**Record of Members**

| Name | Date Received | Birth | By Whom | How | Status | Remarks |
|---|---|---|---|---|---|---|
| Ice, Robert | Apr. 14, 1968 | 12/10/1954 | W. R. Holt | Conf. of Faith | Removed Nov. 27, 1973 | |
| Ice, Ronald E. | Apr. 14, 1968 | 1/13/1928 | W. R. Holt | Lt. Gretna Meth. | Removed Nov. 27, 1973 | |
| Irick, Audrey (Mrs. H.) | Apr. 02, 1961 | | W. R. Holt | Conf. of Faith | TSF May 21, 1970 R.Pk. | |
| Irick, Harold (Dr.) | Apr. 02, 1961 | | W. R. Holt | Tran. EUB, Holton | TSF May 21, 1970 R.Pk | |
| Irvin, Robert | May. 13, 1943 | | W. R. Holt | Conf. of Faith | Removed 4/5/1959 | |
| Irvin, William | May. 13, 1943 | | W. R. Holt | Conf. of Faith | Removed 4/5/1959 | |
| Jacobs, Vincent | | | | | Death 2/21/1959 | |
| Javner, Roy | Jun. 22, 2003 | | Lamberty/ Smart | Other Dem. | | |
| Jella, Karen Lee | Apr. 18, 1954 | | W. R. Holt | Conf. of Faith | TSF Chelsea Baptist | |
| Jella, Russell Howard (Mrs.) | Apr. 18, 1954 | | W. R. Holt | | TSF Chelsea Baptist | |
| Jenkins, Albert | Apr. 21, 1957 | | W. R. Holt | Ltr. LDS | TSF Nov. 1971 AZ | |
| Jenkin, Ruth (Mrs. Al) | Apr. 21, 1957 | | W. R. Holt | Ltr. LDS | TSF Nov. 1971 AZ | |
| Johnson, Anker | Feb. 19, 1933 | | S. B. Williams | Ltr. Methodist | Death Oct. 13, 1981 | DeSpain |
| Johnson, Anna L. (Mrs.) | | | | | Death May 1953 | |
| Johnson, Connie (Gallipeau) | Sept. 26, 1965 | | W. R. Holt | | TSF Oct. 31, 1994 | Lamberty |
| Johnson, Darlene (Simmons/Hoendorf) | 1935 | 7/27/1921 | S. B. Williams | | Simmons & Hoendorf | |
| Johnson, Duane | | | | | Ltr. Oct. 25, 1953 | |
| Johnson, George W. | Apr. 13, 1941 | | W. R. Holt | Conf. of Faith | Removed 4/5/1959 | |

36 - MEMBERS

**Record of Members**

| Name | Date Received | Birth | By Whom | How | Status | Remarks |
|------|------|------|------|------|------|------|
| Johnson, George W. (Mrs.) | Apr. 13, 1941 | | | | Removed 4/5/1959 | |
| Johnson, Harold | | | | | Removed 1/15/1958 | |
| Johnson, Ida Mae (Mrs. J. P.) (Boyd) | 1935 | 09/14/1896 | S. B. Williams | | Death Dec. 22, 1989 | Gasau |
| Johnson, J. Frank (Mrs.) (Maret) | | | | | Marriage 11/1957 | |
| Johnson, J. Richard | Jun. 20, 1975 | | J. R. Harnden | Conf. of Faith | TSF Oct. 31, 2002 | Lamberty |
| Johnson, John Perry | 1935 | 02/27/1894 | S. B. Williams | | Death Apr.1975 | |
| Johnson, Lavone Marie (Hedge/Anglen) | 1935 | 8/28/1934 | S. B. Williams | | TSF Hedge & Anglen | |
| Johnson, Lulu (Mrs. Frank) | Apr. 16, 1922 | | F. W. May | Conf. of Faith | Death Apr. 8, 1988 | West |
| Johnson, Margaret (Mrs. A.) | Feb. 19, 1933 | | S. B. Williams | Ltr. Methodist | Death Jan. 24, 1983 | DeSpain |
| Johnson, Marm Marie (Harmon) | Apr. 09, 1939 | | W. R. Holt | Conf. of Faith | TSF Granted 4/30/1950 | |
| Johnson, Ronald | Aug. 15, 2004 | | L. Lamberty | Conf. of Faith | | |
| Johnson, Vivian (Mrs. David) (Seufert) | | 6/4/1923 | W. R. Holt | Conf. of Faith | Death Oct. 30, 2006 | Lamberty |
| Johnson, William | 1950 | | W. R. Holt | | LTR 10/25/1953 | |
| Johnson, William (Mrs.) | 1950 | | W. R. Holt | | LTR 10/25/1953 | |
| Jones, Carol Shaner (Mrs. Lee) | Jun. 13, 1965 | 6/27/1943 | W. R. Holt | Conf. of Faith | Rem. 12/78 W. Mich. | DeSpain |
| Jones, Howard | 1950 | | W. R. Holt | | 01/06/1956 Parkville | |
| Jones, Howard (Mrs.) | 1950 | | W. R. Holt | | 01/06/1956 Parkville | |
| Jones, Ione (Mrs. Tom) | Feb. 22, 1959 | | W. R. Holt | Ltr. Christian | TSF R.Hgts. Jun.7, 1968 | |

**Record of Members**

| Name | Date Received | Birth | By Whom | How | Status | Remarks |
|------|---------------|-------|---------|-----|--------|---------|
| Jones, Ruth (Mrs. James) (Bushnell) | Feb. 22, 1959 | | W. R. Holt | Conf. of Faith | Removed 12/1978 | Harnden |
| Joseph, Bernice (Mrs. Earl) | Apr. 18, 1954 | | W. R. Holt | TSF | Ltr. Sent 12/07/1955 | |
| Joseph, Earl | Apr. 18, 1954 | | W.R. Holt | TSF | Ltr. Sent 12/07/1955 | |
| Karl, Albert Lyle | May.05, 1957 | | W. R. Holt | | Removed 1967 | |
| Karl, Lyla Marie | Apr. 21, 1957 | | W. R. Holt | Conf. of Faith | Removed 1967 | |
| Karl, Mary | May. 05, 1957 | | W. R. Holt | | Removed 1967 | |
| Keeter, James | | | | | Removed by request | |
| Keeter, James (Mrs.) | Apr. 09, 1944 | | W. R. Holt | Conf. of Faith | Removed by request | |
| Keeter, Janice | | | | | Ltr.Mass., NY 4/4/1966 | |
| Kelley, Gene | Nov. 14, 1926 | | S. B. Williams | Conf. of Faith | Removed 4/5/1959 | |
| Kellog, Dorothy | Sept. 25, 1966 | | W. R. Holt | Ltr. O. Park Bap. | Death Aug. 08, 1977 | Harnden |
| Kelly, Beulah | Oct. 29, 1972 | | R. L. Rayson | Ltr. London Hts. | Death May 1978 | Harnden |
| Kelly, E. N. (Mrs.) (Wright) | | | | Conf. of Faith | TSF to Wright | |
| Kelly, E. N. (Neal) | | | | | Ltr. Welborn Com. | |
| Kelly, Jerry | 1954 | | W. R. Holt | Conf. of Faith | Removed 1967 | |
| Kelly, Leannah (Mrs. E. L.) | Apr. 28, 1968 | 1/4/1906 | W. R. Holt | Conf. of Faith | Death May 13, 1994 | Harper |
| Kelly, Lenora (Mrs.) | | | | | Death May 21,1956 | |
| Kelly, Norma Jean | 1954 | | W. R. Holt | Conf. of Faith | Removed 1967 | |

**Record of Members**

| Name | Date Received | Birth | By Whom | How | Status | Remarks |
|---|---|---|---|---|---|---|
| Kensinger, Alberta (Bass) | May. 26, 1988 | | R. West | Tsf. Stephens Mem | Death Jan. 18, 1994 | Gasau |
| Kensinger, Harold L. | | 6/6/1914 | W. R. Holt | Ltr. Baptist | Death 08/01/2005 | Lamberty |
| Kensinger, Helen (Grubb) | | | W. R. Holt | Conf. of Faith | Mar. Norman Grubb | |
| Kensinger, J. L. (Mrs.) | Nov. 07, 1965 | | W. R. Holt | Conf. of Faith | Death -June 1975 | |
| Kensinger, John L. | Nov. 07,1965 | | W. R. Holt | Conf. of Faith | Death Nov. 20, 1980 | DeSpain |
| Kern, Mildred (Kline) | Apr. 21, 1957 | | W. R. Holt | Conf. of Faith | | |
| Kern, Ruth Mae (Mrs.) | Feb. 19, 1933 | | S. B. Williams | Conf. of Faith | Withdrew 1997 | Lamberty |
| Kern, Will | Feb. 05, 1961 | | W. R. Holt | Ltr. B.Springs, KS | Death | |
| Kerr, Kevin | Apr. 14, 1968 | 4/19/1958 | W. R. Holt | Conf. of Faith | | |
| Kesner, Mae Adams | Mar. 28, 1937 | | W. R. Holt | Conf. of Faith | Removed 1967 | |
| Kile, Henry | Jun. 03, 1979 | | J. R. Harnden | PF | TSF 06/21/83 Wash. Iowa | DeSpain |
| Kile, Kerry | Jun. 03, 1979 | | J. R. Harnden | PF | Removed Nov. 09, 1992 | Gasau |
| Kile, Patsy | Jun. 03, 1979 | | J. R. Harnden | TSF Oskaloosa | TSF 7/22/91 Trinity UMC | Gasau |
| Kimball, William | | | | | Removed 04/05/1959 | |
| King, Eloise Ann | Apr. 09, 1944 | | W. R. Holt | Conf. of Faith | Removed 02/18/1964 | |
| King, James L. | Apr. 07, 1963 | 8/3/1929 | W. R. Holt | Conf. of Faith | Removed1967 | |
| King, James Lee | Apr. 07, 1963 | 2/22/1955 | W. R. Holt | Conf. of Faith | Removed 1967 | |
| King, Lynetta M. | Apr. 07, 1963 | 1/18/1950 | W. R. Holt | Conf. of Faith | Removed 1967 | |

**Record of Members**

| Name | Date Received | Birth | By Whom | How | Status | Remarks |
|------|--------------|-------|---------|-----|--------|---------|
| King, Nellie (Mrs.) | Apr. 09, 1944 | | W. R. Holt | Ltr. | Death Feb. 14, 1970 | |
| King, Wanda Lee (Mrs. J. L.) | Apr. 07, 1963 | 4/9/1933 | W. R. Holt | Conf. of Faith | Removed 1967 | |
| King, Victor H. (Mrs.) | Apr. 09, 1944 | | W. R. Holt | Ltr. | Death 2/14/1970 | |
| Kinsey, Gladys | Oct. 29, 1972 | | R. L. Rayson | Ltr. London Hts. | TSF Trinity Dec. 1978 | Harnden |
| Klock, Judith (Pearson) | Mar. 06, 1960 | | W. R. Holt | TSF London Hts. | Transfer to Pearson | |
| Knisley, C. V. (Mrs.) | | | | | Removed 1967 | |
| Knisley, Wilma (Mrs.) (Grove/Thrall) | | | | | Remarried Wilma Grove | |
| Kramer, Alice ( Mrs. R. L.) | Apr. 02, 1961 | | W. R. Holt | TSF Oliver EUB | Death Aug. 09, 1992 | Gasau |
| Kramer, Roy L. | Apr. 02, 1961 | | W. R Holt | TSF Oliver EUB | Death May 29, 1982 | DeSpain |
| Kresin, Louis | Jul. 18, 1941 | | W. R. Holt | Conf. of Faith | Death Oct. 31, 1980 | DeSpain |
| Kresin, Paula (Lahr) | Sept. 27, 1964 | | W. R. Holt | Conf. of Faith | Married Lahr | |
| Kresin, Pauline (Mrs. L.) (Norgren) | | | W. R. Holt | Conf. of Faith | Death Mar. 30, 2007 MO. | Lamberty |
| Kresin, Richard | Mar. 26, 1960 | | W. R. Holt | Conf. of Faith | Removed Nov. 07/1999 | Lamberty |
| Kroh, Kenneth | | | | | Removed 4/5/1959 | |
| Krone, Wayne (Mrs.) (Dorothy Larsen) | | | | | TSF 05.07/1954 Wic., KS | |
| Krueger, Barbara (Mrs. D.) (Gerber) | 1952 | | W. R. Holt | Conf. of Faith | TSF Mar. 31, 1982 MO. | DeSpain |
| Krueger, Donald | Apr. 06, 1958 | 5/20/1937 | W. R. Holt | Herrington, KS | TSF Death Aug. 07, 2008 | DeSpain |
| Krueger, Gladys (Mrs.) | Apr. 22, 1973 | | R. L. Rayson | Ltr. Trinity UM | Death July 26, 1990 | Gasau |

40 - MEMBERS

**Record of Members**

| Name | Date Received | Birth | By Whom | How | Status | Remarks |
|---|---|---|---|---|---|---|
| Krueger, John Frederick | May. 14, 1978 | | J. R. Harnden | Conf. of Faith | Removed Nov. 07, 1999 | Lamberty |
| Krueger, LaVeta | Apr. 02, 1961 | | W. R. Holt | Conf. of Faith | TSF Catholic 1963 | |
| Krummel, Carolyn (Masters/Day) | Sept. 07, 1986 | | R. West | | TSF 11/10/02 T. KS | Lamberty |
| Krummel, Ethel (Mrs. Richard) | | | W. R. Holt | Ltr. Methodist | Death Nov. 14, 1981 | DeSpain |
| Krummel, Richard | | | W. R. Holt | Ltr. Methodist | Death July 05, 1986 | West |
| Kuhns, Don | | | | | Removed 1959 | |
| Kuhns, Edgar (Mr.) | | | | | Removed 1959 | |
| Kuhns, Edgar (Mrs.) | | | | | Removed 1959 | |
| Kuhns, Philip | Apr. 09, 1944 | | W. R. Holt | Conf. of Faith | Removed 1959 | |
| La Hue, Betty D. (Mrs. W. H.) | Jun. 14, 1959 | | W. R. Holt | Conf. of Faith | TSF Chelsea Apr. 1972 | |
| La Hue, Richard William | Jun. 14, 1959 | 12/19/1949 | W. R. Holt | Conf. of Faith | Withdrew 1976 | |
| La Hue, Victor Dean | May. 12, 1968 | 3/8/1954 | W. R. Holt | Conf. of Faith | TSF Chelsea Apr. 1972 | |
| La Hue, William Henry | Jun. 14, 1959 | 2/8/1924 | W. R. Holt | Conf. of Faith | TSF Chelsea Apr. 1972 | |
| Lacy, Craig, C. | Jun. 15, 1926 | | S. B. Williams | Conf. of Faith | Death Jan. 1977 | |
| Lacy, Craig C. (Mrs.) | Jun. 15, 1926 | | S. B. Williams | Conf. of Faith | Death Aug. 19, 1966 | |
| Lacy, Florence (Mrs. Herschell) | Nov. 28, 1926 | | S. B. Williams | Ltr. | Death Oct. 18, 1971 | |
| Lacy, Harry W. | Apr. 17, 1927 | | S. B. Williams | Conf. of Faith | Death Jun.22, 1991 | Gasau |
| Lacy, Norma Jean (Keeter) | | | | | M. Aug. 12, 1950 Keeter | |

41 - MEMBERS

**Record of Members**

| Name | Date Received | Birth | By Whom | How | Status | Remarks |
|---|---|---|---|---|---|---|
| Lacy, R. Herschell | Nov. 21, 1926 | | S. B. Williams | Conf. of Faith | Death Dec.11, 1967 | |
| Lacy, Viola (Mrs. Harry W. ) | Oct. 25, 1953 | | W. R. Holt | Conf. of Faith | Death May.06, 1967 | |
| Lacy, William | Jun.15, 1926 | | S. B. Williams | Conf. of Faith | Withdrawn Calif. Church | |
| Lacy, William (Mrs.) | | | | | Withdrawn Calif. Church | |
| Lahr, Paula (Kresin, Mrs.) (Norgren) | Sept. 27, 1964 | | W. R. Holt | Conf. of Faith | (See Norgren) | |
| Laidlaw, Ellen (Mrs. J. T. Jr.) | | | | | Removed 1967 | |
| Lamberty, Ligeia (M. H.) | 1997 | | L. Lamberty | TSF Houston, Tx | Death July 09, 2007 | Lamberty |
| Lane, Edith (Pike) | Jan. 11, 1925 | | S. B. Williams | Conf. of Faith | Dropped joined another | |
| Lane , Edith (Mrs.) | Nov. 03, 1957 | | W. R. Holt | Ltr. Baptist | Withdrew 11/13/1986 | West |
| Lane, Ross | Jun. 10, 1962 | | W. R. Holt | Conf. of Faith | Removed Nov. 27, 1973 | |
| Larsen, Dorothy Dorothy | | | | | Married Wayne Krone | |
| Larsen, Jack | | | | | Ltr. | |
| Larsen, Walter (Mrs.) | Apr. 25, 193 | | W. R. Holt | Conf. of Faith | TSF 4/4/1954 Row. Park | |
| Larson, Maude (Mrs.) | Feb. 27, 1955 | | W. R. Holt | Ltr. EU & Reformed | Death May 01, 1984 | DeSpain |
| Laster, Esther (Mrs.) | Mar. 29, 1964 | | W. R. Holt | Conf. of Faith | Death | |
| Laster, Ivory | Jun. 22, 2003 | | Lamberty/ Smart | Conf. of Faith | | |
| Laws, Margaret (Mrs.) (McDaniel) | 1950 | | W. R. Holt | Conf. of Faith | Removed Dec. 1978 | Hamden |
| Lea, Bernard L. | Feb. 13, 1955 | | W. R. Holt | Conf. of Faith | Death 09/08/1983 | DeSpain |

42 - MEMBERS

**Record of Members**

| Name | Date Received | Birth | By Whom | How | Status | Remarks |
|---|---|---|---|---|---|---|
| Lea, Beth (Mrs. Robert) | Mar. 27, 1955 | | W. R. Holt | Ltr. | Removed Nov. 27, 1973 | |
| Lea, Wanda (Crockett) | Jun. 10, 1962 | | W. R. Holt | Conf. of Faith | | |
| Lea, Wanette (Mrs. B. L.) | 1952 | | W. R. Holt | Conf. of Faith | Death Jun. 14, 2001 | Lamberty |
| Leatherwood, Beverly (Mrs. Woodland) | Apr. 17, 1938 | | W. R. Holt | Conf. of Faith | Removed 4/5/1959 | |
| LeClaire, Karen (Mrs. Ralph) (Gicalone) | | | | | Removed 1967 | |
| Ledbetter, Rose (Lamberty) | May. 29, 2005 | | L. Lamberty | Conf. of Faith | L. Lamberty 11/29/2008 | |
| Lee, Franco T. | Dec. 14, 1980 | | I. DeSpain | TSF-Hong Kong | Removed Nov. 21, 1988 | Gasau |
| Lee, Kathy | Dec. 14, 1980 | | I. DeSpain | OD Hong Kong | Removed 11/21/1988 | Gasau |
| Leonard, Harry | Mar. 29, 1959 | 6/11/1947 | W. R. Holt | Conf. of Faith | Removed Oct. 1967 | |
| Leonard, William Paul | Oct. 02, 1955 | | W. R. Holt | Conf. of Faith | Ltr. To 1st Presbyterian | |
| Lero, Carolyn (Mrs. Henry) (Hardsaw) | | | | | Ltr. was Carolyn Hardsaw | |
| Lester, Esther (Mrs.) | Mar. 29, 1964 | | W. R. Holt | Conf. of Faith | Removed Oct. 1967 | |
| Libich, Donna Jean (Morris) | | | | | | |
| Lincoln, John | Apr. 12, 1959 | 6/3/1903 | W. R. Holt | Ltr. | Removed Dec. 1978 | Hamden |
| Lincoln, Lena (Mrs. J) | Apr. 12, 1959 | 8/8/1903 | W. R. Holt | Conf. of Faith | Removed Dec. 1978 | Hamden |
| Liu, Anthony | Apr. 14, 1968 | 9/3/1956 | W. R. Holt | Conf. of Faith | Withdrew Oct. 31, 1994 | Harper |
| Liu, Olive Christine (Perkins) | May. 08, 1966 | 4/1/1955 | W. R. Holt | Conf. of Faith | TSF CA 1977 | Hamden |
| Lloyd, Betty (Mrs. John ) | Oct. 01, 1972 | | R. L. Rayson | TSF London Hgts. | | |

43 - MEMBERS

**Record of Members**

| Name | Date Received | Birth | By Whom | How | Status | Remarks |
|---|---|---|---|---|---|---|
| Lloyd, John | Oct. 01, 1972 | | R. L. Rayson | TSF London Hgts. | Death Apr. 20, 1985 | Stevenson |
| Lloyd, Linda | Oct. 01, 1972 | | R. L. Rayson | TSF London Hgts. | Death June 23, 1973 | |
| Locke, Gail (Mrs. Robert) (Sharp) | | | | | Removed 1967 | |
| Lucas, Amos | Sept. 26, 1937 | | W. R. Holt | Ltr. | Ltr. of Trans. 8/11/1953 | |
| Lucas, Amos (Mrs.) | Sept. 26, 1937 | | W. R. Holt | Ltr. | Ltr. of Trans. 8/11/1953 | |
| Lucas, Frederick | May. 08, 1949 | | W. R. Holt | Ltr. | Ltr. of Trans. 8/11/1953 | |
| Lucas, George | Sept. 26, 1937 | | W. R. Holt | TSF | TSF4/5/1959 Methodist | |
| Lucas, George (Mrs.) | Abt. 1939 | | W. R. Holt | | TSF4/5/1959 Methodist | |
| Lucas, J. Norris | Apr. 20, 1924 | | S. B. Williams | | Death Feb. 03, 1956 | |
| Lucas, J. Norris (Mrs.) | | | | | Death Jan. 15, 1958 | |
| Lucas, Minor L. | | | | | Ltr. of Trans. 8/11/1953 | |
| Lucas, Rhoda Lee (Mrs. Noble) | | | | | Married Mrs. Elton Noble | |
| Maddox, Evelyn | Dec. 14, 1997 | | L. Lamberty | CT | TSF Unitarian, MO 2006 | Lamberty |
| Maertz, Carl F. | | | | | Removed 1967 Tran. Bap. | |
| Maertz, Carl F. (Mrs.) | Apr. 09, 1944 | | W. R. Holt | Trans. | Removed 1967 Tran. Bap. | |
| Main, L. G. | Feb. 09, 1930 | | S. B. Williams | Conf. of Faith | Died Feb. 07, 1957 | |
| Main, L. G. (Mrs.) | Feb. 09, 1930 | | S. B. Williams | Conf. of Faith | Died July 1950 | |
| Main, Luster G. Jr. | Feb. 09, 1930 | | S. B. Williams | Conf. of Faith | TSF joined church 1953 | |

44 - MEMBERS

# Record of Members

| Name | Date Received | Birth | By Whom | How | Status | Remarks |
|---|---|---|---|---|---|---|
| Malott, Margaret (Mrs.) | | | | | Dropped Apr. 30, 1950 | |
| Malott, Merle Margaret | | | | | Dropped Apr. 30, 1950 | |
| Malott, Rhonda Edith | | | | | Dropped Apr. 30, 1950 | |
| Malott, Ronnie Elmer | | | | | Dropped Apr. 30, 1950 | |
| Mann, Linda Lorene | Apr. 12, 1959 | 5/19/1944 | W. R. Holt | Ltr. Transfer | Transfer to Stony Point | |
| Mann, Oscar W. | Apr. 12, 1959 | 1/4/1910 | W. R. Holt | Ltr. Transfer | Transfer to Stony Point | |
| Mann, Virginia A. (Mrs. O. W.) | Apr. 12, 1959 | 6/12/1911 | W. R. Holt | Ltr. Transfer | Transfer to Stony Point | |
| Mann, William | | | | | Ltr. Apr. 19, 1953 | |
| Maret, J. E. (Mrs.) (Johnson) | Apr. 16, 1922 | | | Ltr. | Married Frank Johnson | |
| Maret, Nadine | Apr. 01, 1923 | | F. W. May | Associate | Death 2008 | |
| Mark, Delores Rae (Barrett/Harmon) | Apr. 18, 1954 | | W. R. Holt | Conf. of Faith | TSF to Harmon | |
| Mark, Kevin E. | Apr. 14, 1968 | 6/1/1957 | W. R. Holt | Conf. of Faith | TSF 12/06/1987 Stony Pt. | R. West |
| Mark, Keith LaVerne | Apr. 02, 1972 | | R. L. Rayson | Conf. of Faith | TSF 4/10/84 R. Catholic | DeSpain |
| Mark, Rae (Hannon) | | | | | | |
| Marlow, Ila Mae (Straub) | | | | | Ltr. London Hts. | |
| Marsh, Mildred (Mrs.) | | | | | Death | |
| Marshall, Joanne (Clevenger) | | | | Conf. of Faith | TSF to Marshall | |
| Massey, Briton | Feb. 25, 2006 | | L. Lamberty | | | |

45 - MEMBERS

# Record of Members

| Name | Date Received | Birth | By Whom | How | Status | Remarks |
|---|---|---|---|---|---|---|
| Masters, Carolyn (Krummell/Day) | Sept. 09, 1986 | | R. West | Prince of Peace | TSF 11/11/2002 Tong. K | Lamberty |
| Masters, Rexine | | | R. West | CT Stephen Mem. | Death Sept. 25, 2004 | Lamberty |
| Mathews, Christine (Gentry) | | | | | Married to Gentry | |
| Mathews, Harold R. (Gentry) | | | | | Removed 4/5/1959 | |
| Mathews, Hulda R. (Mrs. Harold) | | | | | Death 1965 | |
| Matthew , Joy | Sept. 11, 1983 | | I. DeSpain | PF | Death Oct. 25, 2006 | Lamberty |
| Mattney , Carolyn (Mrs.) (Endsley) | Jan. 22, 1964 | | | TSF. From Endsley | Removed Oct. 1967 | |
| Mayberry , Joyce (Mrs. Don) (Sackman) | Mar. 29, 1959 | 4/24/1942 | W. R. Holt | Conf. of Faith | TSF . 3/26/80 Bashor, KS | Harnden |
| Mayberry , Margaret Ann (Berve) | Jul. 22, 1962 | | W. R. Holt | Conf. of Faith | TSF. to Berve | |
| Mayswinkle, Dale | Feb. 17, 1924 | | S. B. Williams | Ltr. | TSF Jan.20, 1963 Calif | |
| Mayswinkle, Dale (Mrs.) | Feb. 17, 1924 | | S. B. Williams | Ltr. | TSFJan. 20, 1963 Calif. | |
| Mayswinkle, Dale Jr. | Feb. 09, 1930 | | S. B. Williams | Conf. of Faith | TSF Jan.20, 1963 Calif | |
| McAllister, Barbara (Mrs. John) | Nov. 03, 1963 | | W. R. Holt | Ltr Lee's Summit | TSF Wy. UM Oct. 1975 | |
| McAllister, John Kevin | Apr. 11, 1971 | 12/10/1958 | R. L. Rayson | Conf. of Faith | TSF WY UM 1976 | |
| McAllister, Shawn | Apr. 22, 1973 | 10/23/1961 | R. L. Rayson | Conf. of Faith | TSF Wy. UM 1976 | |
| McBroom, Horace | | | | Ltr. | | |
| McBroom, Horace (Mrs.) | | | | Ltr. | | |
| McBroom, Mabel (Mrs. S. H.) | | | S. B. Williams | Ltr. | Death June 1969 | |

46 - MEMBERS

**Record of Members**

| Name | Date Received | Birth | By Whom | How | Status | Remarks |
|---|---|---|---|---|---|---|
| McBroom, Sam H. | | | S. B. Williams | Ltr. | Death July 1979 | Harnden |
| McCarty, Catherine (Mrs. R. ) | Dec. 06, 1953 | | W. R. Holt | Ltr. Baptist | | Stevenson |
| McCarty, Robert | Jan. 04, 1970 | | R. L. Rayson | Ltr. Grace Lutheran | Death June 1984 | |
| McCarty, Roberta (Lopez) | Jan. 04, 1970 | | R. L. Rayson | Ltr. Grace Lutheran | Withdrew 1996 | Lamberty |
| McClatchey, Ellen (Mrs.) | Aug.27, 1922 | | | Conf. of Faith | Death Oct. 05, 1964 | |
| McClean, Bertha (Mrs. Edm.) (Charles) | 1936 | | W. R. Holt | TSF From Charles | | |
| McClean, Edmond | Apr. 02, 1972 | | R. L. Rayson | Ltr. Wesley UM | Death Dec. 1978 | Harnden |
| McClure, Sue | Oct. 05, 1975 | | J. R. Harnden | CT | TSF10/18/88 Olathe, Ks | Gasau |
| McCoy, Freda | Sept. 27, 1964 | | W. R. Holt | Conf. of Faith | Rcc Dec. 1978 | Harnden |
| McCutcheon, Gertie (Mrs. Russell) | Oct. 01, 1972 | | R. L. Rayson | TSF London Hgts. | TSF Grandview 1974 | |
| McCutcheon, Russell | Oct. 01, 1972 | | R. L. Rayson | TSF London Hgts | TSF Grandview Jan. 1975 | |
| McDaniels, Barbara (Margaret) (Laws) | 1950 | | W. R. Holt | | TSF to Laws. | |
| McDaniels , Bet Bernice (Mrs.) | 1950 | | W. R. Holt | Ltr. Methodist | Death Sept. 1972 | |
| McDaniels, Josephine Elizabeth | Apr. 17, 1966 | 3/27/1938 | W. R. Holt | Conf. of Faith | TSF Trinity Jun. 1975 | |
| McDaniels, Karen Elizabeth | Apr. 18, 1971 | 12/16/1961 | R. L. Rayson | Conf. of Faith | TSF Trinity Jan. 1975 | |
| McDaniels, Kenneth Eugene Jr. | Apr. 17, 1966 | 10/16/1955 | W. R. Holt | Conf. of Faith | TSF Trinity Jun. 1975 | |
| McDaniels, Kenneth Eugene Sr. | 1950 | | W. R. Holt | Conf. of Faith | TSF Trinity Jun. 1975 | |
| McDaniels, Kevin LeRoy | Apr. 17, 1966 | 5/10.1957 | W. R. Holt | Conf. of Faith | TSF Trinity Jun. 1975 | |

47 - MEMBERS

## Record of Members

| Name | Date Received | Birth | By Whom | How | Status | Remarks |
|---|---|---|---|---|---|---|
| McDaniels, Orville (Mrs.) | 1950 | | W. R. Holt | | | |
| McGee, LaResa Nicole | May. 01, 1994 | | M. Gasau | Conf. of Faith | Removed Nov. 07, 1999 | Lamberty |
| McGee, Sacoll Dawauii | May. 01, 1994 | | M. Gasau | Conf. of Faith | Removed Nov. 07, 1999 | Lamberty |
| McGuire, David R. | | | | | Death Feb. 25, 1996 | |
| McGuire, Mary Lee (Mrs. David) (Ellis) | | | | | TSF To Methodist 1962 | |
| McGuire, Sheryl Lynn | Mar. 29, 1959 | 1/31/1949 | W. R. Holt | Conf. of Faith | TSF To Methodist 1962 | |
| McHenry, Larry | Mar. 26, 1967 | 7/5/1951 | W. R. Holt | Conf. of Faith | Withdrew to Ga. | Gasau |
| McKee, Frank | Apr. 17, 1927 | | S. B. Williams | Conf. of Faith | Death Mar. 12, 1981 | DeSpain |
| McKenzie, Carol (Bailey) (Reid) | Mar. 26, 1967 | | W. R. Holt | Cert. of Transfer | TSF Baptist 7/21/1987 | West |
| McKenzie, Vickie (Cunningham) | | | | | | |
| McMaken, Della Mae | Dec. 11, 1960 | 11/1/1916 | W. R. Holt | Ltr. Baptist | TSF 3/21/88 Bonner Sgs. | West |
| McMaken, Janet Ann (Edward)(Dudley) | Dec. 11, 1960 | 11/13/1944 | W. R. Holt | Conf. of Faith | John Edward Dudley | |
| McNerney, Frank J. | | | | | Removed St. Pauls. | |
| McNerney, Frank (Mrs.) | | | | | Removed St. Pauls. | |
| Merriwether, Martha | Jun. 03, 1979 | | J. R. Harnden | TSF Western H. UP | Death Aug. 11, 2003 | Lamberty |
| Miller, John (Mrs.) | Dec. 04, 1960 | | W. R. Holt | Ltr. | TSF Wyandotte 1970 | |
| Miller, Louise (Charles) | Apr. 09, 1939 | | W. R. Holt | Conf. of Faith | TSF Presby. In 1967 | |
| Miller, John | Dec. 04, 1960 | | W. R. Holt | Ltr. | TSF Wyandotte 1970 | |

48 - MEMBERS

**Record of Members**

| Name | Date Received | Birth | By Whom | How | Status | Remarks |
|------|--------------|-------|---------|-----|--------|---------|
| Minckely, O. W. | | | | | TSF Stephens 1/27/1961 | |
| Minckely, O. W. (Mrs.) | | | | | TSF Stephens 1/27/1961 | |
| Minteer, Glen | Mar. 28, 1937 | | W. R. Holt | Conf. of Faith | Removed 4/5/1959 | |
| Moll, Marienne | Oct. 18, 1960 | | W. R. Holt | TSF Hutchinson | TSF to Minn. 11/27/1973 | |
| Moll, Oletha (Mrs. R. A.) | Dec. 18, 1960 | | W. R. Holt | Tran. Hutchinson | TSF Minn. 1/26/1968 | |
| Moll, Roscoe A. | Dec. 18, 1960 | | W. R. Holt | TSF Hutchinson | TSF Minn.1/26/1968 | |
| Moody, Rosemary (Mrs. H.) (Barfield) | Apr. 01, 1956 | | W. R. Holt | Conf. of Faith | TSF 1989 | Gasau |
| Moore, Betty (Mrs.) (Dunivan) | Apr. 05, 1942 | | W. R. Holt | Conf. of Faith | Married Dunivan | |
| Moore, Hugh (Mrs.) (Sharon Nealy) | | | | | Removed without cert. | |
| Moore, John T. | Apr. 09, 1963 | 04/20/1889 | W. R. Holt | Conf. of Faith | Death Apr. 29, 1966 | |
| Moore, Nora (Mrs.) | Dec. 15, 1963 | | W. R. Holt | TSF Grandview | Death Mar. 14, 1981 | DeSpain |
| Moore, W. R. (Mrs.) | Mar. 27, 1932 | | S. B. Williams | Ltr. | Removed without cert. Oct. | |
| Morning, Dorothy | | | | | Removed 1/13/1958 | |
| Morning, James | | | | | Removed 1/13/1958 | |
| Morning, James (Mrs.) | | | | | Removed 1/13/1958 | |
| Morning, Margaret | | | | | Removed 1/13/1958 | |
| Morris, Donna Jean | Apr. 25, 1954 | | W. R. Holt | Transfer | | |
| Morris, Marie (Mrs.) | Apr. 25, 1954 | | W. R. Holt | Ltr. Baptist | Removed Dec. 1978 | Harnden |

# Record of Members

| Name | Date Received | Birth | By Whom | How | Status | Remarks |
|------|---------------|-------|---------|-----|--------|---------|
| Morris, Terry | Apr. 25, 1954 | | W. R. Holt | Conf. of Faith | Removed 1967 | |
| Morrison, Linda Ruth (Bassett) | Apr. 02, 1972 | | R. L. Rayson | Conf. of Faith | TSF May 1980 Leawood | Harnden |
| Morrison, Ruth (Mrs. Wm.) (Bassett) | 1950 | | W. R. Holt | Conf. of Faith | TSF May 1980 Leawood | Harnden |
| Morrison, William | | | W. R. Holt | Conf. of Faith | TSF May 1980 Leawood | Harnden |
| Murphy, Marion (Alexander) | | | | | Married Alexander | |
| Myers, Ethel | | | S. B. Williams | Conf. of Faith | Death Dec. 17, 2005 | |
| Myers, Frances (Mrs. J. T.) | Jan. 15, 1956 | | W. R. Holt | Ltr. | Removed Nov. 27, 1973 | |
| Myers, Henry | Aug. 27, 1922 | | | Conf. of Faith | Death Aug. 1961 | |
| Myers, Henry (Mrs.) | Apr. 16, 1922 | | | Conf. of Faith | | |
| Myers, John Thomas | Nov. 27, 1927 | | S. B. Williams | Conf. of Faith | Removed Nov. 27, 1973 | |
| Myers, Maude (Mrs.) | Apr. 16, 1922 | | F. W. May | Conf. of Faith | Death | |
| Myers, William H. | | | | | | |
| Myers, William H. (Mrs.) | | | | | | |
| Neal, Daniel | 1997 | | L. B. Lamberty | Altersg. 01/15/1998 | | |
| Neal, Lynn (Hollander) (Ellington) | Sept. 27, 1964 | | W. R. Holt | TSF Hollender | | |
| Neal, Niccole | 1997 | | L. B. Lamberty | TSF Altersgate | | |
| Neaves, Candy | Sept. 12, 1976 | | J. R. Harnden | TSF | TSF TX. Jun. 1977 | Harnden |
| Neaves, David | Sept. 12, 1976 | | J. R. Harnden | TSF | TSF TX. Jun. 1977 | Harnden |

50 - MEMBERS

# Record of Members

| Name | Date Received | Birth | By Whom | How | Status | Remarks |
|---|---|---|---|---|---|---|
| Nedrud, Donald George | Apr. 14, 1968 | 2/7/1929 | W. R. Holt | Ltr. Lutheran | Jul. 23, 1971 Irving, TX | |
| Nedrud, Donna Marie | Apr. 14, 1968 | 2/9/1957 | W. R. Holt | Conf. of Faith | Jul. 23, 1971 Irving, TX | |
| Nedrud, Jamie | Apr. 14, 1968 | 4/4/1953 | W. R. Holt | Conf. of Faith | Jul. 23, 1971 Irving, TX | |
| Nedrud, Janice | Mar. 26, 1967 | 4/4/1953 | W. R. Holt | Conf. of Faith | | |
| Nedrud, Mary Dale (Mrs. D. G.) | Apr. 14, 1968 | 6/20/1933 | W. R. Holt | Conf. of Faith | Jul. 23, 1971 Irving, TX | |
| Nedrud, Michael | Apr. 14, 1968 | 7/28/1954 | W. R. Holt | Conf. of Faith | Jul. 23, 1971 Irving, TX | |
| Nedrud, Michael | Mar. 26, 1967 | 7/28/1954 | W. R. Holt | Conf. of Faith | | |
| Neely, Sharon (Moore) | | | | | Married Hugh Moore | |
| Neely, Theodore | | | | | TSF 1st Baptist 1956 | |
| Neely, Theodore (Mrs.) | | | | | TSF 1st Baptist 1956 | |
| Nelson, Darryl | Jan. 05, 1964 | | W. R. Holt | Conf. of Faith | Removed 11/20/1989 | Gasau |
| Nelson, David Lee | Apr. 18, 1954 | | W. R. Holt | Conf. of Faith | Removed 11/20/1989 | Gasau |
| Nelson, David Lee (Mrs.) | Apr. 18, 1954 | | W. R. Holt | Lt London H. Bapt. | Ltr. 04/21/1960 | |
| Nelson, David Roland | Apr. 18, 1954 | | W. R. Holt | Conf. of Faith | Removed 11/20/1989 | |
| Nelson, Dennis | | | W. R. Holt | Conf. of Faith | | |
| Nelson, Dorothy | | | | | Ltr Olive Memorial | |
| Nelson, J. R. | Sept. 1953 | | W. R. Holt | Ltrs. | Death May 1965 | |
| Nelson, Jack | May.13, 1943 | | W. R. Holt | Conf. of Faith | Removed 4/05/1959 | |

51 - MEMBERS

## Record of Members

| Name | Date Received | Birth | By Whom | How | Status | Remarks |
|------|---------------|-------|---------|-----|--------|---------|
| Nelson, Jean (Mrs. J. R.) (Otney) | Sept. 25, 1966 | | W. R. Holt | Ltr. Methodist | | |
| Nelson, John Roland | Nov. 19, 1953 | | W. R. Holt | Ltr. Methodist | Death July 19, 1971 | |
| Nelson, Marion (Mrs. Jack) | Apr. 18, 1954 | | W. R. Holt | Conf. of Faith | Removed Apr. 5, 1959 | |
| Neves, Albert L. (Mrs.) | | | | | TSF Jan. 10, 1954 | |
| Neves, Albert L. (Roy) | | | | | Died Oct. 17, 1949 | |
| Neves, Charles Edwin | | | | | | |
| Newbanks, C. W. | Nov. 1972 | | R. L. Rayson | TSF Oswego UM | TSF Mar. 11, 1985 | Stevenson |
| Newbanks, Joyce Dee (Cunningham) | Mar. 29, 1959 | 12/25/1949 | W. R. Holt | From "C" List | TSF Mar. 11, 1985 | Stevenson |
| Nichelson, Michael | Sept. 06, 1959 | | W. R. Holt | Conf. of Faith | Removed 1967 | |
| Nichols, Charles (Dr.) | Charter Mem. | | Dean Reese | Ltr. | Death June 30, 1952 | |
| Nichols, Charles (Mrs.) | 1926 | | S. B. Williams | Ltr. | | |
| Nichols, Charles (Mrs.) (Hoagland) | | | | | TSF Pilgrim Cong. 1963 | |
| Nichols, Edna (Miss) | Charter Mem. | | Dean Reese | Ltr. | Death 1961 | |
| Nichols, Jenn (Mrs.) | 1926 | | S. B. Williams | Ltr. Methodist | Death 1979 | Harnden |
| Nicklin, John Riley | Jun. 05, 1960 | 4/25/1930 | W. R. Holt | TSF 1st So. Bap. | Removed 1967 | |
| Noah, Clay | | | | | Removed Baptist | |
| Noah, Virgil (Mrs.) | | | | | Removed Baptist | |
| Noble, Rhoda (Mrs. Elton B. ) | | | | Rhoda Lucas | Ltr. Oct. 18, 1953 | |

**Record of Members**

| Name | Date Received | Birth | By Whom | How | Status | Remarks |
|------|---------------|-------|---------|-----|--------|---------|
| Noel, Illa | | | | | Removed 1954 | |
| Noel, Jennice | | | | | Removed 1954 | |
| Noel, Mary | Sept. 24, 1933 | | S. B. Williams | Ltr. | Removed 1954 | |
| Noel, Richard | | | | | Removed 1954 | |
| Noltensmeyer, Betty Lou (Taylor) | | | | TSF Taylor | TSF Parsons Apr. 1975 | |
| Norgren, Pauline (Krisin) | | | | | | |
| Notson, Mary Jane (Mrs.) | Mar. 31, 1963 | 11/18/1910 | W. R. Holt | Conf. of Faith | Withdrew 1996 | Lamberty |
| Novak, Anthony Jr. (Tony) | Apr. 18, 1954 | | W. R. Holt | Conf. of Faith | Jun. 1975 R. Cath. Church | |
| Novak, Robin | Apr. 18, 1954 | | W. R. Holt | Conf. of Faith | Catholic Church 1962 | |
| Novak, Tony (Mrs.) (Zimmer) | Dec. 06, 1953 | | W. R. Holt | Conf. of Faith | Transfer to Zimmer | |
| Obee, Alfred Charles | 1950 | | W. R. Holt | Conf. of Faith | Death Oct. 1998 | Lamberty |
| Obee, Richard | Sept. 27, 1964 | | W. R. Holt | Conf. of Faith | TSF TX. Apr. 1975 | |
| Obee, Robert William | Jun. 14, 1964 | 11/2/1952 | W. R. Holt | Conf. of Faith | T.01/17/1988 Kinsley,KS | Gasau |
| Obee, Ronald Lee | Apr. 10, 1966 | 3/15/1956 | W. R. Holt | Conf. of Faith | TSF Dec. 07, 1986 | West |
| Obee, Rosemary (Mrs. A.) (Halverhout) | Jan. 12, 1941 | | W. R. Holt | Conf. of Faith | Was Halverhout | |
| Odneal, F. C. (Mr.) | | | | | | |
| Odneal, F. C. (Mrs.) | | | | | | |
| Odneal, Florence C. | | | S. B. Williams | Ltr. Methodist | Death July 22, 1971 | |

# Record of Members

| Name | Date Received | Birth | By Whom | How | Status | Remarks |
|---|---|---|---|---|---|---|
| Odneal, Golda | | | S. B. Williams | Ltr. Methodist | Death Sep. 1972 CA. | |
| Odneal, Jack | | | | | Ltr. May 01, 1955 | |
| Odneal, Ralph | 1950 | | W. R. Holt | Ltr. Methodist | Death June 1986 | West |
| Odneal, Ramona (Carmitchell) | 1950 | 4/23/1930 | W. R. Holt | | M.Charles Carmitchell Jr. | |
| Odneal, Robert | 1950 | | W. R. Holt | Conf. of Faith | Death Jun.19, 2003 | Lamberty |
| Odneal, Vona (Mrs. Ralph) | 1950 | | W. R. Holt | Ltr. Methodist | Death Dec.30, 1982 | DeSpain |
| Ogden, Armin C. | 1952 | | W. R. Holt | Conf. of Faith | Death Oct. 27, 1990 | Gasau |
| Ogden, Betty | Apr. 09, 1939 | | W. R. Holt | Conf. of Faith | Removed Jan. 13, 1958 | |
| Ogden, Donald | Apr. 09, 1939 | | W. R. Holt | Conf. of Faith | TSF to Oliver | |
| Ogden, Donald (Mrs) | Apr. 18, 1954 | | W. R. Holt | Tran. Linwood | TSF To Oliver 1957 | |
| Ogden, Frankie Dean (Mrs. K.) (Raw) | Dec. 20, 1959 | | W. R. Holt | Conf. of Faith | TSF Chelsea  Aug. 1972 | |
| Ogden, Gerald | 1952 -1953 | | W. R. Holt | | TSF Welborn June 1955 | |
| Ogden, Gerald (Mrs.) | 1952-1953 | | W. R. Holt | | TSF Welborn June 1955 | |
| Ogden, Julia M. (Mrs. Armin) (Judy) | 1952 | | W. R. Holt | Conf. of Faith | Death Sept. 26,1999 | Lamberty |
| Ogden, Karen (Roberts) | Sept. 27, 1964 | | W. R. Holt | Conf. of Faith | TSF Roberts | |
| Ogden, Kenneth | 1952 | | W. R Holt | Conf. of Faith | TSF Chelsea Aug. 1972 | |
| Ogden, T. E. | | | | | Removed 1953 | |
| Ogden, T. E. (Mrs.) | | | | | Removed 1953 | |

54 - MEMBERS

**Record of Members**

| Name | Date Received | Birth | By Whom | How | Status | Remarks |
|------|---------------|-------|---------|-----|--------|---------|
| O'Hara, H. P. | | | | | Removed without cert. | |
| O'Hara, H. P. (Mrs.) | | | | | Removed without cert. | |
| O'Hara, James A. | | | | | Removed without cert. | |
| Oliver, Ferm (Schilke) (Mrs. J.)(Powers) | Apr. 03, 1927 | | W. R. Holt | From "P" List | Removed Dec. 1978 | Harnden |
| Olson, Betty (Mrs. C. ) | Dec. 23, 1964 | | W. R. Holt | Conf. of Faith | TSF 1997 | Lamberty |
| Olson, Clarence Jr. | Dec. 23, 1962 | | W. R. Holt | Reinstated | TSF 1997 | Lamberty |
| Olson, Eric | Apr. 22, 1973 | 1/8/1961 | R. L. Rayson | Conf. of Faith | Withdrew 1996 | Lamberty |
| Olson, Laura Ann (Stanford) | Apr. 06, 1969 | 1/5/1958 | R. L. Rayson | Conf. of Faith | Withdrew Nov. 24, 1986 | West |
| Otney, James | Mar.   1984 | | I. DeSpain | PF | Death 1990 | Lamberty |
| Otney, Naomi Jean (Mrs. James Nelson) | Sept. 25, 1966 | | W. R. Holt | CT Meth. | | |
| Ott, Dorothy (Mrs. F. P.) | | | W. R. Holt | Conf. of Faith | Aug. 04, 1981 Rowland | DeSpain |
| Ott, Floyd P. | | | W. R. Holt | Conf. of Faith | Death Mar. 1981 | DeSpain |
| Ott, Gordon | | | | | Ltr. 1960 | |
| Ott, Ronald | | | | | Ltr. Southside Pby 1965 | |
| Pack, Robert | | | | | Removed 4/30/1950 | |
| Parker, Bruce | Oct. 18, 1970 | | R. L. Rayson | Grinter Chapel | Withdrew Jan. 30, 1980 | Harnden |
| Parker, Patricia (Mrs. Bruce) (Watson) | Dec. 22, 1957 | | W. R. Holt | Grinter Chapel | Removed Nov. 30, 1980 | Harnden |
| Parsott, James (Mrs.) | Apr. 18, 1954 | | W. R. Holt | Conf. of Faith | | |

55 - MEMBERS

**Record of Members**

| Name | Date Received | Birth | By Whom | How | Status | Remarks |
|------|---------------|-------|---------|-----|--------|---------|
| Patterson, John | | | | | Removed Apr. 30, 1950 | |
| Patterson, Kenneth D. | | | | | Removed Apr. 30, 1950 | |
| Patterson, Kenneth D (Mrs.) | | | | | Removed Apr. 30, 1950 | |
| Patterson, Lynda (Roush) | 1952 | | W. R. Holt | | Mar. 08/29/1955, Roush | |
| Patterson, Mary | | | | | Removed Apr. 30, 1950 | |
| Patty, Betty (Mrs. Donald) | Mar. 26, 1961 | 1/5/1928 | W. R. Holt | Conf. of Faith | Removed 1967 | |
| Patty, Donald S. | Mar. 26, 1961 | 1/20/1928 | W. R. Holt | Conf. of Faith | Removed 1967 | |
| Patty, Marcelene Gay | Mar. 26, 1961 | 09/03.1948 | W. R. Holt | Conf. of Faith | Removed 1967 | |
| Paulson, Ruth Evelyn (Thorp) | Mar. 02, 1958 | 3/16/1934 | W. R. Holt | Conf. of Faith | Married Fred L. Thorp | |
| Paulson, Walter (Throp) | Apr. 02. 1961 | | W. R. Holt | Conf. of Faith | Adopted by Fred Thorp | |
| Pearson, Esther | | | W. R. Holt | Conf. of Faith | Death Dec. 1974 | |
| Pearson, Gilbert | | | W. R. Holt | Ltr. London Height | Death May 20, 1970 | |
| Pearson, Gilbert Ronald | | | W. R. Holt | Conf. of Faith | | |
| Pearson, Judith Ann (Mrs. G. R. ) | Mar. 06, 1960 | | W. R. Holt | Ltr.London Height | Withdrew 1980 | Hamden |
| Pearson, Ronald | 1950 | | W. R. Holt | Conf. of Faith | Withdrew 1980 | Hamden |
| Peat, Barbara | Apr. 22, 1962 | 8/8/1950 | W. R. Holt | Conf. of Faith | TSF Lebo Apr. 1975 | |
| Peat, Helen (Mrs. W. T. ) | Apr. 09, 1939 | | W. R. Holt | Conf. of Faith | Death Sept. 01, 1990 | Gasau |
| Peat, R. T. (Mrs.) | Nov. 16, 1930 | | S. B. Williams | Conf. of Faith | Death 09/16/1969 | |

56 - MEMBERS

**Record of Members**

| Name | Date Received | Birth | By Whom | How | Status | Remarks |
|---|---|---|---|---|---|---|
| Peat, Raymond Leslie | Apr. 02, 1972 | | R. L. Rayson | Conf. of Faith | T. Nov. 18, 1991 Asbury | Gasau |
| Peat, Richard Thomas | Apr. 09, 1939 | | W. R. Holt | W.C. Child | TSF Roland Park 5/9/1965 | |
| Peat, Sharon Lynn (Smith) | 1955 | | W. R. Holt | Conf. of Faith | Transfer to Smith | |
| Peat, Wilbur Thomas | Nov. 14, 1926 | 10/8/1914 | S. B. Williams | Conf. of Faith | Death Nov. 17, 2000 | Lamberty |
| Peel, Dorothy | May. 24, 1981 | | I. DeSpain | TSF UMC | Death Oct. 1998 | Lamberty |
| Peel, Fred | May. 24, 1981 | | I. DeSpain | TSF Central Ave. | Death Feb. 25, 1991 | Gasau |
| Peel, Rosmarie | May. 24, 1981 | | I. DeSpain | TSF K.C. KS | Death Feb. 26, 2002 | Lamberty |
| Pence, Joe Jr. | 1947 | | W. R. Holt | Ltr. | Ltr. Ashbury 04/11/1965 | |
| Pence, Joe Jr. (Mrs.) | 1933 | | S. B. Williams | Conf. of Faith | Ltr. Ashbury 04/11/1965 | |
| Pence, Terry Stephen | Apr. 21, 1957 | 10/23/1947 | W. R. Holt | Conf. of Faith | Ltr.Ashbury 04/11/1965 | |
| Pepperdine, Helen | May. 08, 1977 | | J. R. Harnden | TSF Trinity UMC | | Lamberty |
| Pepperdine, Ralph | May., 08, 1977 | | J. R. Harnden | TSF Trinity UMC | Death 1977 | Harnden |
| Peters, A. C. | | | | | Death 1951 | |
| Peters, A. C. (Mrs.) | | | | | Death 1951 | |
| Peters, John | | | | | Removed 4/5/1959 | |
| Peters, Mildred | Sept. 23, 1984 | | | | TSF11/07/1986 1stPresby | West |
| Peters, Raymond L. | Sept. 11, 1960 | | W. R. Holt | Ltr. 1st United Pres | Removed 1967 | |
| Peters, Raymond L. (Mrs.) | Sept. 11, 1960 | | W. R. Holt | Ltr. 1st United Pres | Removed 1967 | |

57 - MEMBERS

# Record of Members

| Name | Date Received | Birth | By Whom | How | Status | Remarks |
|------|---------------|-------|---------|-----|--------|---------|
| Peters, William Lee | Sept. 11, 1960 | | W. R. Holt | Ltr. 1st United Pres | Removed 1967 | |
| Picknick, John (Mrs.) | | | | | | |
| Picknick, Joyce | | | | | | |
| Pigg, Eleanor Frances (Bukaty) | Dec. 10, 1961 | 3/28/1947 | W. R. Holt | Conf. of Faith | Trans. To Bukaty | |
| Pigg, Glenna (Mrs. Robert) | Mar. 06, 1960 | | W. R. Holt | Ltr. Trinity Meth. | Died Jan. 09, 2006 | Lamberty |
| Pigg, Linda Dianne (Hanigan) | Dec. 10, 1961 | 3/2/1951 | W. R. Holt | Conf. of Faith | TSF Hanigan 3/17/1970 | |
| Pigg, Marilyn Louise (Young) | Dec. 10, 1961 | 7/23/1949 | W. R. Holt | Conf. of Faith | TSF Young 7/12/1969 | |
| Pigg, Robert | Jan. 06, 1957 | 11/17/1913 | W. R. Holt | Conf. of Faith | Death June 27, 1973 | |
| Pike, Austin | | | | | Ltr. Granted 4/30/1950- | |
| Pike, Austin (Mrs.) | | | | | Ltr. Granted 4/30/1950- | |
| Pike, Barbara Elaine | | | | | Ltr. Granted 4/30/1950- | |
| Pike, Edith | Sept. 24, 1933 | | S. B. Williams | Conf. of Faith | Death Mar. 28, 1982 | DeSpain |
| Pike, Keith Allen | Apr. 17, 1938 | | W. R. Holt | Conf. of Faith | Removed 1/13/1958 | |
| Pike, Lucien Robert | Apr. 17, 1938 | | W. R. Holt | Conf. of Faith | TSF Christian | |
| Pike, Lucien Robert Jr. | | | | | TSF St. Paul's Epis | |
| Pike, R. M. | Oct. 08, 1933 | | S. B. Williams | Conf. of Faith | Death 1956 | |
| Pike, R. M. (Mrs.) | Sept. 24, 1933 | | S. B. Williams | Conf. of Faith | | |
| Plakas, Rosemary (Mrs. Chris) (Fry) | Apr. 18, 1954 | | W. R. Holt | Conf. of Faith | TSF May 19, 1991VA | Gasau |

58 - MEMBERS

# Record of Members

| Name | Date Received | Birth | By Whom | How | Status | Remarks |
|------|---------------|-------|---------|-----|--------|---------|
| Porter, Jessie | | | S. B. Williams | Tran. UB | Death removed 1974 | |
| Potter, Bryan Edward | Apr. 06, 1980 | | J. R. Harnden | Conf. of Faith | | |
| Potter, Carol (Mrs. Robert) | Mar. 24, 1963 | 1/17/1938 | W. R. Holt | Ltr. Ch. Of Christ | | |
| Potter, Eldon Robert | May. 14, 1978 | | J. R. Harnden | Conf. of Faith | T. Portland, OR 5/15/2005 | |
| Potter , Robert (Dr.) | Mar. 24, 1963 | 12/2/1938 | W. R. Holt | Ltr.Ch.of Christ | | |
| Potts, Nancy (Mrs.) (Fry) | 1964 | | W. R. Holt | Conf. of Faith | TSF. Fry, Rcc Dec. 1978 | Harnden |
| Powers, Fern (Schilke) (Oliver) | Apr. 03, 1927 | | S. B. Williams | Ltr. | 1972 To "O"list married | |
| Powers, Naomi (Mrs.) (Bishop) | Jun. 14, 1964 | | W. R. Holt | Ltr. Christian | Removed Dec. 1978 | Harnden |
| Price, Cheri | Aug. 17, 2008 | | Seong Lee | | | |
| Price, Helen (VanDyke) | Mar. 28, 1937 | | W. R. Holt | | Removed 4/5/1959 | |
| Puskarick, Michael Lee | Dec. 10, 1961 | 09/04.1949 | W. R. Holt | Conf. of Faith | Removed 1967 | |
| Rader, June (Mrs. Ralph) | Mar. 07, 1965 | | W. R. Holt | Ltr. Grandview Bap. | Death 1978 | Harnden |
| Radotinsky, Edna E. (Mrs. J. W.) | Apr. 09, 1944 | | W. R. Holt | Ltr. | TSF.1976 | |
| Radotinsky, Sandra Gayle (Doane/Dean) | Apr. 09, 1944 | | W. R. Holt | Conf. of Faith | Transfer to Doane/Dean | |
| Rand, Irene (Mrs. Kasper) | Jan. 11, 1925 | | S. B. Williams | TSF UB | Death Dec. 1972 | |
| Rand, Kasper | Jan. 11, 1925 | | S. B. Williams | Ltr. | Death Mar. 13, 1964 | |
| Raw, Frankiedene (Ogden) | Dec. 20, 1959 | | W. R. Holt | Conf. of Faith | Married K. Ogden | |
| Rayson, Carolyn Jean (Mrs. ) | Jun. 01, 1968 | 2/23/1953 | R. L. Rayson | T. Grace Mem. Ind. | Neodesha UM Feb. 1975 | |

**Record of Members**

| Name | Date Received | Birth | By Whom | How | Status | Remarks |
|---|---|---|---|---|---|---|
| Rayson, David Elton | Jun. 01, 1968 | 8/20/1951 | R. L. Rayson | T. Grace Mem. Ind. | TSF Dec. 20, 1979 Indep. | Harnden |
| Rayson, Gary Donn | Apr. 06, 1969 | 4/27/1957 | R. L. Rayson | Conf. of Faith | Neodesha UM June 1974 | |
| Rayson, Muriel (Mrs. LeRoy) | Jun. 01, 1968 | 6/20/1929 | R. L. Rayson | T. Grace Mem. Ind. | Neodesha UM June 1974 | |
| Rayson, Paul Frank | Apr. 06, 1969 | 7/20/1959 | R. L. Rayson | Conf. of Faith | Neodesha UM June 1974 | |
| Rayson, R. LeRoy (Rev.) | Jun. 01, 1968 | 3/29/1928 | Appt. by Conf. | | Conf. Action Jun. 1974 | |
| Reece, Evelyn | Oct. 25, 1992 | | M. Gasau | OD Mission. Bap. | | Gasau |
| Reed, Donna (Szulski) | Feb. 04, 1990 | | M. Gasau | | Removed Nov. 07, 1999 | Lamberty |
| Reeves, James (Mrs.) | Apr. 10, 1925 | | S. B. Williams | Ltr. | Apr. 1957 Death | |
| Reid, Ora (Mrs.) | Aug. 10, 1960 | | W. R. Holt | Conf. of Faith | Death 3/9/1968 | |
| Rhodes, Al | 1952-1953 | | W. R. Holt | Ltr. | TSF Welborn Comm. | |
| Rhodes, Al (Mrs.) | 1952-1953 | | W. R. Holt | Ltr. | TSF Welborn Comm. | |
| Rhodes, Curtis | 1952-1953 | | W. R. Holt | Ltr. | TSF Welborn Comm. | |
| Rich, Joyce Cathell | Apr. 09, 1944 | | W. R. Holt | Conf. of Faith | Ltr Pres. Indp. MO. 1962 | |
| Riley, Bruce | Apr. 06, 1958 | 11/15/1948 | W. R. Holt | Conf. of Faith | Removed Dec. 1978 | Harnden |
| Riley, Charles | 1953 | | W. R. Holt | | Removed 1/13/1958 | |
| Riley, Elizabeth (Mrs.) (Evans/Blevin) | Apr. 23, 1944 | | W. R. Holt | | TSF Blevin Fm. Evans | |
| Riley, Helen | Jun. 12, 1977 | | J. R. Harnden | Conf. of Faith | Withdrew Jan.30, 1980 | Harnden |
| Riley, Janet Kay | Mar. 29, 1959 | | W. R. Holt | Conf. of Faith | To Clyde Listing | |

60 - MEMBERS

**Record of Members**

| Name | Date Received | Birth | By Whom | How | Status | Remarks |
|---|---|---|---|---|---|---|
| Riley, Laura Elaine (Early) | Apr. 21, 1957 | 9/13/1946 | W. R. Holt | Conf. of Faith | Married Marvin Early | |
| Riley, Steven (Steve) | Mar. 26, 1967 | 3/21/1954 | W. R. Holt | Conf. of Faith | Removed Nov. 09, 1992 | Gasau |
| Rinn, Peter | Mar. 26, 1972 | | R. L. Rayson | T. United Meth. | Removed Dec. 1978 | Harnden |
| Roberts, Karen (Odgen) | Sept. 27, 1964 | | W. R. Holt | TSF From "O" list | TSF Dec. 01, 1988 Olathe | Gasau |
| Rogers, Loren | | | | | Removed.4/5/1959 | |
| Ropp, Pamela | Feb. 14, 1962 | | W. R. Holt | Conf. of Faith | Removed 1967 | |
| Rose, Joseph (M Joseph (Mrs.) | | | | | Removed 4/5/1959 | |
| Rose, Nan Lynn (Sturtridge) | Jan. 06, 1957 | 4/1/1940 | W. R. Holt | Ltr. Methodist | "S" , Marriage 8/10/1958 | |
| Roush, Linda I. (Patterson) | 1952 | | W. R. Holt | Conf. of Faith | TSF  Baptist 1956 | |
| Ruby, Wayne | Sept. 13, 1959 | | W. R. Holt | Conf. of Faith | | |
| Ruby, Wayne (Mrs.) | Sept. 13, 1959 | | W. R. Holt | Conf. of Faith | | |
| Russell, George (Mrs.) (Lacy) | | | | | Death 1953 | |
| Russell, Luke | | | | | Feb. 10, 1953 Letter | |
| Russell, Mary | Apr. 28, 1991 | | M. Gasau | CT Baptist | Death Aug. 06, 1996 | Lamberty |
| Rymer, Kent | Mar. 26, 1967 | 11/12/1952 | W. R. Holt | Conf. of Faith | | |
| Sackman, Albert Jr. | Aug. 07, 1960 | | W. R. Holt | Conf. of Faith | TSF. 1976 | |
| Sackman, Janice Carol | Mar. 29, 1959 | 1/11/1944 | W. R. Holt | Conf. of Faith | Removed Dec.03, 1981 | DeSpain |
| Sackman, Joyce Elizabeth (Mayberry) | Mar. 29, 1959 | 4/24/1942 | W. R. Holt | Conf. of Faith | Transfer to Mayberry | |

61 - MEMBERS

**Record of Members**

| Name | Date Received | Birth | By Whom | How | Status | Remarks |
|------|---------------|-------|---------|-----|--------|---------|
| Sackman, Mabel (Mrs. A.) | Aug. 07, 1960 | | W. R. Holt | Conf. of Faith | TSF 1976 | |
| Sackman, Martha J. | Mar. 23, 1975 | | J. R. Harnden | Conf. of Faith | TSF 1976 | |
| Sackman, Virginia Louise (Fry) | Apr. 21, 1957 | 11/13/1945 | W. R. Holt | Conf. of Faith | Transfer to Fry | |
| Sacks, Ethel Jeanne | | | | | Married | |
| Sacks, Clara | Sept. 10, 1986 | | R. West | Reinstated | Death Jul. 1988 | Lamberty |
| Sacks, Claude | Sept. 10, 1986 | | R. West | Reinstated | Death Dec. 05, 1988 | Gasau |
| Sacks, John Richard | Mar. 27, 1941 | | W. R. Holt | | Joined another church | |
| Scheets, Sarah | Dec. 01, 2002 | | L. Lamberty | Conf. of Faith | | |
| Scheloski, Betty | Apr. 03, 1950 | | W. R. Holt | Conf. of Faith | Removed Nov. 21, 1988 | Gasau |
| Scheloski, Donald | Apr. 03, 1950 | | W. R. Holt | Conf. of Faith | Removed Nov. 21, 1988 | Gasau |
| Scheloski, Helen (Mrs.) | 1950 | | W. R. Holt | | Died 1950 | |
| Schilke, Marie (Mrs. Walter F.) | Apr. 03, 1927 | | S. B. Williams | Ltr. Lutheran | Death Mar. 22, 1971 | |
| Schilke, Mildred | Dec. 1972 | | R. L. Rayson | Ltr. Cent. Christian | Dec. 16, 1987 Ctl. Christ. | West |
| Schilke, Walter F. | Apr. 03, 1927 | | S. B. Williams | Ltr. Lutheran | Death Oct. 24, 1982 | DeSpain |
| Schmidt, Albert | Aug. 09, 1959 | | W. R. Holt | Conf. of Faith | | |
| Schmidt, Barbara Dawn (Dunivan) | Aug. 09, 1959 | 7/27/1939 | W. R. Holt | Conf. of Faith | Mar. Dunivan 7/28/1962 | |
| Schmidt, Iona (Mrs.) | Aug. 09, 1959 | | W. R. Holt | Conf. of Faith | T. 10/15/1990 Clearview, | Gasau |
| Schmidt, Joan (Weinert) | Jul. 06, 1980 | | I. DeSpain | PF | TSF 04/12/1998 Smithville | Lamberty |

**Record of Members**

| Name | Date Received | Birth | By Whom | How | Status | Remarks |
|---|---|---|---|---|---|---|
| Schmidt, Linda Lou (Cunningham) | 1952 | 8/4/1940 | W. R. Holt | Conf. of Faith | Married Cunningham | |
| Schmidt, Mark Alan | Apr. 06, 1980 | | J. R. Harnden | | | |
| Schockey, Clyde | Dec. 11, 1960 | 3/20/1993 | W. R. Holt | Ltr. Methodist | Death Oct. 1971 | |
| Schockey, Ethel May (Mrs. C.) | Dec. 11, 1960 | 6/8/1997 | W. R. Holt | Ltr. Methodist | | |
| Schockey, Virginia Pauline | Dec. 11, 1960 | 4/2/1925 | W. R. Holt | Ltr. Methodist | | |
| Schockey, Vivian Jeanette | Dec. 11, 1960 | 3/18/1932 | W. R. Holt | Ltr. Methodist | | |
| Scholl, Grace | | | | | Death May 14, 1968 | |
| Schroeder, Aubrey H. | | | | | Lettered Aug. 11, 1953 | |
| Schroeder, Aubrey H. (Mrs.) | | | | | Lettered Aug. 11, 1953 | |
| Schroeder, Darlene | | | | | Lettered Aug. 11, 1953 | |
| Schroeder, Dona Lou | | | | | Lettered Aug. 11, 1953 | |
| Scott, Carrie B. (Mrs.) | Dec. 15, 1963 | 06/26/1890 | W. R. Holt | Ltr. Methodist | Death May. 1978 | Harnden |
| Scott, Clyde Jr. | Apr. 11, 1971 | 12/28/1929 | R. L. Rayson | Conf. of Faith | Removed Dec. 03, 1981 | DeSpain |
| Scott, Robert Alan | Apr. 2, 1972 | | R. L. Rayson | Conf. of Faith | Removed Dec. 03, 1981 | DeSpain |
| Scott, Rosalie | Apr. 11, 1971 | 2/3/1039 | R. L. Rayson | Conf. of Faith | Removed Dec. 03, 1981 | DeSpain |
| Scott, William Raymon | Apr. 11, 1971 | 3/7/1958 | R. L. Rayson | Conf. of Faith | Removed Dec. 03, 1981 | DeSpain |
| Sears, A. W. | | | | | Return L.D.S. 1/01/1959 | |
| Sears, A. W. (Mrs.) | | | | | Deceased | |

# Record of Members

| Name | Date Received | Birth | By Whom | How | Status | Remarks |
|------|--------------|-------|---------|-----|--------|---------|
| Seitum, Helen | Apr. 18, 1965 | | W. R. Holt | TSF. EUB | T. Nov.27, 1969, C. R. IA. | |
| Seitum, Karl | Apr. 18, 1965 | | W. R. Holt | TSF. EUB | T. Nov.27, 1969, C. R. IA. | |
| Seitum, Karl (Mrs.) | Apr. 18, 1965 | | W. R. Holt | TSF. EUB | T. Nov.27, 1969, C. R. IA. | |
| Self, Carolyn (Mrs. J. L.) | Dec. 31, 1967 | 9/4/1916 | W. R. Holt | Ltr. Presbyterian | Died Apr.09, 2006 M. TN. | Lamberty |
| Self, John Daniel | Apr. 03, 1958 | | W. R. Holt | Ltr. El Toro, Ca. | Ltr. 1960 | |
| Self, John L. | Dec. 31, 1967 | | W. R. Holt | Ltr. Presbyterian | Death Mar. 31, 1984 | DeSpain |
| Self, Leslie | | | W. R. Holt | Ltr. | Ltr. 1960 | |
| Self, Leslie (Mrs.) | Mar. 23, 1937 | | W. R. Holt | Conf. of Faith | Ltr. 1960 | |
| Sell, Mildred | Mar. 09,1975 | | J. R. Harnden | Conf. of Faith | Withdrew Feb. 15, 1979 | Harnden |
| Seufert, Donald | Apr. 17, 1960 | | W. R. Holt | Conf. of Faith | TSF. Jan. 26, 1969 Trinity | |
| Seufert, Ella (Mrs. T. A.) | | | W. R. Holt | Conf. of Faith | Death Nov. 16, 1992 | Gasau |
| Seufert, Marion | Apr. 17, 1960 | 2/10/1920 | W. R. Holt | Conf. of Faith | TSF Jan. 26, 1969 Trinity | |
| Seufert, Tony A. | | | W. R. Holt | Conf. of Faith | Death Mar. 29, 1985 | Stevenson |
| Seufert, Tony M. | Apr. 17, 1960 | 7/13/1917 | W. R. Holt | Conf. of Faith | TSF Jan. 26, 1969 Trinity | |
| Seufert, Vivian (Johnson) | | 6/4/1923 | W. R. Holt | Conf. of Faith | M.Johnson D. 10/30/2006 | Lamberty |
| Sevedge. Cathie (Carter) | | | | Marriage Carter | T.5/8/1967White Church | |
| Sevedge, Roger | Dec.29, 1957 | | W. R. Holt | Conf. of Faith | T.5/8/1967White Church | |
| Sgulski, Mary Ann (Brook) | | | | | Married TSF from Brook | |
| Shaffer, Deana (Wilmoth) | | | | | Removed Armordale Bap. | |

W. R. Holt

64 - MEMBERS

**Record of Members**

| Name | Date Received | Birth | By Whom | How | Status | Remarks |
|---|---|---|---|---|---|---|
| Shaner, Bernie C. | Jun. 13, 1965 | 9/23/1900 | W. R. Holt | Conf. of Faith | T. 08/16/1980 Chelsea Pk. | DeSpain |
| Shaner, Bernie Jr. | Jun. 13, 1965 | 2/11/1948 | W. R. Holt | Conf. of Faith | T.Christian, O. P., KS | |
| Shaner, Carol Dee (Jones) | Jun.13, 1965 | 6/27/1943 | W. R. Holt | Conf. of Faith | Marr. Charles Lee Jones | |
| Shaner, Geneva Daymon (Mrs. B.) | Jun. 13, 1965 | 3/22/1915 | W. R. Holt | Conf. of Faith | T.08/16/1980 Christian | DeSpain |
| Shaner, John Robert | Jun. 13, 1965 | 7/7/1954 | W. R. Holt | Conf. of Faith | Withdrew Nov. 03, 1987 | West |
| Shannon, Dean | Jun. 10, 1962 | | W. R. Holt | Conf. of Faith | Death Apr. 1977 | Harnden |
| Shannon, Mae (Mrs. Dean) | Jun. 10, 1962 | | W. R. Holt | Conf. of Faith | Death June 1986 | Stevenson |
| Sharp, Eli | 1918 | 12/3/1969 | | | Death July 19, 1963 | |
| Sharp, Ellen (Mrs. Eli) | 1939 | | W. R. Holt | Ltr. | Ltr. Granted 1950 | |
| Sharp, Gail/Gayle Ann (Locke) | Aug. 07, 1960 | | W. R. Holt | TSF Baptist | Removed 8/01/1954 | |
| Sharp, Mark | 1918 | | | | Ltr. To Unitarian Church | |
| Sharp, Mark (Mrs.) | | | | | Death 1952 | |
| Sharp, Richard Gale | | | | Child Watch Care | Dropped 4/30/50 in error | |
| Sharp, Ruth Elaine (Maloney) | Apr. 16, 1933 | | S. B. Williams | | Mrs. Jerry Maloney | |
| Shaw, Harry | | | | | Died Apr. 1950 | |
| Shaw , Harry (Mrs.) | Feb. 05, 1928 | | S. B. Williams | Ltr. | Died Nov. 16, 1967 | |
| Shelley, Craig | Apr. 10, 1966 | 4/22/1953 | W. R. Holt | Conf. of Faith | Removed Dec. 1978 | Harnden |
| Shelley, Donvea (Charles/Phillips) | | | | TSF Charles | Ltr. 02/07/1960 Ore. | |

65 - MEMBERS

**Record of Members**

| Name | Date Received | Birth | By Whom | How | Status | Remarks |
|------|--------------|-------|---------|-----|--------|---------|
| Shelley, Joseph | | | | | TSF Mar.13, 1959 Ore. | |
| Shelley, Martha (Addison) | Sept. 27, 1964 | | W. R. Holt | | TSF"A" list, Addison | |
| Sherman, Michael | Apr. 27, 2003 | | Lamberty/ Smart | | | |
| Shevling, Kay | Jun. 01, 2003 | | Lamberty/ Smart | T. Central A. KCK | | |
| Shirley, David | | | W. R. Holt | | Removed 1967 | |
| Shirley, Lois Elaine (Sweney)(Baker) | | | W. R. Holt | TSF from Baker | Removed 1967 | |
| Shockey, Clyde | Dec. 11, 1960 | 03/20/1893 | W. R. Holt | Ltr. Step. Meth. | | |
| Shockey, Ethel May | Dec. 11, 1960 | 06/08/1897 | W. R. Holt | Ltr. Step. Meth. | T. Step. Meth. Dec. 1978 | Harnden |
| Shockey, Virginia Pauline | Dec. 11, 1960 | 4/2/1925 | W. R. Holt | Ltr. Step. Meth. | T. Step.Meth.Dec. 1978 | Harnden |
| Shockey, Vivian Jeannet | Dec. 11, 1960 | 3/18/1932 | W. R. Holt | Ltr. Step. Meth. | T. Step. Meth. Dec. 1978 | Harnden |
| Short, Judy | | | W. R. Holt | Conf. of Faith | | |
| Shultz, Alice (Mrs.) (Neeves) | | | | | Letter 1952 was Neeves | |
| Shumacher, Orene (Mrs.) | Aug. 21, 1966 | | W. R. Holt | Ltr. Christian | TSF Oct. 6, 1973  Baptist | |
| Siak, Ralph E. (Mrs.) | | | W. R. Holt | | Removed 1967 | |
| Sietam, Helen | Apr. 18, 1965 | | W. R. Holt | TSF Waterloo, IA | | |
| Sietam, Karl | Apr. 18, 1965 | | W. R. Holt | TSF Waterloo, IA | | |
| Sietam, Karl (Mrs.) | Apr. 18,1965 | | W. R. Holt | TSF Waterloo, IA | | |
| Simmons, Darlene (Johnson/Hoendorf) | 1935 | 7/27/1921 | S. W. Williams | | Married D. Simmons | |

**Record of Members**

| Name | Date Received | Birth | By Whom | How | Status | Remarks |
|------|---------------|-------|---------|-----|--------|---------|
| Simmons, Daulton | Apr. 18, 1954 | 2/15/1918 | W. R. Holt | Conf. of Faith | Died Dec. 18, 1977 | Harnden |
| Simmons, Nancy (Foster) | Mar. 23, 1975 | | J. R. Harnden | Conf. of Faith | Removed Nov. 21, 1988 | Gasau |
| Simpson, Bob | | | | | Removed 4/5/1959 | |
| Simpson, Danny | | | | | Ltr. Apr. 19, 1953 | |
| Simpson, Mary (Mrs. Robert) | Apr. 01, 1956 | | W. R. Holt | Conf. of Faith | Removed 4/5/1959 | |
| Sisk, Lawrence Eugene (Larry) | Apr. 22, 1973 | 3/17/1960 | R. L. Rayson | Conf. of Faith | | |
| Sisk, Ralph E. (Mrs.) | | | W. R. Holt | | Removed 1967 | |
| Sisk, Randal Lee (Randy) | Apr. 22, 1973 | 10/29/1958 | R. L. Rayson | Conf. of Faith | | |
| Slater, Naomi Irene (Bushnell/Davidson) | May. 06, 1960 | | W. R. Holt | TSF | Bushnell to Davidson | |
| Slawson, Don | Jan. 01,1956 | | W. R. Holt | TSF | Ltr. To Wyandotte1967 | |
| Slawson, Rheta (Harbour) | | | | Mar. 6/4/1954 | Ltr. Wyan. Meth. 1967 | Harnden |
| Smith, Beverly (Mrs.) (Larsen) | Apr. 26, 1943 | | W. R. Holt | Conf. of Faith | Ltr. 4/21/1960 | |
| Smith, Katherine M. (Mrs.) | Apr. 14, 1963 | 4/7/1890 | W. R. Holt | Conf. of Faith | Death Mar. 06, 1972 | |
| Smith, Leatha | Oct. 16, 1977 | | J. R. Harnden | Conf. of Faith | Death | Harnden |
| Smith, Martha (VanDyke) | | | | TSF VanDyke | Removed without cert. | |
| Smith, Maurice R. | Apr. 01, 1956 | | W. R. Holt | Conf. of Faith | Death Mar. 09, 1957 | |
| Smith, Maurice R. (Mrs.) | Apr. 01, 1956 | | W. R. Holt | Conf. of Faith | Ltr. To Meth. In Ill. 1963 | |
| Smith, Robert L. | 1950 | | W. R. Holt | | Ltr. 4/21/1960 | |

**Record of Members**

| Name | Date Received | Birth | By Whom | How | Status | Remarks |
|---|---|---|---|---|---|---|
| Smith, Robert (Mrs.) (Larsen) | | | | | Ltr. 4/21/1960 | |
| Smith, Sharon (Mrs. Donald) | 1955 | | W. R. Holt | Conf. of Faith | T. May 1975 Grandview | |
| Smoyer, Anna (Stakely) (Mrs. Mack) | Sept. 27, 1964 | | W. R. Holt | Tran. From Stakley | Withdrew Oct. 25, 1986 | West |
| Snoderly, Frank | | | W. R. Holt | | Removed 4/5/1959 | |
| Snoderly, Frank (Mrs.) | | | W. R. Holt | | Removed 4/5/1959 | |
| Snodgras, Diane Bolton | Jun. 03, 1973 | | R. L. Rayson | Conf. of Faith | | |
| Snyder, William | Apr. 09, 1944 | | W. R. Holt | Ltr. | Removed 1967 | |
| Snyder, William (Mrs.) | Apr. 09, 1944 | | W. R. Holt | Ltr. | Death 04/30/1957 | |
| Sohn, Tammy | Jan. 28, 2001 | | L. Lamberty | Conf. of Faith | | |
| Sooter, Carl (Mrs.) | | | W. R. Holt | | Withdrawn Feb.1954 | |
| Spandle, Louis R. | 1953 | | W. R. Holt | Conf. of Faith | Death 1978 | Harnden |
| Spandle, Margaret | 1953 | | W. R. Holt | Ltr. Presbyterian | Death Nov. 30, 1990 | Gasau |
| Sparks, Jane (Stakley) | Nov. 26, 1972 | | R. L. Rayson | | TSF 07/18/86 Asbury | West |
| Spatz, Elizabeth (Mrs. LaVerne)(Blevin) | Apr. 23, 1944 | | W. R. Holt | Tran. From Blevin | Removed Dec. 1978 | Harnden |
| Spencer, Ella (Mrs.) | | | W. R. Holt | Tran. UB | Death 12/7/1969 | |
| Spencer, Ernest | | 11/19/1985 | W. R. Holt | Transfer | Apr. 10, 1968 Death | |
| Spencer, Ernest (Mrs.) | | | W. R. Holt | Transfer | | |
| Spencer, Linda | Oct. 23, 1988 | | M. Gasau | TSF Stillwell, KS | Removed Nov. 01, 1998 | Lamberty |

68 - MEMBERS

# Record of Members

| Name | Date Received | Birth | By Whom | How | Status | Remarks |
|---|---|---|---|---|---|---|
| Sprague, Davon Jamaar | May. 08, 1994 | | M. Gasau | Conf. of Faith | Removed Nov. 07, 1999 | Lamberty |
| Sprague, Taja Meshae | May. 08, 1994 | | M. Gasau | Conf. of Faith | Removed Nov. 07, 1999 | Lamberty |
| Spriester , (Mrs. Otto) | Mar. 29, 1970 | | R. L. Rayson | TSF Tuale UM | TSF.1974 | |
| Spurgeon, Ivy (Mrs.) | | | | | Death 1953 | |
| Squlski, Mary Ann (Mrs. P.) (Flander) | Apr. 25, 1954 | | W. R. Holt | Conf. of Faith | Divorced -changed "F". | |
| Squlski, Peter | May. 26,1968 | 4/18/1932 | W. R. Holt | Ltr. Ukeranian Bap. | Divorced, Death | |
| Stakley, Anna (Smoyer) | Sept. 27, 1964 | | W. R. Holt | Conf. of Faith | Married Mack Smoyer | |
| Stakley, Catherine (McCarty) | Dec. 06, 1953 | | W. R. Holt | Ltr. | Married Robert McCarty | |
| Stakley, Jane Marie (Sparks) | Nov. 26, 1972 | 1/25/1954 | R. L. Rayson | Conf. of Faith | TSF To Sparks | |
| Stakley, John | Dec. 06, 1953 | | W. R. Holt | Ltr. | Removed 1967 | |
| Stakley, Laura Jean | Jan. 10, 1982 | | I. DeSpain | Conf. of Faith | TSF 1989 (?) | |
| Stemen, H. G. | | | | | Death -no date | |
| Stemen, H. G. (Mrs.) | | | | | Death Feb. 25, 1958 | |
| Sterrett, Linda (Mrs. Larry) (Cates) | | | | TSF Cotes | TSF Jan.1974 Pratt, KS | |
| Stevens, Florence (Mrs. Maurice) | | | | | Death Apr. 29,1962 | |
| Stevenson, Jane | Sept. 23, 1984 | | E. Stevenson | TSF Aldersgate | TSF1986 Asbury UMC | Gasau |
| Stoddard, Valery | 1950 | | W. R. Holt | | Removed 01/13/1958 | |
| Stoff, Glen | 1950 | | W. R. Holt | Conf. of Faith | Removed Dec. 03, 1981 | DeSpain |

69 - MEMBERS

**Record of Members**

| Name | Date Received | Birth | By Whom | How | Status | Remarks |
|------|------|-------|---------|-----|--------|---------|
| Stoff, Vivian (Mrs. Glenn) | 1950 | | W. R. Holt | Conf. of Faith | Death 1974 | |
| Stoff, William | 1950 | | W. R. Holt | Conf. of Faith | Ltr.Admire 5/12/1964 | |
| Story, Nancy (Swengle) | | | | TSF to Story | Removed 1967 | |
| Stott, Jan | 1958 | | W. R. Holt | Conf. of Faith | Watch Care Roll | |
| Stott, Jan Claire (Baumgart) | Apr. 21, 1957 | 4/23/1945 | W. R. Holt | Conf. of Faith | Married Don Baumgart | |
| Stott, Mildred (Mrs. M. R. ) | Nov. 21, 1926 | | S. B. Williams | Conf. of Faith | Death Jul. 01, 1981 | DeSpain |
| Stott, Milo R. | Nov. 21, 1926 | | S. B. Williams | Conf. of Faith | Death Jul.30, 1982 | DeSpain |
| Stott, Sandra Gail | | | | | | |
| Strandt, Charles | 1961 | | W. R. Holt | Ltr. | Death Sept. 28, 1986 | West |
| Strandt, Leslie | 1961 | | W. R. Holt | Conf. of Faith | TSF Nov. 27, 1973 | |
| Strandt, Lydia (Mrs. C.) | 1961 | | W. R. Holt | Ltr. | | |
| Straub, Illa Mae (Marlow) | Nov. 16, 1958 | | W. R. Holt | TSF Marlow | Watch Care Roll ? 1950 | |
| Strauss, Charles Lee | Oct. 13, 1991 | | M. Gasau | Conf. of Faith | Removed Nov. 07, 1999 | Lamberty |
| Strickel, Bertha Naomi (Mrs. J.) | Mar. 17, 1968 | 09/31/1895 | W. R. Holt | Ltr. Ch. of Christ | Death Oct. 14 1971 | |
| Strickel, John Leonard | Mar. 17, 1968 | 2/4/1885 | W. R. Holt | Ltr. Ch. of Christ | Death May 23, 1972 | |
| Stubbs, Preston B. | Apr. 10, 1960 | | W. R. Holt | Ltr. Wash. Av | Death 1975 | |
| Stubbs, Ruth (Mrs. P. B.) | Apr. 10, 1960 | | W. R. Holt | Ltr. Wash. Av. | Mar. 1972 Death | |
| Studt, Dorothy (Mrs.) | Jan. 02, 1955 | | W. R. Holt | Conf. of Faith | Death Mar. 1988 | West |

70 - MEMBERS

**Record of Members**

| Name | Date Received | Birth | By Whom | How | Status | Remarks |
|------|---------------|-------|---------|-----|--------|---------|
| Studt, George (Mrs.) | Jan. 02. 1955 | | W. R. Holt | Conf. of Faith | | |
| Sturgis, Janet (Mrs. Donald E.) | Apr. 09, 1944 | | W. R. Holt | Conf. of Faith | Death Dec. 1957 | |
| Sturtridge, Gary | | | W. R. Holt | | Removed 1967 | |
| Sturtridge, Nan Lynn (Rose) | | | | Transfer From Rose | To Emanuel Baptist | |
| Sutherland, Lewis M. (Mrs.) | Jul. 27, 1962 | | | TSF Judy Theroff | Removed 1967 | |
| Sutton, William Michael | Apr. 21, 1957 | 9/3/1945 | W. R. Holt | Conf. of Faith | Removed 4/5/1959 | |
| Swanson, Henry Carl | Jan. 21, 1962 | | W. R. Holt | Conf. of Faith | Death Dec. 1970 | |
| Sweney, Lois (Baker) (Shirley) | | | | | Marr. David Shirley | |
| Sweney, Phelma M. (Mrs. William) | 1950 | | W. R. Holt | Conf. of Faith | Death Jan. 06, 1995 | Lamberty |
| Sweney, William M. | Apr. 11, 1971 | | R. L. Rayson | TSF Central Chris. | Death Jan. 12, 1988 | West |
| Swengel, Nancy (Story) | Nov. 16, 1958 | | W. R. Holt | Conf. of Faith | Transfer to Story | |
| Szulski, Peter | May. 26, 1968 | 4/18/1932 | W. R. Holt | T. Ukeranian Bap. | Death June 1979 | Harnden |
| Tapp, Carol | Oct. 17, 1954 | | W. R. Holt | Conf. of Faith | Withdrew Jan. 03, 1989 | Gasau |
| Taylor, Betty Lou (Noltensmeyer) | Dec. 27, 1959 | 8/11/1946 | W. R. Holt | Conf. of Faith | Transfer to N list | |
| Taylor, Demarcus Anthony | May.08,1994 | | M. Gasau | Conf. of Faith | Removed Nov. 7, 1999 | Lamberty |
| Taylor, Dena Jenice | Apr. 02, 1972 | | R. L. Rayson | Conf. of Faith | | |
| Taylor, Errol Dean | Apr. 18, 1954 | | W. R. Holt | Conf. of Faith | Withdrew 1975 | |
| Taylor, Floyd Martin | Dec. 27, 1959 | 5/3/1921 | W. R. Holt | Conf. of Faith | Death Dec. 04, 1981 | DeSpain |

# Record of Members

| Name | Date Received | Birth | By Whom | How | Status | Remarks |
|------|---------------|-------|---------|-----|--------|---------|
| Taylor, Harold R. | Oct. 16, 1966 | | W. R. Holt | Ltr. Grinter Chapel | Rcc Dec. 1978 | Harnden |
| Taylor, Hollis Denise | Apr. 18, 1954 | | W. R. Holt | Conf. of Faith | | |
| Taylor, James Edward | Apr. 02, 1972 | | R. L. Rayson | Conf. of Faith | | |
| Taylor, Joseph | | | W. R. Holt | | Removed 4/05/1959 | |
| Taylor, Karen Joy | Apr. 18, 1954 | | W. R. Holt | Conf. of Faith | | |
| Taylor, Margaret Bea (Brockman) | Dec. 27, 1959 | 2/18/1922 | W. R. Holt | Conf. of Faith | D.9/10/1991 Brockman | Gasau |
| Taylor, Marjorie | Oct. 16, 1966 | | W. R. Holt | Ltr.Grinter Chapel | Removed Dec. 1978 | Harnden |
| Taylor, Maxine Clara (Mrs.) | Apr. 18, 1954 | | W. R. Holt | Conf. of Faith | | |
| Taylor, Melody (Norsworth) | April 14, 1968 | 8/9/1957 | W. R. Holt | Conf. of Faith | TSF 8/13/1986 Austin, Tx | West |
| Taylor, Michael Monroe | Apr. 18, 1954 | | W. R. Holt | Conf. of Faith | | |
| Taylor, Odessa Lucas (Mrs. T. T.) | | | | | 02/17, 1956 Richmond | |
| Taylor, Sharon Jane | Apr. 18, 1954 | | W. R. Holt | Conf. of Faith | | |
| Terry, Millicent (Mrs.) | Jun. 10, 1962 | | W. R. Holt | Ltr.Quindaro Meth. | TSF Trinity 6/30/1967 | |
| Teters, Jennie Lucille | Jun. 10, 1962 | | W. R. Holt | Ltr. From Baptist | Deceased Rcc 12/31/1981 | DeSpain |
| Teters, Jennifer Sue | Jun. 10, 1962 | | W. R. Holt | Conf. of Faith | Death 05/22/1969 | |
| Teters, Larry | | | W. R. Holt | | Removed without cert. | |
| Teters, Nancy June (Byrd) | Jun. 10, 1962 | | W. R. Holt | Conf. of Faith | Married Ronald Byrd | |
| Tevis, Marjorie (Mrs. R.) | Apr. 18, 1954 | | W. R. Holt | Conf. of Faith | Death 03/02/2001 | Lamberty |

72 - MEMBERS

**Record of Members**

| Name | Date Received | Birth | By Whom | How | Status | Remarks |
|------|------|------|---------|-----|--------|---------|
| Tevis, Richard | Apr. 18, 1954 | | W. R. Holt | Conf. of Faith | Withdrew Nov. 18, 1986 | West |
| Theroff, Judy (Sutherland) | Apr. 21, 1957 | | W. R. Holt | Conf. of Faith | Married Sutherland | |
| Thomas, Arthur | | | W. R. Holt | | Death Apr. 16, 1960 | |
| Thomas, Arthur (Mrs.) | | | W. R. Holt | | | |
| Thomas, Constantine | Apr. 29, 2007 | | L. Lamberty | OD | | |
| Thomas, Jacqueline | Oct. 28, 2001 | | L. Lamberty | RF | | |
| Thomas, Joyce Darlene | Mar. 29, 1970 | 5/13/1954 | R. L. Rayson | Conf. of Faith | Removed Dec. 03, 1981 | DeSpain |
| Thomas, Julius (Mrs.) | | | | | Transfer Jan. 10, 1954 | |
| Thompson, Deborah Louise | Feb. 11, 1968 | 12/1/1954 | W. R. Holt | Conf. of Faith | Removed Dec. 1978 | Harnden |
| Thompson, Marilyn Louise (Mary Lyn) | Feb.11, 1968 | 9/8/1934 | W. R. Holt | Ltr. Grandview Bap | Removed Dec. 1978 | Harnden |
| Thompson, Robert | | | W. R. Holt | | Death Aug. 22, 1955 | |
| Thompson, Robert (Mrs.) | | | W. R. Holt | | Death Sept. 1955 | |
| Thompson, Robert Earl Jr. | Feb. 11, 1968 | 11/28/1953 | W. R. Holt | Conf. of Faith | Removed Dec. 1978 | Harnden |
| Throp, F. L. (Mrs.) (Paulson) | Apr. 10. 1960 | | W. R. Holt | TSF Paulson | Ret. to Bap. 09/13/1963 | |
| Throp, Freddie L. | Apr. 10, 1960 | | W. R. Holt | Ltr. 1st South. Bap. | Ret.to Bap. 09/13/1963 | |
| Throp, Walter (Paulson) | Apr. 02, 1961 | | W. R. Holt | TSF From Paulson | Ret.to Bap. 09/13/1963 | |
| Thurman, Edith (Mrs.) | Jul. 06, 1969 | | R. L. Rayson | TSF. Bristol Hills | Death Apr. 30, 1993 | Gasau |
| Tipton, Lawrence | Apr. 22, 1973 | 4/28/1959 | R. L. Rayson | TSF Whitechurch | Removed Dec. 31, 1981 | DeSpain |

73 - MEMBERS

## Record of Members

| Name | Date Received | Birth | By Whom | How | Status | Remarks |
|---|---|---|---|---|---|---|
| Tombaugh, Clarence W. | Feb. 22, 1959 | | W. R. Holt | Supt. D. W. Smith | Death 1962 | |
| Tombaugh, Iona (Mrs. C. A.) | Feb. 22, 1959 | | W. R. Holt | Ltr. Christian Ch. | | |
| Tombaugh, M. K. (Mrs.) | | | | | Dropped 1949 | |
| Tomecal, Frank | Apr. 17, 1938 | | W. R. Holt | Conf. of Faith | June 1975 Catholic Ch | |
| Tomecal, Jewell (Mrs. Frank) | Apr. 17, 1938 | | W. R. Holt | Conf. of Faith | Death Nov. 17, 1963 | |
| Tomecal, Judy (Hattaway) | | | W. R. Holt | Watch Care Roll | TSF Hattaway | |
| Trindle, Debbie Lynn | Apr. 21, 1968 | 6/21/1956 | W. R. Holt | Conf. of Faith | Removed Dec. 1978 | Harnden |
| Trindle, Jesse B. | Jun. 02, 1957 | 9/22/1928 | W. R. Holt | Conf. of Faith | Removed Dec. 1978 | Harnden |
| Trindle, Kathy (Kelly) | Jul. 22, 1962 | 6/21/1953 | W. R. Holt | Conf. of Faith | Removed Dec. 1978 | Harnden |
| Trindle, Ruby (Mrs. J. ) | Jun. 02, 1957 | 7/21/1928 | W. R. Holt | Conf. of Faith | Removed Dec. 1978 | Harnden |
| Triplett, Avonne Danell | Oct. 13, 1991 | | M. Gasau | Conf. of Faith | | |
| Triplett          Pamela | Oct. 13, 1991 | | M. Gasau | CT Lenexa UMC | TSF 10/10/1997 Trinity | Lamberty |
| True, Alice Kaye | Dec. 11, 1960 | 12/10/1947 | W. R. Holt | Ltr.London Hts | Ltr. 1967 | |
| True, Ginger | Mar. 26, 1967 | 3/19/1957 | W. R. Holt | Conf. of Faith | Nov. 27, 1973 Baptist | |
| True, Paul Eugene | Dec.11,1960 | 10/14/1950 | W. R. Holt | Conf. of Faith | | |
| True, Raymond Paul | Dec. 11, 1960 | 10/9/1925 | W. R. Holt | London Hts.Meth. | Nov. 27, 1973 Baptist | |
| True, Raymond Paul Jr. | Dec. 11, 1960 | 10/14/1950 | W. R. Holt | Conf. of Faith | Nov. 27, 1973 Baptist | |
| True, Roy | Apr. 14, 1968 | 8/8/1958 | W. R. Holt | Conf. of Faith | Nov. 27, 1973 Baptist | |

74 - MEMBERS

**Record of Members**

| Name | Date Received | Birth | By Whom | How | Status | Remarks |
|------|---------------|-------|---------|-----|--------|---------|
| True, Virginia (Mrs. R. P.) | Dec.11, 1960 | 11/28/1928 | W. R. Holt | London Hts. Meth | Nov. 27, 1973 Baptist | |
| Truitt, Eva (Mrs.) | Nov. 16, 1930 | | S. B. Williams | Conf. of Faith | Death 12/06/1960 | |
| Tucker, Bobby R. | Apr. 17, 1960 | 11/14/1928 | W. R. Holt | Conf. of Faith | Removed Dec. 1978 | Harnden |
| Tucker, Carol (Day) | Mar. 26, 1967 | 5/25/1957 | W. R. Holt | Conf. of Faith | Removed Nov. 21, 1988 | |
| Tucker, Donald Richard | Apr. 10, 1966 | 1/4/1956 | W. R. Holt | Conf. of Faith | Nov. 01, 1982 Bapt. | |
| Tucker, Dorthea Lucille (Mrs. R.) | Apr. 17, 1960 | 4/7/1931 | W. R. Holt | Ltr.Bap. Drexel,MO | Removed Dec. 1978 | Harnden |
| Tucker, Gwendolyn (Mrs. R. ) | 1961 | | W. R. Holt | Ltr. EU | Lee's Summit 03/ 01/1992 | Gasau |
| Tucker, Jack (Mrs.) | Apr. 17, 1938 | | W. R. Holt | Conf. of Faith | Removed 5/8/1949 | |
| Tucker, Judy Diann | Apr. 10, 1966 | 2/23/1952 | W. R. Holt | Conf. of Faith | Removed Dec. 03, 1978 | Harnden |
| Tucker, Judy | Jun. 16, 1987 | | R. West | Restored | TSF06/16/1987 Stillwell | West |
| Tucker, Kathryn (Mrs. Don) | Dec. 14,1980 | | I. DeSpain | Cath. New York | Nov. 01, 1982 Bap. KS | |
| Tucker, Lana (Taylor) | Sept. 27, 1964 | | W. R. Holt | Conf. of Faith | Dec.27, 1970 Grace Luth. | |
| Tucker, Lois Dianne | Sept. 27, 1964 | | W. R. Holt | Conf. of Faith | Withdrew Nov. 19, 1986 | West |
| Tucker, Martha Ann (Alexander) | Sept. 27, 1964 | | W. R. Holt | Conf. of Faith | Transfer to Alexander | |
| Tucker, Richard | 1961 | | W. R. Holt | Ltr. Epsicopal | Death 12/09/1966 | Gasau |
| Tucker, T. T. (Mrs.) | | | | | Ltr.2/17/1956 Richmond | |
| Turner, Floyd | Dec. 20. 1952 | | W. R. Holt | Conf. of Faith | 3/25/1971 Bethel Pres. | |
| Turner, Margaret | Dec. 20, 1953 | | W. R. Holt | Trans. | 3/25/1971 Bethel Presby. | |

**Record of Members**

| Name | Date Received | Birth | By Whom | How | Status | Remarks |
|------|---------------|-------|---------|-----|--------|---------|
| Usnick, Barbara (Mrs.) (Olson) | | | | | Ltr. Apr. 19, 1953 | |
| VanAlden, Katie (Mrs.) | | | | | Death | |
| VanAlden, Theodore | | | | Conf. of Faith | Dropped by Request | |
| Vandiver, Mary V. (Hill) | | | W. R. Holt | TSF Hill | Removed 1959 | |
| VanDyke, Carolyn | | | | | | |
| VanDyke, Dorothy (Carlson) | Mar. 28, 1937 | | W. R. Holt | Conf. of Faith | Married as Carlson | |
| VanDyke, Elmer | Mar. 28, 1937 | | W. R. Holt | Conf. of Faith | TSF Methodist 1967 | |
| VanDyke, Elmer (Mrs.) | Mar. 28, 1937 | | W. R. Holt | Conf. of Faith | TSF Methodist 1967 | |
| VanDyke, Helen (Price) | Mar. 28, 1937 | | W. R. Holt | Conf. of Faith | Married Price | |
| VanDyke, Martha (Smith) | | | W. R. Holt | TSF to Smith | Removed 1959 | |
| VanDyke, Mary Catherine | Mar. 28, 1937 | | W. R. Holt | Conf. of Faith | Removed 1/13/1958 | |
| Vaughn, C. J. | Apr. 17, 1938 | | W. R. Holt | Conf. of Faith | Removed 5/8/1949 | |
| Vaughn, C. J. (Mrs.) | | | | | | |
| Verser, Albert | May. 16, 2004 | | L. Lamberty | Conf. of Faith | | |
| Vest, J. B. (Mrs.) | Jan. 19, 1930 | | S. B. Williams | Conf. of Faith | Roeland Park 2/18/1964 | |
| Visteen, Victoria Helen | Apr. 06, 1980 | | J. R. Harnden | Conf. of Faith | Removed Nov. 01, 1998 | Lamberty |
| Wagoner, Arthur R. | | | | | | |
| Wagoner, Arthur R. (Mrs.) | | | | | | |

76 - MEMBERS

**Record of Members**

| Name | Date Received | Birth | By Whom | How | Status | Remarks |
|---|---|---|---|---|---|---|
| Wallace, Jack | Dec.06, 1953 | | W. R. Holt | Transfer | Ltr.to Bap. Dallas Tx 1959 | |
| Wallace, William W. | | | | | | |
| Wallace, William W. (Mrs.) | | | | | | |
| Warnick, Dixie Lee (Wingate) | Apr. 09, 1944 | | W. R. Holt | Ltr. Christian Ch. | Death 02/16/2005 | |
| Warnick, Frances (Donahue) | Jan.24, 1932 | | S. B. Williams | Ltr. Baptist | Married Roy Donahue | |
| Warnick, L. Wayne | Jan. 24, 1932 | | S. B. Williams | Ltr. | Death 09/03/1964 | |
| Warnick, Patty Sue (Converse) | | | | | Married Verne Converse | |
| Warren, Etta Mae (Mrs.) (Watson) | | 8/17/1903 | | Married Watson | Ltr. To Meth. TX 1967 | |
| Warren, George | Apr. 12, 1959 | 06/26/1892 | W. R. Holt | Transfer | Death 1961 | |
| Watson, Alfred G. | 1940 | | W. R. Holt | Trans. U.B. | 10/27/1980 Robinson, KS | DeSpain |
| Watson, Anita Fern | | | | | Death 1952 | |
| Watson, Barbara Ann | Jul. 06, 1958 | | W. R. Holt | Conf. of Faith | Ltr. 1968 | |
| Watson, Carol | Sept. 27, 1964 | 10/5/1954 | W. R. Holt | Conf. of Faith | Nov. 27, 1973 Wyandotte | |
| Watson, Carol | Feb. 11, 1991 | | M. Gasau | Reinstated | 1970 Wyandotte | Gasau |
| Watson, Charles | Sept. 27, 1964 | 7/17/1953 | W. R. Holt | Conf. of Faith | Nov. 27, 1973 Wyandotte | |
| Watson, Charles | | | | | 1970 Wyandotte | Gasau |
| Watson, David | Sept. 27, 1964 | 10/1/1956 | W. R. Holt | Conf. of Faith | Nov. 27, 1973 Wyandotte | |
| Watson, David | | | | | 1970 Wyandotte | Gasau |

**Record of Members**

| Name | Date Received | Birth | By Whom | How | Status | Remarks |
|---|---|---|---|---|---|---|
| Watson, Etta Mae (Warren) | | | | | Married George Warren | |
| Watson, Kenneth E. | 1958 | | | | 1970 Wyandotte UMC | Gasau |
| Watson, Kenneth L. | Sept. 27, 1964 | 7/14/1924 | W. R. Holt | Ltr. Christian Ad. | Nov. 27, 1973 Wyandotte | |
| Watson, Louise (Mrs. A. G.) | 1940 | | W. R. Holt | Trans. U.B. | 10/27/1980 Robinson, KS | DeSpain |
| Watson, Patricia (Parker) | Dec. 22, 1957 | | W. R. Holt | Conf. of Faith | Transfer to Parker | |
| Watson, Patricia J. | 1958 | | | | 1970 Wyandotte UMC | Gasau |
| Watson, Patricia (Mrs. K. L. ) (Parker) | Sept. 27, 1964 | 12/5/1931 | W. R. Holt | Ltr. Christian Ad. | Nov. 27, 1973 Wyandotte | |
| Weddell, Heather Lynn | Jul. 28, 1991 | | M. Gasau | Conf. of Faith | Removed Nov. 07, 1999 | Lamberty |
| Wehrer, Fred | | | | | Death 1953 | |
| Wehrer, Karen Ann (Hrgensk) | Apr. 21, 1957 | 10/7/1945 | W. R. Holt | Conf. of Faith | Transfer to Hrgensk | |
| Wehrer, Lois (Mrs. Ralph) | Apr. 24, 1940 | | W. R. Holt | Ltr. Presbyterian | 11/27/1973 Horsesh., AZ | |
| Wehrer, Ralph | May. 08, 1927 | | S. B. Williams | Conf. of Faith | 11/27/1973 Horsesh.AZ | |
| Weinert, Charles Daniel | Jul. 06, 1980 | | I. DeSpain | T 7th St. UMC | 12/03/1989 Westwood | Gasau |
| Weinert, Daniel Carl | Jul. 06, 1980 | | I. DeSpain | T 7th St. UMC | OD 04/12/1998 Smithville | Lamberty |
| Weinert, Joan (Schmidt) | Jul. 06, 1980 | | I. DeSpain | PF | CT 04/12/1998 Smithville | Lamberty |
| Weinert, Rose Darlene | Jul. 06, 1980 | | I. DeSpain | T 7th St. UMC | OD 12/03/1989 Westwood | Gasau |
| Welch, Philip Gerald | Apr. 21, 1957 | 7/21/1948 | W. R. Holt | Conf. of Faith | Nov. 27, 1973 Removed | |
| Wells, W. E. (Mrs.) | Aug. 31, 1924 | | S. B. Williams | | Transfer to California | |

78 - MEMBERS

**Record of Members**

| Name | Date Received | Birth | By Whom | How | Status | Remarks |
|---|---|---|---|---|---|---|
| Werth, Ann (Bernard) | | | | | Mar. Bernard 06/06/1954 | |
| Werth, Jane | | | | | Removed 4/5/1959 | |
| Werth, Marshall L. | | | | | Ltr. Jun. 25, 1956 | |
| Werth, Marshall L. (Mrs.) | | | | | Ltr. Jun. 25, 1956 | |
| Werth, Marshall L. Jr. | | | | | | |
| Werth, Richard | | | | | Removed 1963 | |
| West, Margaret E. | Jul. 07, 1986 | | R. West | TSF Kirksville, MO | Jun. 08, 1988 Lancaster | West |
| Wetherell, Lillie (Mrs. W. T.) | Jun. 11, 1933 | | S. B. Williams | Tran. UB | Death Mar. 27, 1982 | DeSpain |
| Wetherell, W. Ted | Jun. 11, 1933 | | S. B. Williams | Tran. UB | Death May.04, 1995 | Lamberty |
| Wey, Ruth (Mrs.) (Adams) | | | | | Removed 1967 | |
| Wheeler, Barbara Ann | Jul. 06, 1958 | | W. R. Holt | Conf. of Faith | Ltr.1962 | |
| Wheeler, Frank | | | W. R. Holt | | Transfer 1962 | |
| Wheeler, Frank (Mrs.) | | | W. R. Holt | | Transfer 1962 | |
| Wheeler, H. D. | | | | | Death 12/02/1958 | |
| Wheeler, H. D. (Mrs.) | | | | | Death 1960 | |
| White, Brenda | Feb. 04, 1990 | | M. Gasau | OD M. Bap. Church | | |
| White, Chassidy | Oct. 25, 1992 | | M. Gasau | OD M.Bap. Church | | |
| White, Florence (Mrs. Jewell) | Jan. 06, 1957 | 10/17/1928 | W. R. Holt | Ltr. Baptist | Glad Tidings 12/03/1981 | DeSpain |

79 - MEMBERS

**Record of Members**

| Name | Date Received | Birth | By Whom | How | Status | Remarks |
|------|---------------|-------|---------|-----|--------|---------|
| White, Gladys Mae (Donley) | | | | | M. Donley Sept. 05, 1953 | |
| White, Jewell E. | Jan. 06, 1957 | 6/27/1923 | W. R. Holt | Ltr. Methodist | Glad Tidings 12/03/1981 | DeSpain |
| White, Michael Edward | Jul. 16, 1967 | 7/7/1955 | W. R. Holt | Conf. of Faith | Glad Tidings 12/03/1981 | DeSpain |
| White, Raymond | Jan. 06, 1957 | 4/10/1947 | W. R. Holt | Conf. of Faith | Glad Tidings 12/03/1981 | DeSpain |
| Whitlock, C.L. (Mrs.) | Apr. 17, 1927 | | S. B. Williams | | Removed 4/5/1959 | |
| Wienshienk, Viola (Mrs. C.) (Hoatson) | Apr. 09, 1939 | | W. R. Holt | Ltr. Methodist | Death 1978 | Harnden |
| Wiggins, George | | | | | | |
| Wiggins, George (Mrs.) | | | | | Removed without cert. | |
| Wilcox, Archer | | | | | Removed 4/5/1959 | |
| Wilcox, Archie | | | | | Death | |
| Wilcox, Archie (Mrs.) | | | | | Death Sept. 1957 | |
| Willett, Melva | May. 12, 1959 | | W. R. Holt | Conf. of Faith | Dec. 21, 1969 Central | |
| Willett, Ronald E. | May. 12, 1959 | | W. R. Holt | Conf. of Faith | Dec. 21, 1969 Central | |
| Williams, Doris | Sept. 12, 1982 | | I. DeSpain | Conf. of Faith | Death Jun. 10, 2008 | Lee |
| Williams, Pearl (Mrs. S. B.) | May. 09, 1954 | | W. R. Holt | Trans. EUB | Beloit, KS Mar. 28, 1978 | Harnden |
| Williams, Preston | Sept. 12, 1982 | | I. DeSpain | Conf. of Faith | | |
| Williams, Stanley B. (Dr.) | May. 09, 1954 | | W. R. Holt | Trans. EUB | Death 1977 | Harnden |
| Williams, Vickie | Apr. 20, 2003 | | Lamberty/ Smart | Conf. of Faith | | |

80 - MEMBERS

**Record of Members**

| Name | Date Received | Birth | By Whom | How | Status | Remarks |
|---|---|---|---|---|---|---|
| Williamson, Carl | May. 29, 1976 | | J. R. Harnden | C. T. | Death Dec. 22, 1984 | Stevenson |
| Williamson, Sara | May. 29, 1976 | | J. R. Harnden | C. T. | Death Mar. 05, 2003 | Lamberty |
| Willis, Karen (Hunter) | | | | | | |
| Wilmouth, Francis (Mrs.) (Schaffer) | 1950 | | W. R. Holt | Ltr. Congregational | Death March 23, 1971 | |
| Wilson, Anna Jane (Mrs. V.) | | | | | Removed 4/05/1959 | |
| Wilson, Edna (Mrs.) | Apr. 18, 1954 | | W. R. Holt | Conf. of Faith | Removed 4/5/1959 | |
| Wilson, Elaine Olson (Mrs. W. W.) | May. 29, 1926 | | W. R. Holt | Ltr. Methodist | Death Oct. 30, 1986 | West |
| Wingate, Jack | Apr. 18, 1954 | | W. R. Holt | Conf. of Faith | Grandview 3/01/1959 | |
| Wingate, Jack E. (Mr.) | 1950 | | W. R. Holt | | Grandview 3/01/1959 | |
| Wingate, Jack (Mrs.) | Mar. 28, 1937 | | W. R. Holt | Conf. of Faith | Grandview 3/01/1959 | |
| Winn, C. R. | | | | | Letter 09/01/1957 | |
| Winn, C. R. (Mrs.) | | | | | Letter 09/01/1957 | |
| Winterringer, Carl Everett | May. 01, 1960 | 6/3/1929 | W. R. Holt | Conf. of Faith | Removed Dec. 03, 1981 | DeSpain |
| Winterringer, Myrene Mary (Mrs.) | May. 01, 1960 | | W. R. Holt | Ltr. Baptist | Death 1976 | |
| Winterringer, Patricia Margaret | May. 01, 1960 | 10/6/1931 | W. R. Holt | Conf. of Faith | Removed Dec. 03, 1981 | DeSpain |
| Wittenberg, Roberta (Mrs. Charles) | Dec. 1946 | | W. R. Holt | Conf. of Faith | 03/22/1988 Eldorado, KS | West |
| Wolch, Phillip Gerald | Apr. 21, 1957 | 7/21/1948 | W. R. Holt | Conf. of Faith | | |
| Woodland, Carl (Mrs.) | | | | | Removed | |

81 - MEMBERS

**Record of Members**

| Name | Date Received | Birth | By Whom | How | Status | Remarks |
|---|---|---|---|---|---|---|
| Wright, John N. | Apr. 06, 1968 | | W. R. Holt | TSF EUB(Eudora) | Removed Dec. 03, 1981 | DeSpain |
| Wright, Oreta (Mrs. J. N.) (Kelly) | 1939 | | W. R. Holt | Conf. of Faith | Removed Dec/ 03, 1981 | DeSpain |
| Young, Clay | Aug. 21, 1966 | | W. R. Holt | Grandview Meth | Death Sept. 1973 | |
| Young, Elbridge | Sept. 13, 1953 | | W. R. Holt | Ltr. Methodist | Death Oct. 17, 1982 | DeSpain |
| Young, Elbridge (Mrs.) | Sept. 13, 1953 | | W. R. Holt | Ltr. | | |
| Young, Elwood | May. 07, 1933 | | S. B. Williams | Ltr. Baptist | Death Jan. 19, 1990 | Gasau |
| Young, Florette (Mrs. George) | 1950 | | W. R. Holt | Conf. of Faith | Death Feb. 12, 1991 | Gasau |
| Young, George | 1950 | | W. R. Holt | Conf. of Faith | Death Oct. 06, 1983 | DeSpain |
| Young, Helen (Mrs. Elwood) | May. 07, 1933 | | S. B. Williams | Conf. of Faith | | |
| Young, Iona | Aug. 21, 1966 | | W. R. Holt | W. Highlands Pres | Withdrew 1989 | Gasau |
| Young, John F. | Jan. 24, 1932 | | S. B. Williams | Ltr. | Death 1952 | |
| Young, Marilyn (Mrs. Clinton) (Pigg) | Dec. 10, 1969 | | W. R. Holt | TSF from Pigg | Withdrew 1989 | Gasau |
| Young, Mary (Mrs. E.) | Sept. 13, 1953 | | W. R. Holt | Ltr. Congregational | 10/20/1988 Olathe Bible | Gasau |
| Young, Myrtle (Mrs. J. F.) | Jan. 24, 1932 | | S. B. Williams | Ltr. Baptist | Death Oct. 7, 1973 | |
| Youngdoff, Judith (Mr. Larry) | Dec. 15, 1963 | | W. R. Holt | | Old Mission 9/14/1966 | |
| Youngdoff, Larry | Dec. 15, 1963 | | W. R. Holt | | Old Mission 9/14/1966 | |
| Yoxall, Hazel (Mrs. J.) | Oct. 23, 1927 | | S. B. Williams | Trans.UB | Died 5/28/1984/ Dec1949? | DeSpain |
| Yoxall, John | Oct. 23, 1927 | | S. B. Williams | Ltr. | Death Dec. 1977 | Hamden |

**Record of Members**

| Name | Date Received | Birth | By Whom | How | Status | Remarks |
|---|---|---|---|---|---|---|
| Yuille, T. R. (Mrs.) | | | | | | |
| Zane, Wayne | Jan. 24, 1932 | | S. B. Williams | Ltr. | Removed 4/5/1959 | |
| Zane, Wayne W. (Mrs.) | Jan. 24, 1932 | | S. B. Williams | Ltr. | Removed 4/5/1959 | |
| Zimmer, Craig Lee | Apr. 17, 1960 | 7/13/1948 | W. R. Holt | Conf. of Faith | Stony Point June 1977 | Harnden |
| Zimmer, Debra Sue (Hallier) | May. 08, 1966 | | W. R. Holt | Conf. of Faith | TSF Hallier | |
| Zimmer, Deloris (Mrs. Paul) (Novak) | Dec. 06, 1963 | | W. R. Holt | TSF Novak | Cornerst. Bap.06/08/1971 | |
| Zimmer, Linda Sue (Dryer) | Apr. 01, 1956 | 7/13/1944 | W. R. Holt | Conf. of Faith | Married Donald Dryer | |
| Zimmer, Pauline (Mrs. Robert) | | 6/30/1918 | W. R. Holt | Ltr. Methodist | Death 11/11/2004 | Lamberty |
| Zimmer, Robert | | 5/17/1916 | W. R. Holt | Conf. of Faith | Death Oct. 14, 1990 | Gasau |
| Zimmer, Sandra (Mrs. Craig) (Allison) | Jan. 06, 1957 | | W. R. Holt | Conf. of Faith | Stony Point June 1977 | |
| Zimmerman, Ira | Jul. 31, 1966 | | W. R. Holt | Ltr.Presbyterian | Mar. 01, 1981 Trinity | DeSpain |
| Zimmerman, Stella (Mrs. Ira) | Jul. 31, 1966 | | W. R. Holt | Tran. EUB | Deceased Dec. 02, 1975 | |

# RECORD OF BAPTISMS

## 1919 - 2009

**Record of Baptisms**

| Name | Date | Status | Born | Parents | Place | Minister | Remarks |
|---|---|---|---|---|---|---|---|
| Allison, Melvin E. | 1/6/1957 | Adult | 9/3/1928 | | Univ. EUB | Dr. W. R. Holt | |
| Allison, Sandra Sue | 1/6/1957 | Child | 5/15/1952 | Mr. & Mrs. Melvin Allison | Univ. EUB | Dr. W. R. Holt | |
| Atkins, Craig Stevens | 4/1/1956 | Infant | 8/10/1955 | Mr. & Mrs. Clyde Atkins | Univ. EUB | Dr. W. R. Holt | |
| Bailey, Carol Dianne | 3/6/1960 | Child | 2/16/1957 | Robert & Shirley Bailey | Univ. EUB | Dr. W. R. Holt | |
| Bailey, Robert Charles Jr. | 3/6/1960 | Child | 3/22/1959 | Robert & Shirley Bailey | Univ. EUB | Dr. W. R. Holt | |
| Bailey, Shirley Jean | 3/6/1960 | Adult | 11/20/1929 | George & Florence Pearson | Univ. EUB | Dr. W. R. Holt | |
| Baker, David Lawrence | 3/31/1957 | Child | 9/14/1954 | Mr. & Mrs. Lawrence D. Baker | Univ. EUB | Dr. W. R. Holt | |
| Barfield, Rosemary Lee | 4/1/1956 | Child | 5/9/1944 | Mr. & Mrs. Lee Barfield | Univ. EUB | Dr. W. R. Holt | |
| Barrett, Deloris | 4/18/1954 | Adult | | | Univ. EUB | Dr. W. R. Holt | |
| Barton, Airoh | 11/7/2004 | Infant | 1999 | Wayne & Jackie Barton | Univ. UM | L. Lamberty | Preparation |
| Barton, Asha | 11/7/2004 | Infant | 1999 | Wayne & Jackie Barton | Univ. UM | L. Lamberty | Preparation |
| Barton, Wayne | 4/27/2003 | Adult | | | Univ. UM | L. Lamberty | Full mbrshp |
| Bauer, Lisa Marie | 3/19/1967 | Infant | 1/31/1967 | Jesse R. & Dorothy June Bauer | Univ. EUB | Dr. W. R. Holt | |
| Bauer, Scott Wayne | 4/22/1962 | Child | 4/1/1962 | J. Robert & Dorothy June Bauer | Univ. EUB | Dr. W. R. Holt | |
| Becker, Vernon | 7/12/1959 | Adult | | | Univ. EUB | Dr. W. R. Holt | |
| Bennett, Edna (Mrs.) | 7/12/1959 | Adult | 12/6/1910 | Mr. & Mrs. Burl Roberts | Univ. EUB | Dr. W. R. Holt | |
| Berry, Dwight Alan | 3/20/1955 | Infant | 2/7/1953 | Mr. & Mrs. Cleo Berry | Univ. EUB | Dr. W. R. Holt | |

2 - BAPTISMS

| Name | Date | Status | Born | Parents | Place | Minister | Remarks |
|------|------|--------|------|---------|-------|----------|---------|
| Berve, Deborah Lynn | 9/19/1971 | Infant | 2/2/1971 | David & Margaret Berve | Univ. UM | R. L. Rayson | Baptism |
| Berve, John David | 4/24/1960 | Adult | | John & Beatrice Berve | Univ. EUB | Dr. W. R. Holt | |
| Berve, John Leroy | 11/10/1963 | Infant | 7/19/1963 | John D. & Margaret A.Berve | Univ. EUB | Dr. W. R. Holt | |
| Berve, Richard Dean | 1/29/1967 | Infant | 5/3/1966 | John D. & Margaret A. Berve | Univ. EUB | Dr. W. R. Holt | |
| Biggs, Donald Eugene | 10/15/1967 | Child | 1/3/1962 | Emmett W. & Murna M. Biggs | Univ. EUB | Dr. W. R. Holt | |
| Biggs, Edward Wayne | 7/10/1960 | Infant | 8/12/1957 | Emmett W. & Murna M. Biggs | Univ. EUB | Dr. W. R. Holt | |
| Blackaby, Ronald Carl | 3/30/1958 | Infant | 10/11/1957 | Mr. & Mrs. Clyde Blackaby | Univ. EUB | Dr. W. R. Holt | |
| Blevin, Brian Eric | 5/9/1965 | Infant | 12/6/1964 | Richard & Elizabeth Blevin | Univ. EUB | Dr. W. R. Holt | Fath. Died |
| Blevin, Paul Allen | 5/9/1965 | Child | 1/1/1963 | Richard & Elizabeth Blevin | Univ. EUB | Dr. W. R. Holt | Fath. Died |
| Blevin, Richard Elton | 5/9/1965 | Child | 12/4/1959 | Richard & Elizabeth Blevin | Univ. EUB | Dr. W. R. Holt | Fath. Died |
| Blevin, Richard Elton Jr. | 3/29/1970 | Adult | 12/4/1959 | Elizabeth & Richard Blevin | Univ. UM | R. L. Rayson | Sprinkling |
| Blood, David | 5/18/1986 | | | Walter & Pamela Blood | Univ. UM | Stevenson | Preparation |
| Blood, David Andrew | 6/24/1973 | Infant | 2/24/1973 | Walter & Pamela Blood | Univ. UM | R. L. Rayson | Dedication |
| Bolton, Diana Lynn | 6/3/1973 | Youth | 8/1/1955 | George & Rose Bolton | Univ. UM | R. L. Rayson | Sprinkling |
| Bolton, Jeffrey George | 6/3/1973 | Youth | 2/21/1961 | George & Rose Bolton | Univ. UM | R. L. Rayson | Sprinkling |
| Brooks, Mary Ann | 4/25/1954 | Adult | | | Univ. EUB | Dr. W. R. Holt | |
| Brotherton, Charles Duane | 12/24/1989 | | | | Univ. UM | M.Gasau | Full mbrshp |
| Brotherton, Ethan Alexander | 12/24/1989 | | | Chuck & Mary Brotherton | Univ. UM | M.Gasau | Preparation |
| Brotherton, Mary Elizabeth | 12/24/1989 | | | Al & Pat Greenwood | Univ. UM | M. Gasua | Full mbrshp |
| Browne, Serena | 6/24/2007 | | `1988 | Julie Browne | Univ. UM | L. Lamberty | Full mbrshp |

3 - BAPTISMS

| Name | Date | Status | Born | Parents | Place | Minister | Remarks |
|------|------|--------|------|---------|-------|----------|---------|
| Brucker, Todd Edward | 3/30/1969 | Infant | 12/17/1968 | Edward & Ann Brucker | Univ. UM | R. L. Rayson | |
| Bushnell, Duane Jay | 10/13/1957 | Infant | 1/25/1957 | Mr. & Mrs. Wilfred Bushnell | Univ. EUB | Dr. W. R. Holt | |
| Byrd, Bridget Elaine | 4/14/1968 | Infant | 2/14/1968 | Ronald & Nancy Jane Byrd | Univ. EUB | Dr. W. R. Holt | |
| Cain, Alanan | 4/18/1954 | Adult | 11/29/1943 | Mrs. James Parrott | Univ. EUB | Dr. W. R. Holt | |
| Cain, Gary Bryant | 4/18/1954 | Adult | 8/30/1938 | Mrs. James Parrott | Univ. EUB | Dr. W. R. Holt | |
| Cain, Sheryl Lee | 4/18/1954 | Adult | 9/24/1941 | Mrs. James Parrott | Univ. EUB | Dr. W. R. Holt | |
| Canfield, Amy Colleen | 4/16/1967 | Infant | 3/24/1967 | Michael D. & Gayle Canfield | Univ. EUB | Dr. W. R. Holt | |
| Canfield, Sarah Diane | 8/16/1970 | Infant | 7/15/1970 | Michael Duane & Gayle Canfield | Univ. UM | Dr. W. R. Holt | |
| Carmitchell, Allen Lee | 10/26/1955 | Child | | Mr. & Mrs. Charles Carmitchell Jr. | Univ. EUB | Dr. W. R. Holt | |
| Carmitchell, Charles Ralph | 1/6/1957 | Infant | 6/20/1956 | Mr. & Mrs. Charles Carmitchell | Univ. EUB | Dr. W. R. Holt | |
| Carmitchell, Richard Arthur | 1/31/1954 | Infant | 12/14/1953 | Mr. & Mrs. Charles Carmitchell | Univ. EUB | Dr. W. R. Holt | |
| Carmitchell, Steven Douglas | 8/3/1958 | Infant | 3/2/1958 | Mr. & Mrs. Charles Carmitchell Jr. | Univ. EUB | Dr. W. R. Holt | |
| Charles, Debra Ann | 4/18/1954 | Infant | 3/4/1952 | Mr. & Mrs. Eldon Charles | Univ. EUB | Dr. W. R. Holt | GF Wilson |
| Charles, Eldon LeRoy Jr. | 4/18/1954 | | 11/14/1953 | Mr. & Mrs. Eldon Charles | Univ. EUB | Dr. W. R. Holt | GF Wilson |
| Charles, Geoffrey | 4/18/1954 | Sm. Child | 12/17/1946 | Mr. & Mrs. Eldon Charles | | | Baptised Before |
| Charles, Robert Dwaine | 4/6/1958 | Infant | 6/16/1957 | Mr. & Mrs. Buford Charles | Univ. EUB | Dr. W. R. Holt | |
| Charles, Scott Allen | 4/2/1961 | Child | 2/19/1960 | Buford Duaine & Martha Charles | Univ. EUB | Dr. W. R. Holt | |
| Charlson, Reggie Thomas | 2/10/1957 | Child | 10/3/1946 | Mr. & Mrs. Bill Charlson | Univ. EUB | Dr. W. R. Holt | |
| Charlson, Ronnie Eugene | 2/10/1957 | Adult | 9/11/1943 | Mr. & Mrs. Bill Charlson | Univ. EUB | Dr. W. R. Holt | |
| Chisham, William Edward | 4/17/1938 | Infant | 1/15/1932 | Wm. E. & Grace Chisham | Univ. EUB | Dr. W. R. Holt | |

4 - BAPTISMS

| Name | Date | Status | Born | Parents | Place | Minister | Remarks |
|------|------|--------|------|---------|-------|----------|---------|
| Cloughley, Julie | 4/18/1954 | Adult | 9/30/1943 | Mr. & Mrs. Wm. Cloughley | Univ. EUB | Dr. W. R. Holt | |
| Cloughley, Suann | 4/18/1954 | Adult | 1/1/1941 | Mr. & Mrs. Wm. Cloughley | Univ. EUB | Dr. W. R. Holt | |
| Clyde, Gina Marie | Sept. 1970 | Infant | 7/19/1970 | James & Janet Clyde | Univ. UM | R. L. Rayson | |
| Clyde, Lisa Kay | 7/11/1971 | Infant | 5/26/1971 | James & Janet Clyde | Univ. UM | R. L. Rayson | Baptism |
| Cobb, Geffrey Carl | 12/11/1960 | Infant | 4/28/1960 | Lloyd & Betty Cobb | Univ. EUB | Dr. W. R. Holt | |
| Cobb, Matthew Steven | 12/11/1960 | Child | 3/8/1956 | Lloyd & Betty Cobb | Univ. EUB | Dr. W. R. Holt | |
| Cordill, Joyce (Mrs. C.) | 4/14/1968 | Adult | | | Univ. EUB | Dr. W. R. Holt | |
| Crockett, Ginger | 2/14/1954 | Sm. Child | | Mr. & Mrs. David Crockett | | | |
| Cunningham, Kimberly | 5/18/1986 | | | | Univ. UM | Stevenson | No preparation |
| Cunningham, Vickie Sue | 4/17/1960 | Child | 7/28/1951 | John & Marjorie Cunningham | Univ. EUB | Dr. W. R. Holt | |
| Daniels, Rickey DeVaughn | 5/14/1950 | Child | 7/21/1947 | Earl & Marselle Daniels | Univ. EUB | Dr. W. R. Holt | |
| Delich, David Michael Lee | 4/2/1953 | Youth | 10/12/1949 | Michael Eugene & Hazel Delich | Univ. EUB | Dr. W. R. Holt | |
| Delich, Rosemary | 8/25/1963 | Adult | 3/22/1943 | Henry & Mary Delich | Univ. EUB | Dr. W. R. Holt | |
| Divilbiss, Dawn Michele | 12/22/1957 | Infant | 4/18/1957 | Mr. & Mrs. Ronald Divilbiss | Univ. EUB | Dr. W. R. Holt | |
| Divilbiss, James Bradley | 4/2/1961 | Child | 8/2/1960 | Ronald W. & Sandra L.Divilbiss | Univ. EUB | Dr. W. R. Holt | |
| Divilbiss, Ronald Byron | 4/2/1961 | Child | 11/10/1958 | Ronald W. & Sandra L. Divilbiss | Univ. EUB | Dr. W. R. Holt | |
| Dixon, Chris | 4/20/2003 | Adult | `1977 | | Univ. UM | L. Lamberty | Full mbrshp |
| Dodd, James Cody | 9/26/1982 | | | James & Linda Dodd | Univ. UM | Ira DeSpain | Preparation |
| Donnell, Michael Louis | 5/23/2004 | Infant | `2003 | | Univ. UM | L. Lamberty | Preparation |
| Dowd, Nedra Colleen | 2/28/1954 | Infant | 8/14/1953 | Mr. & Mrs. Harry Dowd | Univ. EUB | Dr. W. R. Holt | |

5 - BAPTISMS

| Name | Date | Status | Born | Parents | Place | Minister | Remarks |
|------|------|--------|------|---------|-------|----------|---------|
| Dryer, Shawna Rae | 4/4/1971 | Infant | 6/15/1970 | Daniel & Linda (Zimmer) Dryer | Univ. UM | R. L. Rayson | Baptism |
| Dugan, June (Mrs.) | 4/2/1972 | Adult | | | Univ. UM | R. L. Rayson | Sprinkling |
| Dysert, Brett Robert | 10/26/1955 | Child | 11/14/1954 | Mr. & Mrs. John Dysert | Univ. EUB | Dr. W. R. Holt | |
| Eagle, Robert William | 7/28/1957 | Infant | 12/15/1956 | Mr. & Mrs. John F. Eagle | Univ. EUB | Dr. W. R. Holt | |
| Early, Dale Joseph | 3/22/1970 | Infant | 2/9/1970 | Marvin M. & Laura Elaine Early | Univ. UM | R. L. Rayson | |
| Early, Darryl Lee | 3/26/1967 | Infant | 12/22/1966 | Marion M. & Laura Early | Univ. EUB | Dr. W. R. Holt | |
| Early, Debora Elaine | 8/15/1965 | Infant | 7/14/1965 | Marvin M. & Laura Elaine Early | Univ. EUB | Dr. W. R. Holt | |
| Early, Diana Ellen | 2/20/1972 | Infant | 1/11/1972 | Marvin & Laura Early | Univ. UM | R. L. Rayson | Sprinkling |
| Early, Marvin Milford Jr. | 6/3/1973 | Adult | 6/11/1945 | Marvin & June Early | Univ. UM | R. L. Rayson | Sprinkling |
| Eaton, Edward Anson | 1/19/1958 | Infant | 9/19/1956 | Mr. & Mrs. John Eaton Jr. | Univ. EUB | Dr. W. R. Holt | |
| Eaton, Edward Anton | 1/3/1965 | Child | 9/19/1956 | John A. Eaton Jr. & Virginia Eaton | Univ. EUB | Dr. W. R. Holt | |
| Eaton, Joneen Elaine | 10/24/1954 | Infant | 5/29/1954 | Mr. & Mrs. John E. Eaton Jr. | Univ. EUB | Dr. W. R. Holt | |
| Ellington, Jessica Lynne | 4/12/1981 | | | Dan & Lynne Ellington | Univ. UM | Ira DeSpain | Preparation |
| Evans, Bruce Alvin | 5/14/1950 | Child | 11/15/1948 | Donald D. & Elizabeth Evans | Univ. EUB | Dr. W. R. Holt | Ad. Riley |
| Evans, Janet Kay | 5/14/1950 | Infant | 3/28/1950 | Donald D. & Elizabeth Evans | Univ. EUB | Dr. W. R. Holt | Ad. Riley |
| Evans, Laura Elaine | 11/10/1946 | Infant | 9/10/1946 | Donald D. & Elizabeth Evans | Univ. EUB | Dr. W. R. Holt | Ad. Riley |
| Everhart, Keith | 3/26/1967 | Infant | 6/21/1966 | Richard L. & Margaret Everhart | Univ. EUB | Dr. W. R. Holt | |
| Forbes, Kenneth A. | 1/6/1957 | Child | 3/29/1951 | Mr. & Mrs. Noel Forbes | Univ. EUB | Dr. W. R. Holt | |
| Forbes, Matthew Joel | 11/21/1971 | Infant | 10/11/1971 | Dennis & Peggy Forbes | Univ. UM | R. L. Rayson | Sprinkling |
| Forbes, Michael Leon | 1/6/1957 | Child | 9/10/1955 | Mr. & Mrs. Noel Forbes | Univ. EUB | Dr. W. R. Holt | |

6 - BAPTISMS

| Name | Date | Status | Born | Parents | Place | Minister | Remarks |
|---|---|---|---|---|---|---|---|
| Foster, Georgia Bea (Mrs.) | 4/29/1962 | Adult | 10/31/1936 | Chet & Geneva Smith | Univ. EUB | Dr. W. R. Holt | |
| Foster, Michael Steven | 12/31/1967 | Infant | 9/18/1966 | Ronald Lee & Georgia Bea Foster | Univ. EUB | Dr. W. R. Holt | |
| Foster, Mitchell Scott | 3/31/1963 | Child | 10/7/1962 | Ronald Lee & Georgia Bea Foster | Univ. EUB | Dr. W. R. Holt | |
| Foster, Ronald Lee | 4/29/1962 | Adult | 9/16/1935 | Arte & Gertrude Foster | Univ. EUB | Dr. W. R. Holt | |
| Frazier, Kennice Lymette | 3/23/2008 | Infant | '2008 | Kenya Frazier | Univ. UM | L. Lamberty | Preparation |
| Frazier, Ricky Jr. | 2/25/2006 | Youth | '1989 | Ricky Frazier Sr. | Univ. UM | L. Lamberty | Full mbrshp |
| Gallipeau, Connie Lee | 9/26/1965 | Youth | | | Univ. EUB | Dr. W. R. Holt | |
| Gallipeau, Jerry | 9/26/1965 | Adult | | | Univ. EUB | Dr. W. R. Holt | |
| Gallipeau, Kimberly Lynn | 6/24/1973 | Infant | 4/23/1973 | Michael & Cheryl Gallipeau | Univ. UM | R. L. Rayson | Sprinkling |
| Gallipeau, Maxine | 9/26/1965 | Adult | | | Univ. EUB | Dr. W. R. Holt | |
| Gallipeau, Michael | 9/26/1965 | Youth | | | Univ. EUB | Dr. W. R. Holt | |
| Gerster, Bonnie | 4/14/1968 | Youth | 11/14/1955 | Mr. R. C. Gerster-Mrs. S. Neidholdt | Univ. EUB | Dr. W. R. Holt | |
| Gerster, Robert | 4/14/1968 | Youth | 5/12/1958 | Mr. R. C. Gerster-Mrs. S. Neidholdt | Univ. EUB | Dr. W. R. Holt | |
| Gicalone, Jennifer Sue | 1/2/1972 | Infant | 11/19/1971 | Philip and Julie Gicalone | Univ. UM | R. L. Rayson | |
| Gicalone, Philip Anthony Jr. | 11/3/1968 | Infant | 10/2/1968 | Philip and Julie Gicalone | Univ. UM | R. L. Rayson | |
| Givler, Ailsa Kay | 4/18/1954 | Infant | 3/18/1954 | Mr. & Mrs. E. G. Givles | Univ. EUB | Dr. W. R. Holt | |
| Givler, Gary Wayne | 4/18/1954 | Sm. Child | 9/4/1949 | Mr. & Mrs. E. G. Givles | | | Bp. Before |
| Gordon, David B. | 12/25/1966 | Adult | | | Univ. EUB | Dr. W. R. Holt | |
| Graves, Clifford Elmer | 5/5/1957 | Adult | 9/10/1910 | Mr. & Mrs. George F. Graves | Univ.EUB | Dr. W. R. Holt | |

| Name | Date | Status | Born | Parents | Place | Minister | Remarks |
|---|---|---|---|---|---|---|---|
| Graves, Clifford Frank | 3/2/1958 | Child | 11/30/1950 | Mr. & Mrs. Clifford Graves | Univ. EUB | Dr. W. R. Holt | |
| Graves, Dorothy Lucille | 5/5/1957 | Adult | 9/10/1910 | Mr. & Mr. Andrew Rosentreter | | | |
| Graves, Stephen Louis | 3/2/1958 | Child | 1/12/1953 | Mr. & Mrs. Clifford Graves | Univ. EUB | Dr. W. R. Holt | |
| Green, Shanika | 4/23/2006 | | `1989 | Patricia Green | Univ. UM | L.Lamberty | Full mbrshp |
| Green, Vivian Lynn | 10/20/1957 | Infant | 7/17/1957 | Mr. & Mrs. Arthur Green | Univ. EUB | Dr. W. R. Holt | |
| Greenwood, Patricia | 1/2/1983 | Adult | | | Univ. UM | Ira DeSpain | Full mbrshp |
| Grubb, Corey | 6/3/2007 | Adult | `1988 | | Univ. UM | L.Lamberty | Full mbrshp |
| Gung, Helen Lavon | 4/10/1966 | Youth | | | Univ.EUB | Dr. W. R. Holt | |
| Gung, Pamela Ann | 4/10/1966 | Youth | | | Univ. EUB | Dr. W. R. Holt | |
| Gung, Richard E. | 4/10/1966 | Adult | | | Univ. EUB | Dr. W. R. Holt | |
| Hallier, Bryan Grant | 9/27/1981 | Infant | 12/8/1980 | Steve & Debbie Hallier | Univ. UM | Ira DeSpain | Preparation |
| Hallier, Lisa Renee | 6/26/1983 | Infant | 4/29/1983 | Debra& Steve Hallier | Univ. UM | Ira DeSpain | Preparation |
| Hataway, Deborah Lynne | 6/19/1955 | Infant | 9/4/1954 | Mr. & Mrs. C. A. Hataway | Univ. EUB | Dr. W. R. Holt | |
| Hataway, Deborah Lynne | 5/8/1966 | Youth | 9/4/1954 | Cara Lee Jr. & Marilyn Hataway | Univ. EUB | Dr. W. R. Holt | |
| Hataway, Shawn Rene | 5/13/1956 | Child | 11/4/1955 | Mr. & Mrs. C. L. Hataway | Univ. EUB | Dr. W. R. Holt | |
| Hataway, Shawn Rene | 5/8/1966 | Youth | 11/4/1955 | Cara Lee Jr. & Marilyn Hataway | Univ. EUB | Dr. W. R. Holt | |
| Hataway, Sue Ann | 6/19/1960 | Child | 8/30/1959 | Cara Lee & Marilyn Hataway | Univ. EUB | Dr. W. R. Holt | |
| Hauskins, William Dean | 4/18/1954 | | 10/17/1951 | Harry C. & Julia Hauskins | Univ. EUB | Dr. W. R. Holt | |
| Heathman, Gerald Lee | 6/10/1962 | Infant | 5/6/1962 | Gerald L. & Connie L. Heathman | Univ. EUB | Dr. W. R. Holt | |
| Heilman, Heather Ann | 1/5/1969 | Infant | 11/20/1968 | Michael & Julie Heilman | Univ. UM | R. L. Rayson | |

| Name | Date | Status | Born | Parents | Place | Minister | Remarks |
|---|---|---|---|---|---|---|---|
| Henderson, Johnny | 3/23/2008 | Youth | 4/29/1994 | John Henderson & Lou A. Gosling | Univ. UM | L.Lamberty | Full mbrshp |
| Hershberger, Brian Lee | 4/1/1973 | Infant | 11/20/1972 | Larry Ray & Jill Sue Hershberger | Univ. UM | R. L. Rayson | Sprinkling |
| Hershberger, Gina L. | 1/30/1983 | Infant | 10/18/1982 | Larry & Jill Hershberger | Univ. UM | Ira DeSpain | Preparation |
| Hershberger, Scott Ray | 8/22/1971 | Infant | 8/4/1971 | Larry and Jill Hershberger | Univ. UM | R. L. Rayson | Baptism |
| Hobbs, Jamika Marini | 10/31/1991 | | | Margie Hobbs | Univ. UM | M. Gasau | Full mbrshp |
| Holcomb, Kathy Jane | 4/18/1954 | Infant | 7/10/1953 | Mr. & Mrs. Gene Holcomb | Univ. EUB | Dr. W. R. Holt | |
| Hollander, Amy Jean | 12/22/1985 | | | Bill & Candy Hollander | Univ. UM | Stevenson | Preparation |
| Hollander, Gregory Louis | Easter 1950 | Infant | 3/5/1949 | William & Geneva Hollander | Univ. EUB | Dr. W. R. Holt | |
| Hollander, Julie Ann | 6/3/1956 | Infant | 2/27/1956 | Mr. & Mrs. William Hollander | Univ. EUB | Dr. W. R. Holt | |
| Hollander, Lynn Marie | 12/21/1952 | Infant | 9/11/1952 | William & Geneva Hollander | Univ. EUB | Dr. W. R. Holt | |
| Hollander, William Dustin | 12/21/1980 | | | William & Candy Hollander | Univ. UM | Ira DeSpain | |
| Hollander, William George | 11/10/1957 | Infant | 9/13/1957 | Mr. & Mrs. William Hollander | Univ. EUB | Dr. W. R. Holt | |
| Holsapple, Mary Katherine | 12/26/1948 | Infant | 6/12/1948 | Fred W. & Arlene Edna Holsapple | Univ. EUB | Dr. W. R. Holt | |
| Hoover, Allen Scott | 7/1/1962 | Child | 7/7/1961 | Wm. Carl & Sherry Gail Hoover | Univ. EUB | Dr. W. R. Holt | |
| Hoover, Annie Lee | 7/1/1962 | Child | 6/7/1959 | Wm. Carl & Sherry Gail Hoover | Univ. EUB | Dr. W. R. Holt | |
| Hoover, William Carl Jr. | 4/21/1957 | Infant | 11/2/1956 | Mr. & Mrs. William Carl Hoover | Univ. EUB | Dr. W. R. Holt | |
| Hunt, Kimberly Sue | 7/6/1958 | Infant | 1/5/1958 | Mr. & Mrs. Bryce E. Hunt | Univ. EUB | Dr. W. R. Holt | |
| Jella, Karen Lee | 4/18/1954 | Adult | 9/3/1944 | Mr. & Mrs. Howard M. Jella | Univ. EUB | Dr. W. R. Holt | |
| Jella, Russell Howard | 4/18/1954 | Adult | 9/16/1946 | Mr.& Mrs. Howard M. Jella | Univ. EUB | Dr. W. R. Holt | |
| Johnson, David Milton Jr. | 9/29/1957 | Infant | 8/7/1957 | Mr. & Mrs. David Johnson | Univ.EUB | Dr. W. R. Holt | |

9 - BAPTISMS

| Name | Date | Status | Born | Parents | Place | Minister | Remarks |
|------|------|--------|------|---------|-------|----------|---------|
| Johnson, Duane William | 4/17/1949 | Child | 9/3/1944 | William & Gola Johnson | Univ. EUB | Dr. W. R. Holt | |
| Johnson, Evan Lawrence | 4/17/1949 | Infant | 11/23/1948 | William & Gola Johnson | Univ. EUB | Dr. W. R. Holt | |
| Johnson, James Nicholas | 2/15/1981 | Infant | 10/27/1980 | Richard & Connie Johnson | Univ. UM | Ira DeSpain | Preparation |
| Johnson, Kevin Eugene | 6/12/1960 | Child | 4/24/1960 | David & Vivian Johnson | Univ. EUB | Dr. W. R. Holt | |
| Johnson, Laura Elizabeth | 4/20/1986 | Infant | 1/15/1986 | Richard & Connie Johnson | Univ. UM | Stevenson | Preparation |
| Johnson, Pamella Ann | 4/14/1963 | Infant | 9/27/1962 | David M. & Vivian Johnson | Univ. EUB | Dr. W. R. Holt | |
| Karl, Albert Lyle | 5/5/1957 | Adult | 9/16/1911 | | Univ. EUB | Dr. W. R. Holt | |
| Keeter, Juanette (Mrs.) | 3/7/1954 | | | | Univ. EUB | Dr. W. R. Holt | |
| Keeter, Kay Ellen | 4/17/1960 | Infant | 5/11/1959 | James & Norma Jeanne Keeter | Univ. EUB | Dr. W. R. Holt | |
| Kelly, Leannah (Mrs.) | 4/28/1968 | Adult | 1/4/1906 | | Univ. EUB | Dr. W. R. Holt | |
| Kerr, Kevin | 4/14/1968 | Youth | 4/19/1958 | Mr. & Mrs. George Kerr | Univ. EUB | Dr. W. R. Holt | |
| Kieter, Mark David | 9/13/1953 | Infant | 8/16/1953 | Mr. & Mrs. James Kieter | Univ. EUB | Dr. W. R. Holt | |
| King, James L. | 4/7/1963 | Adult | | | Univ. EUB | Dr. W. R. Holt | |
| King, James Lee | 4/7/1963 | Child | 2/22/1955 | James & Wanda King | Univ. EUB | Dr. W. R. Holt | |
| King, Lynette M. | 4/7/1963 | Youth | 1/18/1950 | James & Wanda King | Univ. EUB | Dr. W. R. Holt | |
| King, Wanda L. | 4/7/1963 | Adult | | | Univ. EUB | Dr. W. R. Holt | |
| Krueger, John Frederick | 5/24/1964 | Infant | 3/7/1964 | Donald P. & Barbara K. Krueger | Univ. EUB | Dr. W. R. Holt | |
| Lacy, Hershall Wm. | 10/25/1953 | Infant | 8/25/1953 | Mr. & Mrs. Harry Lacy | Univ. EUB | Dr. S. B. Williams | |
| LaHue, Betty Dean | 6/14/1959 | Adult | 12/21/1925 | Neal Matney & Mildred Matney | Univ. EUB | Dr. W. R. Holt | |
| LaHue, Nic Monroe | 4/22/1962 | Child | 3/17/1962 | William & Betty LaHue | Univ. EUB | Dr. W. R. Holt | |

10 - BAPTISMS

| Name | Date | Born | Status | Parents | Place | Minister | Remarks |
|---|---|---|---|---|---|---|---|
| LaHue, Richard Willam | 6/14/1959 | 12/19/1949 | Adult | Mr. & Mrs. Wm. H. LaHue | Univ. EUB | Dr. W. R. Holt | |
| LaHue, Victor Dean | 6/14/1959 | 3/8/1954 | Child | Mr. & Mrs. Wm. H. LaHue | Univ. EUB | Dr. W. R. Holt | |
| LaHue, Wm. Henry | 6/14/1959 | 2/8/1924 | Adult | Orville Richard & Hope A LaHue | Univ. EUB | Dr. W. R. Holt | Lawrence, KS |
| Lane, Willard Ross Jr. | 6/10/1962 | 11/20/1950 | Youth | Willard Ross Sr. & Edith Viola | Univ. EUB | Dr. W. R. Holt | |
| Lange, Barbara Jean | 5/31/1959 | 1/1/1959 | Infant | Mr. Glen & Mrs.Bernice Lange | Univ. EUB | Dr. W. R. Holt | |
| Lea, Dorothy Darlene | 8/19/1956 | 7/26/1956 | Child | Mr. & Mrs. Robert Lea | Univ. EUB | Dr. W. R. Holt | |
| Lea, Roberta Jean | 5/2/1965 | 8/22/1963 | Infant | Robert L. & Dorothy E. Lea | Univ. EUB | Dr. W. R. Holt | |
| Lea, Wanetta Marie | 6/24/1962 | 11/20/1961 | Infant | Robert L. & Dorothy E. Lea | Univ. EUB | Dr. W. R. Holt | |
| Lee, Eugene Paul | 12/14/1980 | | | Franco & Kathy Lee | Univ. UM | Ira DeSpain | Preparation |
| Leonard, Harry Charles | 3/29/1959 | 6/11/1947 | Child | Mr. & Mrs. William B. Leonard | Univ. EUB | Dr. W. R. Holt | To Reg. Roll |
| Leonard, William Paul | 10/2/1955 | 11/20/1942 | Child | Mr. & Mrs. Leonard | Univ. EUB | Dr. W. R. Holt | |
| Lincoln, John (Mrs.) | 4/12/1959 | 8/8/1903 | Adult | | Univ. EUB | Dr. W. R. Holt | |
| Liu, Anthony | 4/14/1968 | 9/3/1956 | Youth | Dr. & Mrs. Chien Liu | Univ. EUB | Dr. W. R. Holt | |
| Liu, Olive Christine | 5/8/1966 | 4/1/1955 | Child | Dr.& Mrs. Cien Liu | Univ. EUB | Dr. W. R. Holt | |
| Lohr, Loren | ? | | | | Univ. UM | L.Lamberty | No preparation |
| Lucas, George Hoyt Jr. | 4/18/1954 | 11/7/1953 | Infant | Mr. & Mrs. George Hoyt Lucas | Univ. EUB | Dr. W. R. Holt | |
| Mark, Keith LaVerne | 12/18/1960 | 1/5/1959 | Child | Robert & Delores Rae Mark | Univ. EUB | Dr. W. R. Holt | |
| Mark, Kevin Eugene | 12/18/1960 | 6/1/1957 | Child | Robert & Delores Rae Mark | Univ. EUB | Dr. W. R. Holt | |
| Massey, Briton | 2/25/2006 | `1990 | Youth | Rhonda Forrest | Univ. UM | L.Lamberty | Full mbrshp |
| McAllister, Darren Taylor | 3/26/1967 | 5/18/1960 | Infant | JohnTaylor & Barbara McAllister | Univ. EUB | Dr. W. R. Holt | |

11 - BAPTISMS

| Name | Date | Status | Born | Parents | Place | Minister | Remarks |
|---|---|---|---|---|---|---|---|
| McAllister, John Kevin | 3/26/1967 | Infant | 12/10/1958 | JohnTaylor & Barbara McAllister | Univ. EUB | Dr. W. R. Holt | |
| McAllister,Pamela Elaine | 3/26/1967 | Infant | 10/25/1964 | JohnTaylor & Barbara McAllister | Univ. EUB | Dr. W. R. Holt | |
| McAllister, Paula June | 3/26/1957 | Infant | 10/25/1964 | JohnTaylor & Barbara McAllister | Univ. EUB | Dr. W. R. Holt | |
| McAllister, Penny Sue | 3/26/1967 | Infant | 10/25/1964 | JohnTaylor & Barbara McAllister | Univ. EUB | Dr. W. R. Holt | |
| McAllister, Shawn Michael | 3/26/1967 | Infant | 10/23/1961 | JohnTaylor & Barbara McAllister | Univ. EUB | Dr. W. R. Holt | |
| McCoy, Freda (Mrs.) | 9/27/1964 | Adult | | | Univ. EUB | Dr. W. R. Holt | |
| McDaniels, Josephine Eliz. | 4/17/1966 | Adult | | | Univ. EUB | Dr. W. R. Holt | |
| McDaniels, Karen Elizabeth | 4/17/1966 | Child | 12/19/1961 | Kenneth & Josephine McDaniels | Univ. EUB | Dr. W. R. Holt | |
| McDaniels, Keven Leroy | 4/17/1966 | Youth | | Kenneth & Josephine McDaniels | Univ. EUB | Dr. W. R. Holt | |
| McDaniels, Kenneth Eugene | 4/17/1966 | Youth | | Kenneth & Josephine McDaniels | Univ. EUB | Dr. W. R. Holt | |
| McGee, LaRosa Nicole | 5/1/1994 | | | Lisa McGee | Univ. UM | M. Gasau | Full mbrshp |
| McGee, Sacou Dawaun | 5/1/1994 | | | Lisa McGee | Univ. UM | M. Gasau | Full mbrshp |
| McGuire, James Robert | 7/20/1958 | Infant | 11/6/1957 | David R. & Mary Lee McGuire | Univ. EUB | Dr. W. R. Holt | |
| McGuire, Kathleen Marie | 1/1/1956 | Child | 8/14/1952 | Mr. & Mrs. David McGuire | Univ. EUB | Dr. W. R. Holt | |
| McGuire, Walter Lee | 1/1/1956 | Infant | 1/30/1954 | Mr. & Mrs. David McGuire | Univ. EUB | Dr. W. R. Holt | |
| McMaken, Janet Ann | 12/11/1960 | Adult | 11/13/1944 | H. G. & Della Mae McMaken | Univ. EUB | Dr. W. R. Holt | |
| Morris, Terry | 4/18/1954 | Adult | | Mrs. Marie Morris | Univ. EUB | Dr. W. R. Holt | |
| Morrison, Linda Ruth | 8/2/1959 | Infant | 3/7/1959 | Mr. & Mrs. Wm. Kline Morrison | Univ. EUB | Dr. W. R. Holt | |
| Morrison, Lisa Anne | 4/14/1968 | Infant | 6/2/1967 | William & Ruth Morrison | Univ. EUB | Dr. W. R. Holt | |
| Morrison, Lori Jeanne | 10/20/1963 | Infant | 1/14/1963 | William & Ruth Morrison | Univ. EUB | Dr. W. R. Holt | |

12 - BAPTISMS

| Name | Date | Status | Born | Parents | Place | Minister | Remarks |
|---|---|---|---|---|---|---|---|
| Morrison, Wm. Kline | 8/2/1959 | Adult | 11/19/1931 | Mr. & Mrs. Wm. K. Morrison Sr. | Univ. EUB | Dr. W. R. Holt | |
| Neal, Allison Elizabeth | 5/19/2002 | Infant | 2/11/2002 | Dan & Niccole Neal | Univ. UM | L.Lamberty | Preparation |
| Neal, Jackson Mitchell | 5/19/2002 | Infant | 2/11/2002 | Dan & Niccole Neal | Univ. UM | L.Lamberty | Preparation |
| Nedrud, Donna | 4/14/1968 | Youth | 2/9/1957 | Mr. & Mrs. D. G. Nedrud | Univ. EUB | Dr. W. R. Holt | |
| Nedrud, Janice | 4/14/1968 | Youth | 4/4/1953 | Mr. & Mrs. D. G. Nedrud | Univ. EUB | Dr. W. R. Holt | |
| Nedrud, Michael | 4/14/1968 | Youth | 7/28/1954 | Mr. & Mrs. D. G. Nedrud | Univ. EUB | Dr. W. R. Holt | |
| Nelson, Cheryl Lynn | 3/2/1958 | Infant | 12/2/1957 | Mr. & Mrs. J. R. Nelson | Univ. EUB | Dr. W. R. Holt | Death 1958 |
| Nelson, David Richard | 4/18/1954 | | | Mr. & Mrs. David Nelson | Univ.EUB | Dr. W. R. Holt | |
| Nelson, David Roland | 10/10/1954 | Adult | | Mr. & Mrs. John Nelson | Univ. EUB | Dr. W. R. Holt | |
| Nelson, Dorothy Andrea | 10/26/1955 | Child | | Mr. & Mrs. David Nelson | Univ. EUB | Dr. W. R. Holt | |
| Nelson, Jack Dillard Jr. | 4/18/1954 | | | Mr. & Mrs. David Nelson | Univ. EUB | Dr. W. R. Holt | |
| Nelson, Lee Ann Beth | 4/18/1954 | | | Mr. & Mrs. David Nelson | Univ. EUB | Dr. W. R. Holt | |
| Nelson, Marion (Mrs.) | 4/25/1954 | Adult | | | Univ. EUB | Dr. W. R. Holt | |
| Nelson, Roy Franklin | 1/19/1958 | Infant | 9/23/1957 | Mr. & Mrs. David Nelson | Univ. EUB | Dr. W. R. Holt | |
| Nelson, Timothy Wayne | 4/18/1954 | | | Mr. & Mrs. Jack D. Nelson | Univ. EUB | Dr. W. R. Holt | |
| Newbanks, Doris Jane | 4/4/1982 | Infant | 8/12/1981 | C. W. & Joyce Newbanks | Univ. UM | Ira DeSpain | Preparation |
| Newbanks, Ryan Christopher | 4/22/1973 | Infant | 1/29/1973 | C. W. & Joyce Newbanks | Univ. UM | R. L. Rayson | Sprinkling |
| Nichols, Karen Elaine | 4/17/1960 | Infant | 1/22/1960 | Charles & Janet Nichols | Univ. EUB | Dr. W. R. Holt | |
| Noteon, Mary Jane | 3/31/1963 | Adult | 11/18/1910 | James & Katherine Cutler | Univ. EUB | Dr. W. R. Holt | |
| Novak, Robin | 4/18/1954 | Adult | | Mr. & Mrs. Tony Novak | Univ. EUB | Dr. W. R. Holt | |

13 - BAPTISMS

| Name | Date | Status | Born | Parents | Place | Minister | Remarks |
|------|------|--------|------|---------|-------|----------|---------|
| Novak, Tony Jr. | 4/18/1954 | Adult | | Mr. & Mrs. Tony Novak | Univ. EUB | Dr. W. R. Holt | |
| Obee, Elizabeth Hassig | 12/23/1984 | | | Ron & Marilyn Obee | Univ. UM | Stevenson | |
| Obee, Ronald Lee | 4/15/1956 | Child | 3/15/1956 | Mr. & Mrs. Al Obee | Univ. EUB | Dr. W. R. Holt | |
| Odneal, Timothy Parul | 3/14/1954 | Infant | 8/19/1953 | Mr. & Mrs. Jack Odneal | Univ. EUB | Dr. W. R. Holt | |
| Ogden, Armin Kevin | 1/20/1963 | Child | 12/29/1962 | Armin K.& Frances G.Ogden | Univ. EUB | Dr. W. R. Holt | |
| Olson, Laura Ann | 10/5/1958 | Infant | 1/5/1958 | Clarence A. Jr. & Betty Mae Olson | Univ. EUB | Dr. W. R. Holt | |
| Olson, Laura Ann | 4/6/1969 | Youth | 1/5/1958 | Mr. & Mrs. Clarence Olson Jr. | Univ. UM | R. L. Rayson | |
| Parrott, James (Mrs.) | 4/18/1954 | Adult | | | Univ. EUB | Dr. W. R. Holt | |
| Paulson, Keith Andrew | 3/2/1958 | Child | 11/30/1955 | Mr. Oliver & Ruth Paulson | Univ. EUB | Dr. W. R. Holt | |
| Paulson, Ruth Evelyn | 3/2/1958 | Adult | 3/16/1934 | Mr. & Mrs. Clifford Graves | Univ. EUB | Dr. W. R. Holt | |
| Paulson, Walter Neal | 3/2/1958 | Child | 12/22/1952 | Mr. Oliver & Ruth Paulson | Univ. EUB | Dr. W. R. Holt | |
| Pearson, Susan Elaine | 4/10/1966 | Infant | 2/2/1966 | Gilbert R. & Judith A. Pearson | Univ. EUB | Dr. W. R. Holt | |
| Peat, Barbara Jean | 5/1/1951 | Infant | 8/8/1950 | Wilbur T. & Helen Peat | Univ. EUB | Dr. W. R. Holt | |
| Peat, Raymond Leslie | 5/1/1960 | Infant | 3/6/1960 | Wilbur T. & Helen Peat | Univ. EUB | Dr. W. R. Holt | |
| Peat, Sharon Lynn | 5/13/1943 | Infant | 3/4/1943 | Wilbur T. & Helen Peat | Univ. EUB | Dr. W. R. Holt | |
| Pence, Patti Lynn | 11/7/1954 | Infant | 6/1/1954 | Mr. & Mrs. Joseph F. Pence Jr. | Univ. EUB | Dr. W. R. Holt | |
| Potter, Bryan | 4/6/1980 | | `1968 | Robert & Carol Potter | Univ. UM | J. Hamden | No preparation |
| Rayson, Gary Donn | 4/6/1969 | Youth | 4/27/1957 | Rev. & Mrs. R. L. Rayson | Univ. UM | R. L. Rayson | |
| Rayson, Paul Frank | 5/25/1969 | Youth | 7/21/1959 | Rev. & Mrs. R. L. Rayson | Roeland Pk | R. L. Rayson | Immersion |
| Rayson, Philip Joel | `1971 | Infant | 5/16/1971 | LeRoy & Murial Rayson | Univ. UM | R. L. Rayson | Dedication |

14 - BAPTISMS

| Name | Date | Status | Born | Parents | Place | Minister | Remarks |
|---|---|---|---|---|---|---|---|
| Reynolds, Gordon Armstrong | 6/19/1955 | Infant | 10/8/1954 | Capt. & Mrs. G. A. Reynolds | Univ. EUB | Dr. W. R. Holt | Gs. Of Holt |
| Reynolds, Martha Jane | 6/19/1955 | Infant | 7/26/1951 | Capt. & Mrs. G. A. Reynolds | Univ. EUB | Dr. W. R. Holt | Gd. Of Holt |
| Rich, Steven Ellis | 4/6/1958 | Infant | 6/25/1957 | Mr. & Mrs. Howard Rich | Univ. EUB | Dr. W. R. Holt | |
| Riley, Steven Alfred | 5/9/1954 | Infant | 3/21/1954 | Mrs. Charles Riley | Univ. EUB | Dr. W. R. Holt | |
| Roberts, Nicholas | 9/23/1984 | | | Steve & Karen Roberts | Univ. UM | Stevenson | Preparation |
| Ropp, Kevin Shawn | 4/22/1962 | Child | 7/23/1960 | Leonard Neal & Pamela J. Ropp | Univ. EUB | Dr. W. R. Holt | |
| Ruby, Diana Lee (Mrs. W.) | 9/13/1959 | Adult | 3/21/1941 | Mr. & Mrs. Claude Staton | Univ. EUB | Dr. W. R. Holt | |
| Ruby, Gregory Eugene | 4/16/1961 | Child | 1/4/1961 | Wayne Eugene & Diana Lee Ruby | Univ. EUB | Dr. W. R. Holt | |
| Ruby, Mark Allen | 3/27/1960 | Infant | 12/2/1959 | Wayne & Dianne Ruby | Univ. EUB | Dr. W. R. Holt | |
| Ruby, Wayne | 9/13/1959 | Adult | 6/8/1939 | Mr. & Mrs. Paul Ruby | Univ. EUB | Dr. W. R. Holt | |
| Sackman, Janice Carol | 3/29/1959 | Adult | 1/11/1944 | Mr. & Mrs. Albert Sackman | Univ. EUB | Dr. W. R. Holt | |
| Sackman, Joyce Elizabeth | 3/29/1959 | Adult | 4/24/1942 | Mr. & Mrs. Albert Sackman | Univ. EUB | Dr. W. R. Holt | |
| Sackman, Martha Jane | 8/7/1960 | Child | 7/17/1959 | Albert Jr. & Mable Eliz. Sackman | Univ. EUB | Dr. W. R. Holt | |
| Scheets, Corey | 4/20/2003 | Child | `1997 | Sarah Scheets | Univ. UM | L.Lamberty | Preparation |
| Schmidt, Barabara Dawn | 8/9/1959 | Adult | 7/27/1939 | Iona Schmidt (W. W. Schmidt) | Univ. EUB | Dr. W. R. Holt | |
| Schmidt, Iona Dawn (Mrs.) | 8/9/1959 | Adult | 1/23/1919 | | Univ. EUB | Dr. W. R. Holt | |
| Schmidt, Joan Ellen | 7/2/1961 | Child | 2/9/1961 | Wm. Albert & Linda Lou Schmidt | Univ. EUB | Dr. W. R. Holt | |
| Schmidt, Mark Alan | 5/12/1968 | Infant | 4/10/1968 | Wm. Albert & Linda Lou Schmidt | Univ. EUB | Dr. W. R. Holt | |
| Schmidt, William Albert | 8/9/1959 | Adult | 8/19/1938 | Iona Schmidt (W. W. Schmidt) | Univ. EUB | Dr. W. R. Holt | |
| Scott, Clyde Jr. | 4/11/1971 | Adult | 12/28/1929 | | Univ. UM | R. L. Rayson | Sprinkling |

15 - BAPTISMS

| Name | Date | Status | Born | Parents | Place | Minister | Remarks |
|------|------|--------|------|---------|-------|----------|---------|
| Scott, Donald Lee | 4/11/1971 | Child | 7/31/1962 | Clyde Jr. & Rosalie Scott | Univ. UM | R. L. Rayson | Baptism |
| Scott, Donna Lynn | 4/11/1971 | Child | 12/23/1963 | Clyde Jr. & Rosalie Scott | Univ. UM | R. L. Rayson | Baptism |
| Scott, Robert Alan | 4/11/1971 | Child | 6/4/1959 | Clyde Jr. & Rosalie Scott | Univ. UM | R. L. Rayson | Baptism |
| Scott, Ronald Dean | 4/11/1971 | Child | 12/3/1964 | Clyde Jr. & Rosalie Scott | Univ. UM | R. L. Rayson | Baptism |
| Scott, Rosalie (Mrs. C. Jr.) | 4/11/1971 | | | | | | |
| Scott, William Raymond | 4/11/1971 | Youth | 3/7/1958 | Clyde & Rosalie Scott | Univ. UM | R. L. Rayson | Sprinkling |
| Self, Christopher Garrett | 10/22/1972 | Infant | 1/25/1972 | John Daniel & Jacqueline Self | Univ. UM | R. L. Rayson | Dedication |
| Seufert, Bethany Ann | 7/2/1961 | Child | 3/2/1957 | Tony M. & Marion Lois Seufert | Univ. EUB | Dr. W. R. Holt | |
| Seufert, Don Arthur | 7/2/1961 | Child | 6/14/1951 | Tony M. & Marion Lois Seufert | Univ. EUB | Dr. W. R. Holt | |
| Sevedge, Kathleen Amy | 5/14/1961 | Child | 8/30/1960 | Roger & Kathleen Sevedge | Univ. EUB | Dr. W. R. Holt | |
| Sevedge, Keith Carter | 5/10/1959 | Infant | 1/23/1959 | Mr. & Mrs. Roger W. Sevedge | Univ. EUB | Dr. W. R. Holt | |
| Sevedge, Roger | 12/29/1957 | Adult | | | Univ. EUB | Dr. W. R. Holt | |
| Sgulski, Diana Jo | 5/26/1968 | Child | 8/10/1956 | Peter & Mary Ann Sgulski | Watch Care | Dr. W. R. Holt | |
| Sgulski, Donna Lee | 5/26/1968 | Child | 3/9/1959 | Peter & Mary Ann Sgulski | Watch Care | Dr. W. R. Holt | |
| Shelley, Bruce Lynn | 3/28/1948 | Infant | 9/1/1947 | Joseph F. Jr. & Doneva M. Shelley | Univ. EUB | Dr. W. R. Holt | |
| Shelley, Craig | 4/10/1966 | Youth | | | Univ. EUB | Dr. W. R. Holt | |
| Shelley, Dennis Stewart | 12/26/1948 | Infant | 10/16/1948 | Joseph F. Jr. & Doneva M. Shelley | Univ. EUB | Dr. W. R. Holt | |
| Sherman, Michael | 4/27/2003 | Youth | '1992 | Jackie Barton | Univ. UM | L. Lamberty | Full mbrshp |
| Simmons, Daulton | 4/18/1954 | Adult | | | Univ. EUB | Dr. W. R. Holt | |
| Sisk, Lawrence | 5/6/1973 | Youth | 3/17/1960 | | Roeland Pk | R. L. Rayson | Immersion |

16 - BAPTISMS

| Name | Date | Status | Born | Parents | Place | Minister | Remarks |
|------|------|--------|------|---------|-------|----------|---------|
| Sisk, Randal Lee | 5/6/1973 | Youth | 10/29/1958 | | Roeland Pk | R. L. Rayson | Immersion |
| Slawson, Constance Elaine | 4/30/1961 | Child | 12/23/1960 | Donald & Rheta Slawson | Univ. EUB | Dr. W. R. Holt | |
| Slawson, Diane Elizabeth | 6/14/1959 | Infant | 3/11/1959 | Mr. & Mrs. Donald Slawson | Univ. EUB | Dr. W. R. Holt | |
| Slawson, Robert Erie | 4/19/1964 | Infant | 11/9/1963 | Donald E. & Rheta Eliz.Slawson | Univ. EUB | Dr. W. R. Holt | |
| Smith, Ashley Nicole | 10/30/1983 | Infant | 9/10/1983 | Kenneth & Pamela Smith | Univ. UM | Ira DeSpain | No preparation |
| Smith, David James | 12/26/1948 | Child | 2/23/1943 | Merlin F. & Mary Edna Smith | Univ. EUB | Dr. W. R. Holt | |
| Smith, Jay Bradley | 5/13/1970 | Infant | 5/6/1970 | Donald & Sharon Peat Smith | Beth. Hosp. | R. L. Rayson | |
| Sprague, Davon Jamaar | 5/8/1994 | | | Shelly Taylor | Univ. UM | M. Gasau | Full mbrshp |
| Sprague, Taja Meshae | 5/8/1994 | | | Shelly Taylor | Univ. UM | M. Gasau | Full mbrshp |
| Stakley, Jane Marie | 11/26/1972 | Youth | 1/25/1954 | Catherine McCarty | Univ. UM | R. L. Rayson | Sprinkline |
| Stakley, Laura Jean | 1/10/1982 | Adult | 11/29/1958 | | Univ. UM | Ira DeSpain | No preparation |
| Strauss, Charles Lee | 10/31/1991 | | | | Univ. UM | M. Gasau | Full mbrshp |
| Studt, Dorothy Rose | 1/2/1955 | Adult | 5/16/1904 | Jack & Grace Furman | Univ. EUB | Dr. W. R. Holt | |
| Taylor, Betty Lou | 12/27/1959 | Adult | 8/11/1946 | Floyd & Margaret Taylor | Univ. EUB | Dr. W. R. Holt | |
| Taylor, Demarcus Anthony | 5/8/1994 | | | Shelly Taylor | Univ. UM | M. Gasau | Full mbrshp |
| Taylor, Dennis Hollis | 4/18/1954 | | 6/4/1952 | Mrs. Maxine Taylor | Univ. EUB | Dr. W. R. Holt | |
| Taylor, Errol Dean | 4/18/1954 | Child | 6/26/1939 | Holdeen M. & Maxine Taylor | Univ. EUB | Dr. W. R. Holt | |
| Taylor, Floyd Martin | 12/27/1959 | Adult | 5/3/1921 | M. R. & Adella Taylor | Univ. EUB | Dr. W. R. Holt | |
| Taylor, Karen Joy | 4/18/1956 | Child | 10/25/1941 | Holdeen M. & Maxine Taylor | Univ. EUB | Dr. W. R. Holt | |
| Taylor, Margaret Bee | 12/27/1959 | Adult | 2/18/1922 | Morris & Leatha Smith | Univ. EUB | Dr. W. R. Holt | |

17 - BAPTISMS

| Name | Date | Status | Born | Parents | Place | Minister | Remarks |
|------|------|--------|------|---------|-------|----------|---------|
| Taylor, Maxine | 4/18/1954 | Adult | 12/19/1916 | Alfred Moore & Mary Jane Peck | Univ. EUB | Dr. W. R. Holt | |
| Taylor, Melody Bee | 12/27/1959 | Child | 8/9/1957 | Floyd & Margaret Taylor | Univ. EUB | Dr. W. R. Holt | |
| Taylor, Michael Monroe | 4/18/1954 | Child | 6/29/1945 | Holdeen M. & Maxine Taylor | Univ. EUB | Church | |
| Taylor, Michael Monroe | 4/18/1954 | Adult | 6/29/1945 | Mr. & Mrs. Taylor (Maxine) | Univ. EUB | Dr. W. R. Holt | |
| Taylor, Sharon Jane | 4/18/1954 | Adult | 11/19/1936 | Holdeen M. & Maxine Taylor | Univ. EUB | Dr. W. R. Holt | |
| Teters, Jennifer Sue | 6/10/1962 | Youth | 6/6/1944 | Clarence L. & Jennie Lucille Teters | Univ. EUB | Dr. W. R. Holt | |
| Teters, Nancy Jane | 6/10/1962 | Youth | 2/16/1949 | Clarence L. & Jennie Lucille Teters | Univ. EUB | Dr. W. R. Holt | |
| Tevis, Marjorie (Mrs.) | 4/18/1954 | Adult | | | Univ. EUB | Dr. W. R. Holt | |
| Tevis, Randy Eugene | 1/6/1957 | Infant | 7/19/1956 | Mr. & Mrs. Robert Tevis | Univ. EUB | Dr. W. R. Holt | |
| Tevis, Richard | 4/18/1954 | Adult | | Mr. & Mrs. Robert Tevis | Univ. EUB | Dr. W. R. Holt | |
| Thomas, Dlynn | 4/20/2003 | Child | `1994 | Sarah Scheets | Univ. UM | L. Lamberty | Preparation |
| Thomas, Joyce Darlene | 3/29/1970 | Adult | 5/13/1954 | Wilbert E. & Daurice L. Thomas | Univ. UM | R. L. Rayson | Sprinkling |
| Thompson, Deborah Louise | 2/11/1968 | Youth | 12/1/1954 | Robert E. Sr. & Marilyn Thompson | Univ. EUB | Dr. W. R. Holt | |
| Thompson, Robert Earl Jr. | 2/11/1968 | Youth | 1/28/1953 | Robert E. Sr. & Marilyn Thompson | Univ. EUB | Dr. W. R. Holt | |
| Tombaugh, Clarence W. | 9/13/1959 | Adult | | | Univ. EUB | Dr. W. R. Holt | |
| Tombaugh, Iona (Mrs. C. W. | 9/13/1959 | Adult | | | Univ. EUB | Dr. W. R. Holt | |
| Trindle, Cathie Lorraine | 6/2/1957 | | | Mr. & Mrs. J. B. Trindle | Univ. EUB | Dr. W. R. Holt | |
| Trindle, Cathy | 4/21/1968 | Youth | 6/21/1953 | Mr. & Mrs. Jesse Trindle | Univ. EUB | Dr. W. R. Holt | |
| Trindle, Debbie Lynn | 6/2/1957 | | | Mr. & Mrs. J. B. Trindle | Univ. EUB | Dr. W. R. Holt | |

18 - BAPTISMS

| Name | Date | Status | Born | Parents | Place | Minister | Remarks |
|------|------|--------|------|---------|-------|----------|---------|
| Trindle, Debbie Lynn | 4/21/1968 | Youth | 6/21/1956 | Mr. & Mrs. Jesse Trindle | Univ. EUB | Dr. W. R. Holt | |
| Trindle, Jesse Burl | 3/15/1959 | Infant | 7/12/1958 | Jesse Burl & Ruby Trindle | Univ. EUB | Dr. W. R. Holt | |
| Triplett, Avonne Danell | 10/31/1991 | | | Pam Triplett | Univ. UM | M. Gasau | Full mbrshp |
| True, Ginger Lee | 12/11/1960 | Child | 3/19/1957 | Raymond P & Virginia True | Lon. Hts.　Me. | V. Becker | |
| True, Roy Lynn | 12/11/1960 | Child | 8/8/1958 | Raymond P. & Virginia True | Lon. Ht. Me Me. | V. Becker | |
| Tucker, Bobby R. | 4/17/1960 | Adult | 11/20/1928 | Lester & Aline Tucker | Univ. EUB | Dr. W. R. Holt | |
| Tucker, Carol Susanne | 10/20/1957 | Infant | 5/25/1957 | Mr. & Mrs. Richard Tucker | Univ. EUB | Dr. W. R. Holt | |
| Tucker, Curtis Edward | 5/13/1962 | Child | 2/17/1962 | R. J. Dryson & Martha G.Tucker | Univ. EUB | Dr. W. R. Holt | |
| Tucker, Donald Richard | 4/15/1956 | Infant | 1/4/1956 | Mr. & Mrs. Richard Tucker | Univ. EUB | Dr. W. R. Holt | |
| Tucker, Judy Dianna | 4/17/1960 | Child | 2/23/1954 | Bobby R. & Lucille Tucker | Univ. EUB | Dr. W. R. Holt | |
| Tucker, Lana Joyce | 4/17/1960 | Child | 8/14/1950 | Bobby R. & Lucille Tucker | Univ. EUB | Dr. W. R. Holt | |
| Tucker, Lois Dianne | 10/24/1954 | Infant | 6/17/1954 | Mr. & Mrs. Richard Tucker | Univ. EUB | Dr. W. R. Holt | |
| Varner, Darren Kent | 3/27/1960 | Infant | 12/27/1959 | Donald & Joan Varner | Univ. EUB | Dr. W. R. Holt | |
| Verser, Albert Jr. | 2/3/2008 | Youth | '1997 | Albert Verser Sr. & Dina Johnson | Univ. UM | L. Lamberty | Preparation |
| Wagner, John | 4/3/1955 | Infant | | Art & Carolyn Wagner | Univ. EUB | Dr. W. R. Holt | |
| Watson, Carol | 10/11/1964 | Child | | Mr. & Mrs. Kenneth Watson | Univ. EUB | Dr. W. R. Holt | |
| Watson, Charles | 10/11/1964 | Child | | Mr. & Mrs. Kenneth Watson | Univ. EUB | Dr. W. R. Holt | |
| Watson, David | 10/11/1964 | Child | | Mr. & Mrs. Kenneth Watson | Univ. EUB | Dr. W. R. Holt | |
| Weddell, Andrew Stevem | 7/28/1991 | | | Heather Weddell | Univ. UM | M. Gasau | |
| Weddell, Heather Lynn | 7/28/1991 | | | | Univ. UM | M. Gasau | Full mbrshp |

19 - BAPTISMS

| Name | Date | Status | Born | Parents | Place | Minister | Remarks |
|---|---|---|---|---|---|---|---|
| Wehrer, Karen Ann | 4/21/1946 | Infant | 10/7/1945 | Ralph K. & Lois Wehrer | Univ. EUB | Dr. W. R. Holt | |
| Weinert, Daniel Shane | 10/5/1986 | Infant | 7/5/1986 | Danny & Joan Weinert | Univ. UM | R. West | Preparation |
| Weinert, Joni Michele | 3/26/1989 | Infant | 12/28/1988 | Danny & Joan Weinert | Univ. UM | M. Gasau | Preparation |
| Wheeler, Barbara Ann | 7/6/1958 | Child | | Mr. & Mrs. Frank Wheeler | Univ. EUB | Dr. W. R. Holt | To Reg. Roll |
| Whillock, James Robert | 4/28/1946 | Infant | 1/14/1946 | Clyde & Lillian Whitlock | Univ. EUB | Dr. W. R. Holt | |
| White, Jeffrey Michael | 4/11/1971 | Infant | 6/20/1970 | Raymond & Diana White | Univ. UM | R. L. Rayson | Dedication |
| White, Michael Edward | 1/6/1957 | Child | 7/7/1955 | Mr. & Mrs. Jewell White | Univ. EUB | Dr. W. R. Holt | |
| White, Michael Edward | 7/16/1967 | Youth | 7/7/1958 | Jewell & Florence White | Univ. EUB | Dr. W. R. Holt | |
| White , Raymond | 1/13/1957 | Child | 4/10/1947 | Mr. & Mrs. Jewell E. White | Univ. EUB | Dr. W. R. Holt | |
| Willett, Heidi Suzanne | 4/18/1965 | Infant | 10/30/1964 | Ronald & Melva Willett | Univ. EUB | Dr. W. R. Holt | |
| Willett, Jeffrey Blake | 4/6/1955 | Infant | 11/3/1954 | Mr. & Mrs. Ronald L. Willett | Univ. EUB | Dr. W. R. Holt | |
| Willett, Kimberly June | 4/6/1958 | Child | 8/14/1956 | Mr. & Mrs. Ronald Willett | Univ. EUB | Dr. W. R. Holt | |
| Willett, Melva Jean | 7/12/1959 | Adult | 7/20/1934 | Mr. & Mrs. Carl Winterringer | Univ. EUB | Dr. W. R. Holt | |
| Willett, Ronald Lee | 7/12/1959 | Adult | 7/19/1932 | Mr. & Mrs. Francis Lee Willett | Univ. EUB | Dr. W. R. Holt | |
| Willett, Shari Ann | 4/18/1954 | | | Mr. & Mrs. Ronald L. Willett | Univ. EUB | Dr. W. R. Holt | |
| Williams, Doris | 9/12/1982 | Adult | | | Univ. UM | I. DeSpain | Full mbrshp |
| Williams, Preston | 9/12/1982 | Adult | | | Univ. Um | I. DeSpain | Full mbrshp |
| Wilson, Edna (Mrs.) | 4/18/1954 | Adult | | | Univ. EUB | Dr. W. R. Holt | |
| Wingate, Jack Ernest | 4/18/1954 | Adult | 8/24/1940 | Mr. & Mrs. John Wingate | Univ. EUB | Dr. W. R. Holt | |
| Winterringer, Carl Everett | 5/1/1960 | Adult | 6/3/1929 | Carl E. Sr. & Mary M. Winterringer | Univ. EUB | Dr. W. R. Holt | |

| Name | Date | Status | Born | Parents | Place | Minister | Remarks |
|------|------|--------|------|---------|-------|----------|---------|
| Winterringer, Dan Alden | 5/1/1960 | Child | 9/8/1955 | Carl E. & Patricia Winterringer | Univ. EUB | Dr. W. R. Holt | |
| Winterringer, Dana Sue | 5/1/1960 | Child | 11/20/1958 | Carl E. & Patricia Winterringer | Univ. EUB | Dr. W. R. Holt | |
| Winterringer, Gayle Lynn | 5/1/1960 | Child | 1/4/1952 | Carl E. & Patricia Winterringer | Univ. EUB | Dr. W. R. Holt | |
| Winterringer, Patricia Marga | 5/1/1960 | Adult | 10/6/1931 | Wm. John Horstor & Alexandria | Univ. EUB | Dr. W. R. Holt | |
| Wolch, Phillip Gerald | 5/5/1957 | Child | 7/21/1948 | Mr. & Mrs. Gerald Wolch | Univ. EUB | Dr. W. R. Holt | |
| Wright, Daniel Alexander | 3/16/2008 | Infant | | | Univ. UM | L.Lamberty | No preparation |
| Young, Mary Elizabeth | 4/21/1968 | Adult | 12/27/1912 | | Univ. EUB | Dr. W. R. Holt | |
| Youngdoff, David Lawrence | 6/21/1964 | Infant | 1/26/1964 | Larry and Judith Youngdoff | Univ. EUB | Dr. W. R. Holt | |
| Youngdoff, Julie Ann | 5/14/1961 | Child | 3/12/1961 | Lawrence & Judith A. Youngdoff | Univ. EUB | Dr. W. R. Holt | |
| Zimmer, Craig Lee | 4/17/1960 | Child | 7/13/1948 | Robert & Pauline Zimmer | Univ. EUB | Dr. W. R. Holt | |
| Zimmer, Debra Sue | 11/7/1954 | Infant | 8/31/1954 | Mr. & Mrs. Robert Zimmer | Univ. EUB | Dr. W. R. Holt | |
| Zimmer, Debra Low | 5/8/1966 | Youth | 8/31/1955 | Robert & Pauline Zimmer | Univ. EUB | Dr. W. R. Holt | |
| Zimmer, Linda Sue | 4/1/1956 | Child | 7/13/1944 | Mr. & Mrs. Robert Zimmer | Univ. EUB | Dr. W. R. Holt | |
| Zimmer, Traci Leigh | 4/22/1973 | Infant | 3/2/1973 | Craig & Sandra Zimmer | Univ. UM | R. L. Rayson | Sprinkling |

# RECORD OF MARRIAGES BY GROOM SURNAME

## 1919 - 2009

**Record of Marriages**

| Groom Name | Date | Age | Residence | Bride Name | Age | Residence |
|---|---|---|---|---|---|---|
| Alexander, Sidney D. | 6/10/1966 | 58 | Kansas City, KS | Kangig, Jean M. | 40 | Kansas City, KS |
| Allsire, Neal Farrell | 10/12/1959 |  | Kansas City, KS | Luschen, Leona Maude |  | Kansas City, MO |
| Amstutz, William E. | 12/1/1956 | 22 | Kansas City, KS | Picknick, Joyce Lee | 19 | Kansas City, KS |
| Anderson, John William | 9/27/1958 | 49 | Kansas City, MO | Carlson, Helen | 51 | Kansas City, KS |
| Bailey, Jon Gordon | 4/17/1959 | 23 | Kansas City, KS | Nicholson, Marjorie Ann | 20 | Kansas City, KS |
| Baines, John L. | 12/19/1970 | 24 | Kansas City, KS | Bailey, Denise Ann | 17 | Kansas City, KS |
| Baker, Lawrence B. | 9/12/1953 |  | Kansas City, KS | Sweeney, Lois Elaine |  | Kansas City, KS |
| Ballard, William Howard ll | 12/26/1959 | 17 | Kansas City, MO | Keeter, Janice Leah | 22 | Kansas City, KS |
| Bayne, Herbert E. | 12/26/1957 | 60 | Parkville, MO | Swazick, Marie K. | 54 | Kansas City, KS |
| Bernard, Dewey D. | 6/6/1954 |  | Kansas City, KS | Werth, Ann Rita |  | Kansas City, KS |
| Berve, David J. | 9/1/1962 |  | Kansas City, KS | Mayberry, Margaret Ann |  | Bethel, KS |
| Blackburn, Robert Neal | 8/31/1957 | 20 | Kansas City, KS | Hartig, Jo Donna | 18 | Kansas City, KS |
| Bradley, James H. | 9/29/1956 | 20 | Kansas City, KS | Stott, Sandra Gail | 19 | Kansas City, KS |
| Brinkmeyer, Harry G. Jr. | 10/13/1956 | 20 | Grandview, MO | Taylor, Sharon Jane | 19 | Kansas City, KS |
| Brotherton, Thomas H. | 9/2/1967 | 20 | Kansas City, KS | Weldon, Carol F. | 18 | Kansas City, KS |
| Bustard, Ralph | 11/21/1969 | 48 | Kansas City, KS | Thompson, Ivy | 46 | Kansas City, KS |
| Byers, Donald E. | 10/25/1955 | 23 | Kansas City, KS | Wyman, Vanita E. | 21 | Kansas City, KS |

| Groom Name | Date | Age | Residence | Bride Name | Age | Residence |
|---|---|---|---|---|---|---|
| Byrd, Ronald Eugene | 7/14/1967 | 18 | Kansas City, KS | Teters, Nancy Jane | 18 | Kansas City, KS |
| Cain, Gary Bryant | 5/8/1964 | 25 | Kansas City, KS | Poole, Sylvia Jean | 21 | Kansas City, KS |
| Canfield, Michael Q. | 9/26/1964 | 19 | Kansas City, KS | Dowd, Gayle Ann | 19 | Kansas City, KS |
| Charles, Buford D. | 4/25/1956 | 20 | Kansas City, KS | West, Martha A. | 19 | Overland Park, KS |
| Couch, William D. | 8/17/1956 | 21 | Kansas City, KS | Grigsby, Betty Jo | 18 | Kansas City, KS |
| Daniels, Earl C. | 6/21/1954 | | Piper, KS | Reeves, Edith O. | | Kansas City, KS |
| Davis, Alreco | 11/8/2006 | | Kansas City, KS | Cuellar, Julie | | Kansas City, KS |
| Davis, Harry C. Sr. | 9/22/1971 | 72 | Kansas City, KS | Black, Mildred L. | 68 | Kansas City, KS |
| Deay, Lewis Everett | 8/31/1954 | | Linwood, KS | Lietzen, Geraldine A. | | Linwood, KS |
| Debus, Vernon Ralph | 12/25/1954 | | Kansas City, Ks | Piliey, Mary Ann | | Kansas City, KS |
| Divilbiss, Roderick William | 10/19/1956 | 21 | Kansas City, KS | Morrell, Phyllis Barbara | 18 | Kansas City, KS |
| Divilbiss, Ronald W. | 9/7/1956 | 21 | Kansas City, KS | Harrod, Sandra Lee | 16 | Kansas City, KS |
| Dixon, Chris | 5/3/2003 | | Kansas City, MO | Scheets, Sarah | | Kansas City, KS |
| Doane, Lloyd A. | 11/4/1961 | | Carbondale, KS | Radotinsky, Sandra Gail | | Kansas City, KS |
| Donley, Jackie D. | 9/5/1953 | | Kansas City, KS | White, Gladys Mae | | Kansas City, KS |
| Donohue, Roy | 9/18/1971 | | Kansas City, MO | Warnick, Frances | | Kansas City, KS |
| Dryer, Daniel Ray | 8/20/1966 | 21 | Liberal, KS | Zimmer, Linda S. | 22 | Kansas City, KS |
| Dudley, John Edward | 5/1/1965 | 23 | Kansas City, KS | McMahen, Janet Ann | 20 | Kansas City, KS |
| Duffett, Charles M. | 9/3/1966 | 41 | Lexington, MO | Webb, Rose Mary | 24 | Lexington, MO |
| Dunivan, Charles | 12/27/1950 | | | Hardsaw, Betty Jean | | Kansas City, KS |

3 - MARRIAGES BY GROOM

| Groom Name | Date | Age | Residence | Bride Name | Age | Residence |
|---|---|---|---|---|---|---|
| Dunivan, Charles J. | 7/28/1962 | | Linwood, KS | Schmidt, Barbara Dawn | | Bonner Springs, KS |
| Eagle, John P. | 9/24/1955 | 24 | Kansas City, KS | Sambol, Alma Suzanne | 24 | Kansas City, KS |
| Emert, Harold L. | 8/10/1956 | 30 | Sebatha, KS | Brant, Delia Ferne | 39 | Robinson, KS |
| Evans, LeRoy E. | 8/5/1967 | 22 | Kansas City, KS | Catlett, Bertha A. | 25 | Kansas City, KS |
| Fanto, John J. | 5/29/1964 | 35 | Topeka, KS | Reynolds, Ann | 38 | Kansas City, KS |
| Forbes, Dennis LeRoy | 8/9/1969 | | Kansas City, KS | Lloyd, Peggy Joyce | | Kansas City, KS |
| Fray, Harry H. | 4/15/1955 | 33 | Sioux Falls, SD | White, Helen E. | 43 | Kansas City, KS |
| Freeman, Henry | 12/12/1964 | 67 | Bethel, KS | Boylan, Carrie M. | 66 | Kansas City, KS |
| Frye, Harold B. | 6/14/1964 | 20 | Kansas City, KS | Hoagland, Nancy Ann | 20 | Kansas City, KS |
| Fulmer, Rolla Augustus | 12/8/1964 | 73 | Chetopa, KS | Pester, Della T. | 74 | Fresno, CA |
| Gragg, Thomas W. | 5/18/1973 | 36 | Kansas City, KS | Garner, Maurine F. | 29 | Kansas City, KS |
| Grauberger, Albert Eugene | 2/17/1955 | 21 | Kansas City, KS | Ellis, Eva Lou | 19 | Kansas City, KS |
| Greiner, John D. | 5/21/1955 | 23 | Kansas City, KS | Halverhout, Anna Mae | 22 | Kansas City, KS |
| Hammett, Michael | 12/25/1962 | | Kansas City, KS | (No Name) | | |
| Hanigan, Leslie Dee | 4/17/1970 | 22 | KS | Pigg, Linda Diane | 19 | Kansas City, KS |
| Harmon, Richard D. | 1/2/1955 | 19 | Kansas City, KS | Henley, LaDoris Y. | 18 | Kansas City, KS |
| Hataway, Cara Lee | 2/14/1954 | | Kansas City, KS | Holt, Marilyn | | Kansas City, KS |
| Hattaway, Raymond Lee | 7/12/1958 | 19 | Kansas City, KS | Tomecal, Judith Ann | 18 | Kansas City, KS |
| Hawkins, James G. | 8/11/1972 | 21 | Kansas City, KS | Placke, Kathy N. | 20 | Kansas City, KS |

| Groom Name | Date | Age | Residence | Bride Name | Age | Residence |
|---|---|---|---|---|---|---|
| Hedge, Ramon Hunter | 6/18/1960 | 25 | Kansas City, KS | Johnson, Lavone Marie | 25 | Kansas City, KS |
| Helm, John M. | 10/27/1967 | 20 | Lexington, MO | Phillips, Mary Ann | 16 | Kansas City, KS |
| Hershberger, Larry Ray | 12/27/1969 | | Kansas City, KS | Gicalone, Jill Sue | | Kansas City, KS |
| Hoendorf, Billie | 1/21/1995 | 75 | Parkville, MO | Simmons, Darlene | 73 | Kansas City, KS |
| Hollander, Gregory | 4/17/1971 | | Kansas City, KS | Freidell, Linda | | Kansas City, KS |
| Hoyt, Walter Lewis Jr. | 6/10/1967 | 21 | Kansas City, KS | Berry, Patricia Ann | 20 | Kansas City, KS |
| Hunt, Bryce | 11/7/1950 | | Welborn, KS | Wilderman, Eugena Lee | | Kansas City, KS |
| Johnson, David Milton | 5/9/1954 | | Kansas City, KS | Seufert, Vivian Marie | | Kansas City, KS |
| Johnson, Donald E. | 2/14/1954 | | Kansas City, KS | Brizendine, Ivah Justine | | Kansas City, MO |
| Jolloff, Walter L. | 5/17/1954 | 28 | Kansas City, KS | Schultz, Wanda L. | 40 | Kansas City, KS |
| Jones, Charles Lee | 6/1/1968 | 24 | Kansas City, MO | Shaner, Carol Dee | 24 | Kansas City, KS |
| Jones, James | 8/13/1960 | | Kansas City, KS | Bushnell, Ruth | | Kansas City, KS |
| Keeter, James | 8/12/1950 | 19 | Kansas City, KS | Lacy, Norma Jean | 18 | Kansas City, KS |
| Kettwig, D. Randall | 8/21/1954 | | Kansas City, KS | McSorley, Mildred Margaret | | Kansas City, KS |
| Knapp, Everett E. | 9/25/1963 | | Kansas City, KS | Fessler, Eloise E. | | Kansas City, KS |
| Knighton, Joseph | 10/19/2002 | | Overland Park, KS | Harwick, Susan | | Mission, KS |
| Krueger, Donald Paul | 5/29/1958 | 21 | Kansas City, KS | Gerber, Barbara Kay | 20 | Kansas City, KS |
| Lash, Kent | 1/20/1962 | | Wichita, KS | Arnold, Laverne | | Mission, KS |
| Laws, Carrol | 10/15/1957 | 21 | Kansas City, KS | McDaniel, Margaret | 17 | Kansas City, KS |

| Groom Name | Date | Age | Residence | Bride Name | Age | Residence |
|---|---|---|---|---|---|---|
| Lea, Robert Leslie | 6/13/1954 | | Kansas City, KS | Flaggard, Dorothy Elizabeth | | Bethel, KS |
| Libich, V. A. | 8/3/1957 | | | Morris, Donna Jean | | Kansas City, KS |
| Long, John Albert | 4/27/1962 | | Kansas City, KS | Dale, Neva Irene | | Kansas City, KS |
| Luckey, Phillip R. | 7/15/1967 | 25 | Kansas City, MO | Lustig, Jean L. | 22 | Kansas City, KS |
| Mark, Robert E. | 8/7/1954 | | Kansas City, KS | Barrett, Delores Rae | | Kansas City, KS |
| Marlow, Phillip W. | 10/20/1961 | | Kansas City, KS | Straub, Ila Mae | | Kansas City, KS |
| Masters, Kenneth William | 2/21/1961 | | Kansas City, KS | Krummel, Carolyn | | Kansas City, KS |
| McCarty, Robert E. | 6/18/1966 | 43 | Kansas City, KS | Stakley, Catherine E. | 36 | Kansas City, KS |
| McCurley, Eugene | 6/1/1957 | 47 | Kansas City, MO | Jolliff, Wanda | 42 | Kansas City, KS |
| McDaniel, Leon James | 6/5/1965 | 19 | Kansas City, KS | Hough, Linda Gay | 22 | Kansas City, MO |
| McDaniel, Orville L. | 6/30/1962 | | Kansas City, KS | Hasenbook (?), Ella M. | | Kansas City, KS |
| Meyer, James Joseph | 11/7/2003 | | Overland Park, KS | McDaniel, Josephine Elizabeth | | Overland Park, KS |
| Mikjanis (?), William | 7/10/1956 | 18 | Kansas City, KS | Bock, Diana | 17 | Kansas City, KS |
| Milburn, Russell Thomas | 2/23/1974 | 20 | Kansas City, KS | Moore, Jane Terese | 16 | Kansas City, KS |
| Moody, Harold Jerome | 12/26/1970 | 28 | Overland Park, KS | Barfield, Rosemary L. | 26 | Kansas City, KS |
| Morrison, William K. | 4/21/1957 | 25 | Kansas City, KS | Bassett, Ruth M. | 20 | Kansas City, KS |
| Neal, Dan | 9/4/1997 | | Kansas City, KS | Burns, Niccole | | Kansas City, KS |
| Newbanks, Charles W. | 8/23/1969 | | Oswego, KS | Cunningham, Joyce Dee | | Kansas City, KS |
| Nichols, Charles Wayne | 7/28/1957 | 21 | Kansas City, KS | Hoagland, Janet Faye | 20 | Kansas City, KS |

| Groom Name | Age | Residence | Date | Bride Name | Age | Residence |
|---|---|---|---|---|---|---|
| Noack, Frank H. | 21 | Kansas City, KS | 9/12/1958 | Spears, Sharon R. | 18 | Kansas City, MO |
| Noltensmeyer, John | | | Mar. 1970 | Taylor, Betty | | |
| Obee, Alfred | 25 | Kansas City, KS | 8/18/1947 | Halverhout, Rosemary | 24 | Kansas City, KS |
| Ogden, Kenneth | | Kansas City, KS | 1/19/1961 | Raw, Frances | | Kansas City, KS |
| Parker, Bruce G. | | Muncie, KS | 8/12/1962 | Watson, Patricia A. | | Kansas City, KS |
| Payne, Steven D. | 25 | Kansas City, KS | 10/5/1968 | Brewer, Cynthia L. | 20 | Kansas City, KS |
| Pearson, Ronald Gilbert | | Kansas City, KS | 4/2/1960 | Klock, Judith Ann | | Kansas City, KS |
| Pence, John Robert | 26 | Kansas City, MO | 8/28/1954 | Heerwald, Ruby | 22 | Kansas City, MO |
| Peterson, Terry L. | | Kansas City, KS | 6/7/1963 | Peerson, Judith L. | | Kansas City, KS |
| Pickens, Ray Dean | 17 | Kansas City, KS | 8/21/1969 | Taylor, Michelle Elaine | 18 | Kansas City, KS |
| Pierce, Ronald C. | 23 | Kansas City, KS | 1/14/1956 | Reed, Carole Ann | 18 | Kansas City, MO |
| Purdy, David Edward | 20 | Kansas City, KS | 12/24/1968 | Hodden, Pearl Martha | 19 | Kansas City, KS |
| Purvis, Charles R. | 27 | Kansas City, MO | 7/13/1956 | Huffman, Violet | 26 | Kansas City, KS |
| Raidesel, Raymond Jr. | 23 | Kansas City, KS | 3/12/1955 | McGowan, Dollie June | 19 | Mountain Grove, MO |
| Reedy, Jerry Ray | 17 | Kansas City, KS | 4/28/1967 | Riley, Doris Erlene | 18 | Liberty, MO |
| Renollet, Raymond Eugene | 23 | Sterling, KS | 4/3/1966 | True, Alice Raye | 18 | Sterling, KS |
| Rich, Howard | 26 | Independence, MO | 8/20/1955 | Cathell, Joyce | 21 | Kansas City, KS |
| Rodenbaugh, Don | 18 | Kansas City, KS | 6/19/1964 | Sargent, Mary | 18 | Kansas City, KS |
| Roush, Robert James | 34 | Indianapolis, IN | 8/27/1955 | Patterson, Linda Iris | 16 | Kansas City, KS |

| Groom Name | Date | Age | Residence | Bride Name | Age | Residence |
|---|---|---|---|---|---|---|
| Sanders, Robert Carl | 7/17/1965 | 23 | Los Angeles,CA | Deoner, Barbara Jean | 22 | Kansas City, KS |
| Schiller, Larry Robert | 7/10/1964 | 22 | Kansas City, KS | Malcolm, Betty Louise | 17 | Kansas City, KS |
| Schmidt, Albert | 4/23/1960 | 21 | Kansas City, KS | Cunningham, Linda Lou | 19 | Kansas City, KS |
| Schwartz, Frank L. ll | 8/23/2003 | | Overland Park, KS | George, Nicole R. | | Overland Park, KS |
| Sevedge, Roger W. | 6/8/1957 | 20 | Kansas City, KS | Carter, Kathleen R. | 20 | Kansas City, KS |
| Shelley, Dennis Stuart | 6/6/1969 | 20 | Kansas City, KS | Horn, Janice Kay | 24 | Kansas City, KS |
| Sheppard, E. Gerald | 9/16/1954 | | Kansas City, KS | Bruning, Ruth Kathleen | | Kansas City, MO |
| Shirley, Don David | 9/5/1958 | 24 | Agnew, CA | Baker, Lois Elaine | 26 | Kansas City, KS |
| Short, Harold LeRoy | 6/1/1958 | 21 | Kansas City, KS | Eversole, Judith Kay | 17 | Kansas City, KS |
| Shuck, Roy Richard | 6/21/1957 | 19 | Kansas City, KS | McMahen, Charlotte Lenore | 18 | Kansas City, KS |
| Simmons, Daulton | 10/1/1950 | 32 | Kansas City, KS | Johnson, Darlene | 28 | Kansas City, KS |
| Simpson, Bob G. | 7/31/1954 | | Kansas City, KS | Nicely, Mary E. | | Kansas City, KS |
| Sisk, Edward S. | 7/21/1957 | 21 | Kansas City, MO | Jacobs, Julia L. | 18 | Kansas City, KS |
| Slater, Gary Allen | 5/6/1960 | 19 | Kansas City, KS | Bushnell, Naomi Irene | 18 | Kansas City, KS |
| Slawson, Donald Earl | 6/6/1954 | | | Harbour, Rhita Elizabeth | | |
| Smith, Arnold L. | 3/25/1965 | 24 | Waterloo, IA | Sietam, Betty K. | 20 | Kansas City, KS |
| Smith, Howard Dean | 2/20/1960 | 22 | Kansas City, KS | Donaldson, Mary Lou | 19 | Kansas City, KS |
| Smith, Michael Garrett | 6/7/1964 | 22 | Lawrence, KS | Delich, Rose Mary | 21 | Lawrence, KS |
| Spatz, LaVerne | 2/16/1973 | | Topeka, KS | Blevin, Elizabeth | | Kansas City, KS |

| Groom Name | Date | Age | Residence | Bride Name | Age | Residence |
|---|---|---|---|---|---|---|
| Spradlen, Robert Cecil Sr. | 4/9/1965 | 32 | Kansas City, KS | Phillips, Ann Marie | 34 | Kansas City, KS |
| Stamp, Harris LeRoy | 9/5/1964 | 29 | Kansas City, KS | Anderson, Letha Mae | 36 | Kansas City, KS |
| Stark, William C. | 12/29/1967 | 21 | Kansas City, KS | Leadington, Cathy Ann | 16 | Kansas City, KS |
| Stoff, William Glenn | 4/5/1958 | 24 | Kansas City, KS | DuBois, Janice Virginia | 20 | Bethel, KS |
| Strickel, Jackson LeRoy | 1/21/1961 | | Kansas City, KS | Nunan, Eldora | | Kansas City, KS |
| Stump, Jerry Lee | 4/20/1974 | 22 | Ft. Riley, KS | Alderman, Pamala Audrey | 20 | Kansas City, KS |
| Sturgis, Donald E. | 12/2/1955 | | | Cathell, Janet Louise | | Kansas City, KS |
| Sturtridge, John Gary | 8/10/1958 | 20 | St. Joseph, MO | Rose, Nan Lynn | 18 | Kansas City, KS |
| Sutherland, Lewis M. | 7/27/1962 | | Kansas City, KS | Theroff, Judith Ann | | Kansas City, KS |
| Szulski, Peter | 11/20/1955 | | Kansas City, KS | Brooks, Mary Ann | | Kansas City, KS |
| Teters, Donald Eugene | 3/17/1957 | 21 | Kansas City, KS | Gardner, Mary Lou | 20 | Kansas City, KS |
| Thomas, Michael | 3/4/2006 | | Kansas City, KS | Baskin, Shelia | | Kansas City, MO |
| Totten, Joseph | 7/13/1963 | | Kansas City, KS | Ridenour, Edith | | Kansas City, KS |
| Turpin, John Lee | 5/20/1964 | 51 | St. Joseph, MO | Christensen, Myrtle Marie | 35 | St. Joseph, MO |
| Varner, Donald L. | 3/28/1959 | 22 | Lansing, KS | Sacks, Joan A. | 19 | Kansas City, KS |
| Wagner, Russell E. | 4/28/1959 | 48 | Kansas City, KS | McGineu (?), Mildred C. | 40 | Kansas City, KS |
| Warnick, James E. | 10/15/1956 | 76 | Kansas City, KS | Ward, Nellie B. | 74 | Decatur, IL |
| Warren, George H. | 7/10/1956 | 64 | Kansas City, KS | Watson, Etta Mae | 52 | Kansas City, KS |
| Werneke, Edwin Morgan | 8/30/1959 | 21 | Arkansas City, KS | Noel, Carolyn Irene Delich | 20 | Kansas City, KS |

| Groom Name | Date | Age | Residence | Bride Name | Age | Residence |
|---|---|---|---|---|---|---|
| Willett, Francis Lee | 7/3/1957 | 57 | Kansas City, KS | Broddle, Dorothy | 52 | Kansas City, KS |
| Wingate, Stanley Eugene | 12/22/1957 | 23 | Pretty Prairie, KS | Warnick, Dixie Lee | 21 | Kansas City, KS |
| Wittenberg, Gerald L. | 6/11/1967 | 27 | Kansas City, KS | Morgan, Maxine | 22 | Kansas City, MO |
| Wittenberg, Hermon E. Jr. | 9/17/1970 | 31 | Kansas City, KS | Baker, Neva J. | 22 | Kansas City, KS |
| Wright, Jack J. | 10/14/1960 | | Kansas City, KS | Haberkorn, Virginia Hope | | Kansas City, KS |
| Wright, John N. | 2/16/1958 | 39 | Kansas City, KS | Kelly, Oreta R. | 38 | Kansas City, KS |
| Young, Clinton Alan | 7/12/1969 | 20 | Kansas City, KS | Pigg, Marilynn Lewise | 19 | Kansas City, KS |
| Young, H. Clay | 4/16/1966 | 63 | Bethel, KS | Everett, Iona L. | 59 | Kansas City, KS |
| Zimmer, Craig | - | - | - | Allison, Sandra | - | - |
| Zimmer, Paul F. | 9/5/1964 | 40 | Kansas City, KS | Novak, Delores | 39 | Kansas City, KS |

# RECORD OF MARRIAGES BY BRIDE'S MAIDEN NAME

## 1919 - 2009

## Record of Marriages

| Bride Name | Date | Age | Residence | Groom Name | Age | Residence |
|---|---|---|---|---|---|---|
| Alderman, Pamala Audrey | 4/20/1974 | 20 | Kansas City, KS | Stump, Jerry Lee | 22 | Ft. Riley, KS. |
| Allison, Sandra | - | - | - | Zimmer, Craig | - | - |
| Anderson, Letha Mae | 9/5/1964 | 36 | Kansas City, KS | Stamp, Harris LeRoy | 29 | Kansas City, KS |
| Arnold, Lavene | 1/20/1962 | | Mission, KS | Lash, Kent | | Wichita, KS |
| Baker, Lois Elaine | 9/5/1958 | 26 b | Kansas City, KS | Shirley, Don David | 24 | Agnew, CA |
| Baker, Neva J. | 9/17/1970 | 22 | Kansas City, KS | Wittenberg, Hermon E. Jr. | 31 | Kansas City, KS |
| Bailey, Denise Ann | 12/19/1970 | 17 | Kansas City, KS | Baines, John L. | 24 | Kansas City, KS |
| Barfield, Rosemary L. | 12/26/1970 | 26 | Kansas City, KS | Moody, Harold Jerome | 28 | Overland Park, KS |
| Barrett, Delores Rae | 8/7/1954 | | Kansas City, KS | Mark, Robert E. | | Kansas City, KS |
| Baskin, Shelia | 3/4/2006 | | Kansas City, MO | Thomas, Michael | | Kansas City, KS |
| Bassett, Ruth M. | 4/21/1957 | 20 | Kansas City, KS | Morrison, William K. | 25 | Kansas City, KS |
| Berry, Patricia Ann | 6/10/1967 | 20 | Kansas City, KS | Hoyt, Walter Lewis Jr. | 21 | Kansas City, KS |
| Black, Mildred L. | 9/22/1971 | 68 | Kansas City, KS | Davis, Harry C. Sr. | 72 | Kansas City, KS |
| Blevin, Elizabeth | 2/16/1973 | | Kansas City, KS | Spatz, LaVerne | | Topeka, KS |
| Brant, Delia Ferne | 8/10/1956 | 39 | Robinson, KS | Emert, Harold L. | 30 | Sebatha, KS |
| Brewer, Cynthia L. | 10/5/1968 | 20 | Kansas City, KS | Payne, Steven D. | 25 | Kansas City, KS |
| Brizendine, Ivah Justine | 2/14/1954 | | Kansas City, MO | Johnson, Donald E. | | Kansas City, KS |

| Bride Name | Date | Age | Residence | Groom Name | Age | Residence |
|---|---|---|---|---|---|---|
| Boylan, Carrie M. | 12/12/1964 | 66 | Kansas City, KS | Freeman, Henry | 67 | Bethel, KS |
| Bock, Diana | 7/10/1956 | 17 | Kansas City, KS | Mikikanis (?), William | 18 | Kansas City, KS |
| Broddle, Dorothy | 7/3/1957 | 52 | Kansas City, KS | Willett, Francis Lee | 57 | Kansas City, KS |
| Brooks, Mary Ann | 11/20/1955 | | Kansas City, KS | Szulski, Peter | | Kansas City, KS |
| Bruning, Ruth Kathleen | 9/16/1954 | | Kansas City, MO | Sheppard, E. Gerald | | Kansas City, KS |
| Burns, Niccole | 9/4/1997 | | Kansas City, KS | Neal, Dan | | Kansas City, KS |
| Bushnell, Naomi Irene | 5/6/1960 | 18 | Kansas City, KS | Slater, Gary Allen | 19 | Kansas City, KS |
| Bushnell, Ruth | 8/13/1960 | | Kansas City, KS | Jones, James | | Kansas City, KS |
| Carlson, Helen | 9/27/1958 | 51 | Kansas City, KS | Anderson, John William | 49 | Kansas City, MO |
| Carter, Kathleen R. | 6/8/1957 | 20 | Kansas City, KS | Sevedge, Roger W. | 20 | Kansas City, KS |
| Cathell, Janet Louise | 12/2/1955 | | Kansas City, KS | Sturgis, Donald E. | | |
| Cathell, Joyce | 8/20/1955 | 21 | Kansas City, KS | Rich, Howard | 26 | Independence, MO |
| Catlett, Bertha A. | 8/5/1967 | 25 | Kansas City, KS | Evans, LeRoy E. | 22 | Kansas City, KS |
| Christensen, Myrtle Marie | 5/20/1964 | 35 | St. Joseph, MO | Turpin, John Lee | 51 | St. Joseph, MO |
| Cuellar, Julie | 11/8/2006 | | Kansas City, KS | Davis, Alreco | | Kansas City, KS |
| Cunningham, Joyce Dee | 8/23/1969 | | Kansas City, KS | Newbanks, Charles W. | | Oswego, KS |
| Cunningham, Linda Lou | 4/23/1960 | 19 | Kansas City, KS | Schmidt, Albert | 21 | Kansas City, KS |
| Dale, Neva Irene | 4/27/1962 | | Kansas City, KS | Long, John Albert | | Kansas City, KS |
| Delich, Rose Mary | 6/7/1964 | 21 | Lawrence, KS | Smith, Michael Garrett | 22 | Lawrence, KS |

3 - MARRIAGES BY BRIDE'S MAIDEN NAME

| Bride Name | Date | Age | Residence | Groom Name | Age | Residence |
|---|---|---|---|---|---|---|
| Deoner, Barbara Jean | 7/17/1965 | 22 | Kansas City, KS | Sanders, Robert Carl | 23 | Los Angeles, CA |
| Donaldson, Mary Lou | 2/20/1960 | 19 | Kansas City, KS | Smith, Howard Dean | 22 | Kansas City, KS |
| Dowd, Gayle Ann | 9/26/1964 | 19 | Kansas City, KS | Canfield, Michael Q. | 19 | Kansas City, KS |
| Ellis, Eva Lou | 2/17/1955 | 19 | Kansas City, KS | Grauberger, Albert Eugene | 21 | Kansas City, KS |
| Everett, Iona L. | 4/16/1966 | 59 | Kansas City, KS | Young, H. Clay | 63 | Bethel, KS |
| Eversole, Judith Kay | 6/1/1958 | 17 | Kansas City, KS | Short, Harold LeRoy | 21 | Kansas City, KS |
| Fessler, Eloise E. | 9/25/1963 | | Kansas City, KS | Knapp, Everett E. | | Kansas City, KS |
| Flaggard, Dorothy Elizabeth | 6/13/1954 | | Bethel, KS | Lea, Robert Leslie | | Kansas City, KS |
| Freidell, Linda | 4/17/1971 | | Kansas City, KS | Hollander, Gregory | | Kansas City, KS |
| Gardner, Mary Lou | 3/17/1957 | 20 | Kansas City, KS | Teters, Donald Eugene | 21 | Kansas City, KS |
| Garner, Maurine F. | 5/18/1973 | 29 | Kansas City, KS | Gragg, Thomas W. | 36 | Kansas City, KS |
| George, Nicole R. | 8/23/2003 | | Overland Park, KS | Schwartz, Frank L. ll | | Overland Park, KS |
| Gerber, Barbara Kay | 5/29/1958 | 20 | Kansas City, KS | Krueger, Donald Paul | 21 | Kansas City, KS |
| Gicalone, Jill Sue | 12/27/1969 | | Kansas City, KS | Hershberger, Larry Ray | | Kansas City, KS |
| Grigsby, Betty Jo | 8/17/1956 | 18 | Kansas City, KS | Couch, William D. | 21 | Kansas City, KS |
| Haberkorn, Virginia Hope | 10/14/1960 | | Kansas City, KS | Wright, Jack J. | | Kansas City, KS |
| Halverhout, Anna Mae | 5/21/1955 | 22 | Kansas City, KS | Greiner, John D. | 23 | Kansas City, KS |
| Halverhout, Rosemary | 8/18/1947 | 24 | Kansas City, KS | Obee, Al | 25 | Kansas City, KS |
| Harbour, Rhita Elizabeth | 6/6/1954 | | | Slawson, Donald Earl | | |

4 - MARRIAGES BY BRIDE'S MAIDEN NAME

| Bride Name | Date | Age | Residence | Groom Name | Age | Residence |
|---|---|---|---|---|---|---|
| Hardsaw, Betty Jean | 12/27/1950 | | Kansas City, KS | Dunivan, Charles | | |
| Harrod, Sandra Lee | 9/7/1956 | 16 | Kansas City, KS | Divilbliss, Ronald W. | 21 | Kansas City, KS |
| Hartig, Jo Donna | 8/31/1957 | 18 | Kansas City, KS | Blackburn, Robert Neil | 20 | |
| Hasenbook (?), Ella M. | 6/30/1962 | | Kansas City, KS | McDaniel, Orville L. | | Kansas City, KS |
| Harwick, Susan | 10/19/2002 | | Mission, KS | Knighton, Joseph | | Overland Park, KS |
| Heerwald, Ruby | 8/28/1954 | 22 | Kansas City, MO | Pence, John Robert | 26 | Kansas City, MO |
| Henley, LaDoris Y. | 1/2/1955 | 18 | Kansas City, KS | Harmon, Richard D. | 19 | Kansas City, KS |
| Hoagland, Janet Faye | 7/28/1957 | 20 | Kansas City, KS | Nichols, Charles Wayne | 21 | Kansas City, KS |
| Hoagland, Nancy Ann | 6/14/1964 | 20 | Kansas City, KS | Frye, Harold B. | 20 | Kansas City, KS |
| Hodden, Pearl Martha | 12/24/1968 | 19 | Kansas City, KS | Purdy, David Edward | 20 | Kansas City, KS |
| Holt, Marilyn | 2/14/1954 | | Kansas City, KS | Hataway, Cara Lee | | Kansas City, KS |
| Horn, Janice Kay | 6/6/1969 | 24 | Kansas City, KS | Shelley, Dennis Stuart | 20 | Kansas City, KS |
| Hough, Linda Gay | 6/5/1965 | 22 | Kansas City, MO | McDaniel, Leon James | 19 | Kansas City, KS |
| Huffman, Violet | 7/13/1956 | 26 | Kansas City, KS | Purvis, Charles R. | 27 | Kansas City, MO |
| Jacobs, Julia L. | 7/21/1957 | 18 | Kansas City, KS | Sisk, Edward S. | 21 | Kansas City, KS |
| Johnson, Darlene Alice | 10/1/1950 | 28 | Kansas City, KS | Simmons, Daulton | 32 | Kansas City, KS |
| Johnson, Lavone Marie | 6/18/1960 | 25 | Kansas City, KS | Hedge, Ramon Hunter | 25 | Kansas City, KS |
| Jolliff, Wanda | 6/1/1957 | 42 | Kansas City, KS | McCurley, Eugene | 47 | Kansas City, MO |
| Kangig, Jean M. | 6/10/1966 | 40 | Kansas City, KS | Alexander, Sidney D. | 58 | Kansas City, KS |
| Keeter, Janice Leah | 12/26/1959 | 22 | Kansas City, KS | Ballard, William Howard ll | 17 | Kansas City, MO |

5 - MARRIAGES BY BRIDE'S MAIDEN NAME

| Bride Name | Date | Age | Residence | Groom Name | Age | Residence |
|---|---|---|---|---|---|---|
| Kelly, Oreta R. | 2/16/1958 | 38 | 6 Kansas City, KS | Wright, John N. | 39 | Kansas City, KS |
| Klock, Judith Ann | 4/2/1960 | | Kansas City, KS | Pearson, Ronald Gilbert | | Kansas City, KS |
| Krummel, Carolyn | 2/21/1961 | | Kansas City, KS | Masters, Kenneth William | | Kansas City, KS |
| Lacy, Norma Jean | 8/12/1950 | 18 | Kansas City, KS | Keeter, James | 19 | Kansas City, KS |
| Leadington, Cathy Ann | 12/29/1967 | 16 | Kansas City, KS | Stark, William C. | 21 | Kansas City, KS |
| Lietzen, Geraldine A. | 8/31/1954 | | Linwood, KS | Deay, Lewis Everett | | Linwood, KS |
| Lloyd, Peggy Joyce | 8/9/1969 | | Kansas City, KS | Forbes, Dennis LeRoy | | Kansas City, KS |
| Luschen, Leona Maude | 10/12/1959 | | Kansas City, KS | Allsire, Neal Farrell | | Kansas City, MO |
| Lustig, Jean L. | 7/15/1967 | 22 | Kansas City, KS | Luckey, Phillip R. | 25 | Kansas City, MO |
| Malcomb, Betty Louise | 7/10/1964 | 17 | Kansas City, KS | Schiller, Larry Robert | 22 | Kansas City, KS |
| Mayberry, Margaret Ann | 9/1/1962 | | Bethel, KS | Berve, David J. | | Bethel, KS |
| McDaniel, Josephine Eliz. | 11/7/2003 | | Overland Park, KS | Meyer, James Joseph | | Overland Park, KS |
| McDaniel, Margaret | 10/15/1957 | 17 | Kansas City, KS | Laws, Carrol | 21 | Kansas City, KS |
| McGineu (?), Mildred C. | 4/28/1959 | 40 | Kansas City, KS | Wagner, Russell E. | 48 | Kansas City, KS |
| McGowan, Dollie June | 3/12/1955 | 19 | Mt. Grove, MO | Raidesel, Raymond Jr. | 23 | Kansas City, KS |
| McMahen, Charlotte L. | 6/21/1957 | 18 | Kansas City, KS | Shuck, Roy Richard | 19 | Kansas City, KS |
| McMahen, Janet Ann | 5/1/1965 | 20 | Kansas City, KS | Dudley, John Edward | 23 | Kansas City, KS |
| McSorley, Mildred Marg. | 8/21/1954 | | Kansas City, KS | Kettwig, D. Randall | | Kansas City, KS |
| Moore, Jane Terese | 2/23/1974 | 16 | Kansas City, KS | Milburn, Russell Thomas | 20 | Kansas City, KS |

6 - MARRIAGES BY BRIDE'S MAIDEN NAME

| Bride Name | Date | Age | Residence | Groom Name | Age | Residence |
|---|---|---|---|---|---|---|
| Morgan, Maxine | 6/11/1967 | 22 | Kansas City, MO | Wittenberg, Gerald L. | 27 | Kansas City, KS |
| Morris, Donna Jean | 8/3/1957 | | Kansas City, KS | Libich, V. A. | | |
| Nicely, Mary E. | 7/31/1954 | | Kansas City, KS | Simpson, Bob G. | | Kansas City, KS |
| Nicholson, Marjorie Ann | 4/17/1959 | 20 | Kansas City, KS | Bailey, Jon Gordon | 23 | Kansas City, KS |
| (No Name) | 12/25/1962 | | | Hammett, Michael | | Kansas City, KS |
| Noel, Carolyn Irene Delich | 8/30/1959 | 20 | Kansas City, KS | Werneke, Edwin Morgan | 21 | Arkansas City, KS |
| Novak, Delores | 9/5/1964 | 39 | Kansas City, KS | Zimmer, Paul F. | 40 | Kansas City, KS |
| Nunan, Eldora | 1/21/1961 | | Kansas City, KS | Strickel, Jackson LeRoy | | Kansas City, KS |
| Patterson, Linda Iris | 8/27/1955 | 16 | Kansas City, KS | Roush, Robert James | 34 | Indianapolis, IN |
| Peerson, Judith L. | 6/7/1963 | | Kansas City, KS | Peterson, Terry L. | | Kansas City, KS |
| Pester, Della T. | 12/8/1964 | 74 | Fresno, CA | Fulmer, Rolla Augustus | 73 | Chetopa, KS |
| Phillips, Mary Ann | 10/27/1967 | 16 | Kansas City, KS | Helm, John M. | 20 | Lexington, MO |
| Picknick, Joyce Lee | 12/1/1956 | 22 | Kansas City, KS | Amstutz, William E. | 19 | Kansas City, KS |
| Pigg, Linda Diane | 4/17/1970 | 19 | Kansas City, KS | Hanigan, Leslie Dee | 22 | Mission, KS |
| Pigg, Marilynn Lewise | 7/12/1969 | 19 | Kansas City, KS | Young, Clinton Alan | 20 | Kansas City, KS |
| Placke, Kathy N. | 8/11/1972 | 20 | Kansas City, KS | Hawkins, James G. | 21 | Kansas City, KS |
| Pliley, Mary Ann | 12/25/1954 | | Kansas City, KS | Debus, Vernon Ralph | | Kansas City, KS |
| Poole, Sylvia Jean | 5/8/1964 | 21 | Kansas City, KS | Cain, Gary Bryant | 25 | Kansas City, KS |
| Radotinsky, Sandra Gail | 11/4/1961 | | Kansas City, KS | Doane, Lloyd A. | | Carbondale, KS |

7 - MARRIAGES BY BRIDE'S MAIDEN NAME

| Bride Name | Date | Age | Residence | Groom Name | Age | Residence |
|---|---|---|---|---|---|---|
| Raw, Frances | 1/19/1961 | | Kansas City, KS | Ogden, Kenneth | | Kansas City, KS |
| Reed, Carole Ann | 1/14/1956 | 18 | Kansas City, MO | Pierce, Ronald C. | 23 | Kansas City, KS |
| Reeves, Edith O. | 6/21/1954 | | Kansas City, KS | Daniels, Earl C. | | Piper, KS |
| Reynolds, Ann | 5/29/1964 | 38 | Kansas City, KS | Fanto, John J. | 35 | Topeka, KS |
| Ridenour, Edith | 7/13/1963 | | Kansas City, KS | Totten, Joseph | | Kansas City, KS |
| Riley, Doris Earlene | 4/28/1967 | 18 | Liberty, MO | Reedy, Jerry Ray | 17 | Kansas City, KS |
| Rose, Nan Lynn | 8/10/1958 | 18 | Kansas City, KS | Sturtridge, John Gary | 20 | St. Joseph, MO |
| Sacks, Joan A. | 3/28/1959 | 19 | Kansas City, KS | Varner, Donald L. | 22 | Lansing, KS |
| Sambol, Alma Suzanne | 9/24/1955 | 24 | Kansas City, KS | Eagle, John P. | 24 | Kansas City, KS |
| Sargent, Mary | 6/19/1964 | 18 | Kansas City, KS | Rodenbaugh, Don | 18 | Kansas City, KS |
| Scheets, Sarah | 5/3/2003 | | Kansas City, KS | Dixon, Chris | | Kansas City, KS |
| Schmidt, Barbara Dawn | 12/27/1950 | | Bonner Springs, KS | Dunivan, Charles J. | | Linwood, KS |
| Schultz, Wanda L. | 5/17/1954 | 40 | Kansas City, KS | Jolloff, Walter L. | 28 | Kansas City, KS |
| Seufert, Vivian Marie | 5/9/1954 | | Kansas City, KS | Johnson, David Milton | | Kansas City, KS |
| Shaner, Carol Dee | 6/1/1968 | 24 | Kansas City, KS | Jones, Charles Lee | 24 | Kansas City, MO |
| Sietam, Betty K. | 3/25/1965 | 20 | Kansas City, KS | Smith, Arnold L. | 24 | Waterloo, IA |
| Simmons, Darlene Alice | 1/21/1995 | 73 | Kansas City, KS | Hoendorf, Billie | 75 | Parkville, MO |
| Spears, Sharon R. | 9/12/1958 | 18 | Kansas City, MO | Noack, Frank H. | 21 | Kansas City, KS |

| Bride Name | Date | Age | Residence | Groom Name | Age | Residence |
|---|---|---|---|---|---|---|
| Stakley, Catherine E. | 6/18/1966 | 36 | Kansas City, KS | McCarty, Robert E. | 43 | Kansas City, KS |
| Stott, Sandra Gail | 9/29/1956 | 19 | Kansas City, KS | Bradley, James H. | 20 | Kansas City, KS |
| Straub, Ila Mae | 10/20/1961 | | Kansas City, KS | Marlow, Phillip W. | | Kansas City, KS |
| Swazick, Marie K. | 12/26/1957 | 54 | Kansas City, KS | Bayne, Herbert E. | 60 | Parkville, MO |
| Sweeney, Lois Elaine | 9/12/1953 | | Kansas City, KS | Baker, Lawrence B. | | Kansas City, KS |
| Taylor, Betty | Mar. 1970 | | | Noltensmeyer, John | | |
| Taylor, Michelle Elaine | 8/21/1969 | 18 | Kansas City, KS | Pickens, Ray Dean | 17 | Kansas City, KS |
| Taylor, Sharon Jane | 10/13/1956 | 19 | Kansas City, KS | Brinkmeyer, Harry G. Jr. | 20 | Grandview, MO |
| Teters, Nancy Jane | 7/14/1967 | 18 | Kansas City, KS | Byrd, Ronald Eugene | 18 | Kansas City, KS |
| Theroff, Judith Ann | 7/27/1962 | | Kansas City, KS | Sutherland, Lewis M. | | Kansas City, KS |
| Thompson, Ivy | 11/21/1969 | 46 | Kansas City, KS | Bustard, Ralph | 48 | Kansas City, KS |
| Tomecal, Judith Ann | 7/12/1958 | 18 | Kansas City, KS | Hattaway, Raymond Lee | 19 | Kansas City, KS |
| True, Alice Raye | 4/3/1966 | 18 | Sterling, KS | Renollet, Raymond Eugene | 23 | Sterling, KS |
| Ward, Nellie B. | 10/15/1956 | 74 | Decatur, IL | Warnick, James E. | 76 | Kansas City, KS |
| Warnick, Dixie Lee | 12/22/1957 | 21 | Kansas City, KS | Wingate, Stanley Eugene | 23 | Pretty Prairie, KS |
| Warnick, Frances | 9/18/1971 | | Kansas City, KS | Donohue, Roy | | Kansas City, MO |

9 - MARRIAGES BY BRIDE'S MAIDEN NAME

| Bride Name | Date | Age | Residence | Groom Name | Age | Residence |
|---|---|---|---|---|---|---|
| Watson, Etta Mae | 7/10/1956 | 52 | Kansas City, KS | Warren, George H. | 64 | Kansas City, KS |
| Watson, Patricia A. | 8/12/1962 | | Kansas City, KS | Parker, Bruce G. | | Muncie, KS |
| Webb, Rose Mary | 9/3/1966 | 24 | Lexington, MO | Duffett, Charles M. | 41 | Lexington, MO |
| Weldon, Carol F. | 9/2/1967 | 18 | Kansas City, KS | Brotherton, Thomas H. | 20 | Kansas City, KS |
| Werth, Ann Rita | 6/6/1954 | | Kansas City, KS | Bernard, Dewey D. | | Kansas City, KS |
| West, Martha A. | 4/25/1956 | 19 | Overland Park, KS | Charles, Buford D. | 20 | Kansas City, KS |
| White, Gladys Mae | 9/5/1953 | | Kansas City, KS | Donley, Jackie D. | | Kansas City, KS |
| White, Helen E. | 4/15/1955 | 43 | Kansas City, KS | Fray, Harry H. | 33 | Sioux Falls, SD |
| Wilderman, Eugena Lee | 11/7/1950 | | Kansas City, KS | Hunt, Bryce | | Welborn, KS |
| Wyman, Vanita E. | 10/25/1955 | 21 | Kansas City, KS | Byers, Donald E. | 23 | Kansas City, KS |
| Zimmer, Linda S. | 8/20/1966 | 22 | Kansas City, KS | Dryer, Daniel Ray | 21 | Liberal, KS |

# RECORD OF DEATHS

## 1919 - 2009

**Record of Deaths**

| Last Name | Death Date | Place of Death | Burial | Burial Date | Minister | Birthdate | Birthplace |
|---|---|---|---|---|---|---|---|
| Adams, Fay (Mrs.) | 6/3/1963 | Kansas City, KS | Mt. Hope | 6/5/1963 | W. R Holt | | |
| Adams, Fayette | 10/22/1968 | Kansas City, KS | Kansas City, KS | 10/25/1968 | Holt/Rayson | 11/13/1892 | Belleverde, ILL |
| Adams, Oscar E. | 5/17/1966 | Kansas City, KS | Memorial Park | 5/20/1966 | W. R. Holt | 11/19/1919 | Robinson, KS |
| Alleman, Birdie | 1/12/1966 | Kansas City, KS | Mt. Hope | 1/15/1966 | W. R. Holt | | |
| Allison, Frank | 4/10/1966 | Gardner, KS | Pleasant Hill | 4/13/1966 | W. R. Holt | | Stanley, KS |
| Baettg (sp?), Frank William | 8/7/1966 | Kansas City, KS | Mt. Hope | 8/10/1966 | W. R. Holt | 4/2/1940 | |
| Bailey, James | 1964 | Kansas City, KS | | | W. R. Holt | | |
| Ballemeir, Sophia (Miss) | 2/20/1968 | Kansas City, KS | Memorial Park | 2/23/1968 | W. R. Holt | | |
| Barfield, Lee | 3/30/1960 | Kansas City, KS | Chapel Hills | 4/2/1960 | W. R. Holt | | |
| Bassett, George | 5/18/1960 | Kansas City, KS | Memorial Park | 5/20/1960 | W. R. Holt | | |
| Beaumont, Firman R. | 11/24/1966 | Overland Park, KS | Memorial Park | 11/26/1966 | W. R. Holt | 11/24/1903 | |
| Beeves, Edward C. | 12/5/1967 | Kansas City, KS | Highland Park | 12/8/1967 | W. R. Holt | 01/16/1899 | |
| Belt, Walter | 12/26/1964 | | | | W. R. Holt | | |
| Blevin, Richard | 12/1/1964 | | | | W. R. Holt | 6/13/1930 | |
| Boston, J. Frank | 10/10/1966 | Kansas City | Mt. Hope | 10/13/1966 | W. R. Holt | 11/12/1906 | |
| Brown, Roy | 10/24/1970 | Kansas City,KS | Kansas City, KS | 10/26/1970 | Holt/Rayson | | |
| Bumgartner, Harold V. | 10/11/1958 | Kansas City, KS | Kansas City, KS | 10/14/1958 | W. R. Holt | | |

2 - DEATHS

| Last Name | Death Date | Place of Death | Burial | Date | Minister | Birthdate | Birthplace |
|---|---|---|---|---|---|---|---|
| Bumgartner, Hulda | 1/18/1969 | Kansas City, KS | Kansas City, KS | 1/20/1969 | Holt/Rayson | 04/26/1885 | |
| Charles, Eldon (Mrs.) | 11/21/1956 | Kansas City, KS | Mount Hope | 11/24/1956 | W. R. Holt | | |
| Charles, Ray (Mr.) | 9/22/1965 | Wadsworth Vet. | Mt. Hope | 9/24/1965 | W. R. Holt | | |
| Chisham, Russel | 7/22/1964 | Kansas City,KS | Ft. Leavenworth | 7/27/1964 | W. R. Holt | 7/27/1930 | Kansas City, KS |
| Christy, H.C.(Mrs.) | 11/1/1963 | Kansas City, KS | Mt. Hope | 11/4/1963 | W. R. Holt | | |
| Clay, Martha (Mrs.) | 3/31/1961 | Kansas City, KS | Raymore, MO | 4/4/1961 | C. O. Bickel | | |
| Clevenger , Lee (Mrs.) | 04/1957 | Kansas City, KS | Highland Park | 4/8/1957 | W. R. Holt | | |
| Cloughley, Joseph | 5/2/1966 | Kansas City, KS | Memorial Park | 5/5/1966 | W. R. Holt | | |
| Coffman, Erma (Mrs.) | `1957 | | | `1957 | | | |
| Crawford, James Lewis | 2/13/1967 | Kansas City, KS | Chapel Hills | 2/15/1967 | W. R. Holt | 03/15/1898 | |
| Crawford, Louis Arthur | 12/22/1966 | Kansas City, KS | Mt. Hope | 12/26/1966 | W. R. Holt | 07/21/1882 | |
| Creed, Lena (Mrs.) | 2/3/1958 | Kansas City, KS | Topeka, KS | 2/6/1958 | W. R. Holt | | |
| Daniels, E. G. (Mr.) | 3/24/1959 | Kansas City, KS | Luray, KS | 3/27/1959 | W. R. Holt | | |
| Daniels, Gertie (Mrs.) | 12/21/1969 | Kansas City, KS | Kansas City, KS | 12/24/1969 | W. R. Holt | | |
| Davenport, Lily (Mrs.) | 1/15/1961 | Kansas City, MO | Mt. Hope | 1/17/1961 | W. R. Holt | | |
| Davis, Roy | 3/29/1965 | | Leavenworth,KS | 4/1/1965 | W. R. Holt | 10/25/1905 | |
| Davis, Bert L. | 10/1/1966 | Kansas City, MO | Forest Hills | 10/5/1966 | W. R. Holt | 03/27/1890 | |
| Davis, Harry Sr. (Mr.) | 10/18/1971 | Kansas City, KS | Kansas City, KS | 10/22/1971 | R. L. Rayson | | |
| Day, Irba R. | 9/25/1958 | Kansas City, KS | | 9/27/1958 | W. R. Holt | | |
| Divilbiss, Lillian (Mrs.) | 4/30/1962 | Gardner, KS | Pleasant Valley | 5/1/1962 | W. R. Holt | | |

3 - DEATHS

| Last Name | Death Date | Place of Death | Burial | Date | Minister | Birthdate | Birthplace |
|---|---|---|---|---|---|---|---|
| Divilbiss, May C. (Mrs.) | 10/9/1966 | Olathe, KS | Pleasant Valley | 10/11/1966 | W. R. Holt | 07/20/1876 | Stanley, KS |
| Dougan, Ella M. (Mrs.) | 11/6/1964 | Stanley, KS | | | W. R. Holt | 12/01/1873 | Wyan. Co., KS |
| Dowd, Harry | 2/17/1971 | Kansas City, KS | Kansas City, KS | 2/20/1970 | Holt/Rayson | | |
| Dowers, John J. | 3/18/1965 | Kansas City, KS | Highland Park | 3/22/1965 | W. R. Holt | 10/13/1938 | |
| Duvall, Mary B. (Mrs.) | 2/29/1968 | Kansas City, KS | Memorial Park | 3/2/1968 | W. R. Holt | 05/22/1875 | |
| Eagle, Elizabeth A. | 9/25/1964 | Kansas City, KS | Quindaro Cem. | 9/27/1964 | W. R. Holt | 08/04/1890 | |
| Eker, Mildred (Mrs.) | 10/11/1966 | Kansas City, KS | Mt. Hope | 10/14/1966 | W. R. Holt | 12/2/1912 | |
| Emge, Andrew F. | 6/3/1965 | Kansas City, KS | Leavenworth, KS | 6/5/1965 | W. R. Holt | | |
| Endsley, Myron (Mrs.) | 12/00/1969 | Kansas City, KS | Kansas City, KS | 12/00/1969 | W. R. Holt | | |
| Eversole, Homer | 8/10/1956 | Kansas City, KS | | 8/12/1956 | W. R. Holt | | |
| Fath, Nellie M. | 1/8/1964 | Kansas City, KS | Quindaro Cem. | 1/10/1969 | W. R. Holt | 07/30/1874 | |
| Feigner, Ella (Mrs.) | 8/24/1965 | Kansas City, KS | Chapel Hills | 8/26/1965 | W. R. Holt | | |
| Ferguson, Marie | 01/00/1970 | Kansas City, KS | Kansas City, KS | Jan. 1970 | W. R. Holt | | |
| Flecher, Matilda Elizabeth | 1/9/1966 | Kansas City, KS | Mt. Hope | 1/12/1966 | W. R. Holt | 09/22/1871 | |
| Foster, Hattie F. | 12/12/1966 | Kansas City, KS | Mt. Hope | 12/14/1966 | W. R. Holt | 7/24/1907 | |
| French, Clifford | 12/3/1964 | | | | W. R. Holt | | |
| Gaffney, Bernard | 5/9/1966 | Kansas City, KS | Wolsey, SD | 5/12/1966 | W. R. Holt | 2/21/1903 | |
| Geory, John | 11/2/1966 | Kansas City, KS | Mt. Calvary | 11/4/1966 | W. R. Holt | | |
| Gingrey | 1/13/1966 | Kansas City, KS | Highland Park | 1/15/1966 | W. R. Holt | | |
| Gingrey, May (Mrs.) | 1/5/1965 | | | 1/7/1965 | W. R. Holt | | |

4 - DEATHS

| Last Name | Death Date | Place of Death | Burial | Date | Minister | Birthdate | Birthplace |
|---|---|---|---|---|---|---|---|
| Goff, Jennie F. (Mrs.) | 2/24/1965 | | Quindaro Cem. | 2/26/1965 | W. R. Holt | 10/13/1877 | |
| Green, Ella (Mrs.) | 11/26/1965 | Garnett Nurs. Home | Mt. Hope | 11/29/1965 | W. R. Holt | | |
| Grigsby, (Mrs. ) | 1/1/1962 | Kansas City, Ks | Mt. Hope | 1/3/1962 | W. R. Holt | | |
| Gung, Frank | 1/10/1967 | Wadsworth, KS | Highland Park | 1/12/1967 | W. R. Holt | 8/21/1900 | Kansas City, MO |
| Harbour, Jack | 12/'1956 | Germany | Nat. Ce. Denver | | | | |
| Hardsaw, David (Mr.) | 2/13/1964 | Kansas City, KS | Memorial Park | 2/15/1964 | W. R. Holt | | |
| Hardsaw, Jerry | 2/22/1970 | Kansas City, MO | Kansas City, KS | 2/24/1970 | Holt/Rayson | | |
| Heinzman, Margaret (Mrs.) | 12/'1957 | Kansas City, KS | Mount Hope | | W. R. Holt | | |
| Hiatt, Simeon | 3/29/1962 | Olathe, KS | Pleasant Valley | 3/31/1962 | W. R. Holt | | |
| Hoffman, Lena (Mrs.) | 11/21/1964 | | | | W. R. Holt | | |
| Holbert, Dave | 10/8/1964 | Kansas City, KS | | 10/12/1964 | W. R. Holt | 08/28/1899 | |
| Holt, Freda (Mrs.) | 4/29/1970 | Kansas City, KS | Kansas City, KS | 5/1/1970 | R/W/Hayes/B | | |
| Horseman, Louise | 6/16/1970 | Kansas City, KS | Kansas City, KS | 6/18/1970 | Holt/Rayson | | |
| Howard, Joseph | 5/12/1966 | Kansas City, MO | Quindaro Cem. | 5/14/1966 | W. R. Holt | | |
| Howard, Kenneth (Mrs.) | 11/12/1965 | Home | Chapel Hills | 11/15/1965 | W. R. Holt | | |
| Hunt, Bryce | 10/21/1958 | Kansas City, KS | | 10/4/1958 | W. R. Holt | | |
| Jacobs, Vincent | 2/20/1959 | Kansas City, KS | Mount Hope | 2/23/1959 | W. R. Holt | | |
| Kelley, E. Neal | 2/10/1968 | Kansas City, KS | Chapel Hills | 2/10/1968 | W. R. Holt | | Kansas City, KS |
| Kelley, Jessie M. (Mrs.) | 5/1/1966 | Kansas City, KS | Maple Hill | 5/4/1966 | W. R. Holt | 03/12/1890 | |
| Kellog, Earnest | 7/21/1966 | Kansas City, KS | Stanley, KS | 7/24/1966 | W. R. Holt | | |

5 - DEATHS

| Last Name | Death Date | Place of Death | Burial | Date | Minister | Birthdate | Birthplace |
|-----------|------------|----------------|--------|------|----------|-----------|------------|
| Kern, Mary (Mrs. Clay) | 12/29/1964 | | | | W. R. Holt | | |
| King, Harry | 12/28/1964 | | | | W. R. Holt | | |
| King, Victor (Mrs.) | 2/14/1970 | Kansas City, KS | Kansas City, KS | 2/16/1970 | R. L. Rayson | | |
| Kluge, Fred (Mr.) | 11/9/1964 | Kansas City, KS | | | W. R. Holt | | |
| Lacy, Florence (Mrs.) | 10/18/1971 | California | Kansas City, KS | 10/22/1971 | Holt/Rayson | | |
| Lacy, Lillian (Mrs.) | 8/19/1966 | Kansas City, KS | Memorial Park | 8/22/1966 | W. R. Holt | 08/27/1896 | Plane, IL |
| Lacy, R. Hershal | 12/11/1967 | Kansas City, KS | Chapel Hills | 12/14/1967 | W. R. Holt | 11/12/1895 | Nevada, MO |
| Lacy, Viola (Mrs. Harry) | 5/16/1967 | Kansas City, KS | Chapel Hills | 5/9/1967 | W. R. Holt | 11/3/1915 | Georgia, IA |
| Lagen (?), John Frieden | 12/2/1964 | | | | W. R. Holt | | |
| LaHue, Orville R. | 10/9/1966 | California | Wadsworth, KS | 10/14/1966 | W. R. Holt | 1890 | |
| Lile, Charles | 11/14/1966 | Kansas City, KS | Mt. Hope | 11/17/1966 | W. R. Holt | 07/05/1883 | |
| Lloyd, Alvey | 3/29/1958 | Kansas City, MO | Chapel Hills | 4/1/1958 | W. R. Holt | | |
| Lowman, Essie (Mrs.) | 4/12/1968 | Gardner, KS | Stanley, KS | 4/14/1968 | W. R. Holt | 11/23/1876 | Harris, MO |
| Lucas, Bernice (Mrs. J.) | 1/15/1958 | Kansas City, KS | Mount Hope | 1/17/1958 | W. R. Holt | | |
| Marsh, Harry W. | 3/15/1967 | Dallas, TX | Highland Park | 3/18/1967 | W. R. Holt | | Hagerstown, MD |
| Martin, Frank L. | 7/1/1967 | Kansas City, KS | Highland Park | 7/11/1967 | W. R. Holt | 10/11/1885 | |
| Matthews, Hulda (Mrs.) | 1965 | Kansas City, KS | Mt. Hope | | W. R. Holt | | |
| Maulding, Estley | 8/14/1966 | Kansas City, KS | Mt. Hope | 8/17/1966 | W. R. Holt | 11/18/1889 | |
| McChauncy, Ruby | 1/12/1968 | Kansas City, KS | Chapel Hills | 1/16/1968 | W. R. Holt | 05/8/1894 | Diaginal, IA |
| McClatchey, Ella (Mrs.) | 10/5/1964 | Kansas City, KS | Mt. Hope | 10/7/1964 | W. R. Holt | 11/20/1867 | |

6 - DEATHS

| Last Name | Death Date | Place of Death | Burial | Date | Minister | Birthdate | Birthplace |
|---|---|---|---|---|---|---|---|
| McClatchey, Oliver R. | 8/10/1967 | Kansas City, KS | Mt. Hope | 8/12/1967 | W. R. Holt | 09/07/1891 | York, NE |
| McDaniels, Bernice | 09/00/1972 | | | | | | |
| Miller, Grant C. | 9/7/1967 | Kansas City, KS | Highland Park | 9/9/1967 | W. R. Holt | | |
| Miller, Mima Pearl | 10/12/1966 | Kansas City, KS | Highland Park | 10/15/1966 | W. R. Holt | | |
| Milligan, Howard G. | 12/30/1964 | | | | W. R. Holt | | Kansas City, KS |
| Moore, Arthur L. | 1/8/1962 | Kansas City, KS | Mt. Hope | 1/10/1962 | W. R. Holt | | |
| Moore, John T. | 4/29/1966 | Kansas City, KS | Memorial Park | 5/2/1966 | W. R. Holt | 04/20/1889 | |
| Mullies, Claude | 12/12/1964 | | | | W. R. Holt | | |
| Murphy, Sybil Irene (Mrs.) | 7/13/1967 | Kansas City, KS | Highland Park | 7/15/1967 | W. R. Holt | 8/13/1904 | Kansas City, KS |
| Nelson, Cheryl Lynn | 3/29/1958 | Kansas City, KS | Mount Hope | 3/31/1958 | W. R. Holt | 12/2/1957 | |
| Nelson, John R. | 7/19/1971 | Kansas City, KS | Kansas City, KS | 7/21/1971 | Holt/Rayson | | |
| Nelson, Thelma | 5/22/1965 | Cleveland, OH | Mt. Hope | 5/26/1965 | W. R. Holt | | |
| Neyman, Ray (Mrs.) | 1/1/1962 | Kansas City, KS | Highland Park | 1/2/1962 | W. R. Holt | 04/09/1899 | |
| Odneal, Florence C. | 7/22/1971 | Kansas City, KS | Kansas City, KS | 7/24/1971 | Holt/Rayson | | |
| Oehring, Orin O. | 1/2/1965 | | Bonner Sp.KS | 1/4/1965 | W. R. Holt | | |
| O'Nan, William Ray | 12/8/1967 | | Rock Hse Prairie | 12/11/1967 | W. R. Holt | 11/23/1890 | |
| Oviott, Al | 1/8/1962 | Kansas City, KS | Highland Park | 1/10/1962 | W. R. Holt | | |
| Pearson, Gilbert | 5/20/1970 | Kansas City, KS | Tonganoxie, KS | 5/23/1970 | Holt/Rayson | | |
| Peat, R. T. | 1/12/1965 | Kansas City, KS | Chapel Hills | 1/14/1965 | W. R. Holt | | |
| Peat, Effie H. (Mrs.) | 9/16/1967 | Kansas City, KS | Chapel Hills | 9/20/1967 | W. R. Holt | 08/14/1884 | |

7 - DEATHS

| Last Name | Death Date | Place of Death | Burial | Date | Minister | Birthdate | Birthplace |
|---|---|---|---|---|---|---|---|
| Peck, Frank P. | 1/12/1967 | Kansas City, KS | Chapel Hills | 1/14/1967 | W. R. Holt | 12/28/1896 | |
| Priestly | 3/30/1966 | Kansas City, KS | Maple Hill | 4/1/1966 | W. R. Holt | | |
| Purdum, James H. | 5/23/1965 | Kansas City, MO | Suoard, NE | 5/26/1965 | W. R. Holt | 02/23/1873 | Kerthburg, IL |
| Rand, Kasper (Mr.) | 3/13/1964 | Kansas City, KS | Valley Falls, KS | 3/17/1964 | W. R. Holt | 12/1/1891 | Valley Falls, KS |
| Reeves, Carrie (Mrs.) | | | | | | | |
| Reid, Ora (Ms.) | 3/9/1968 | Kansas City, KS | Chapel Hills | 3/11/1968 | W. R. Holt | | White Church, KS |
| Rhines, Anna Marie (Mrs.) | 1/18/1967 | Kansas City, KS | Chapel Hills | 1/21/1967 | W. R. Holt | 04/19/1889 | |
| Rickey, Leslie H. | 12/29/1966 | Kansas City, KS | Chapel Hills | 1/3/1967 | W. R. Holt | | Trinidad, CO |
| Rosentrotter, A. P. | 1/20/1962 | Kansas City, KS | Memorial Park | 1/22/1962 | W. R. Holt | | |
| Schilke, Marie (Mrs.) | 2/22/1971 | Kansas City, KS | Kansas City, KS | 2/25/1970 | Holt/Ray/Wil | | |
| Scholl, Grace (Mrs.) | 5/14/1968 | Liberty, MO | Kansas City, KS | 5/17/1968 | W. R. Holt | 01/16/1882 | Wellsville, KS |
| Sebree, Robert Marion Jr. | 1/8/1966 | Kansas City, KS | Highland Park | 1/11/1966 | W. R. Holt | 11/12/1905 | |
| Seckler, Leslie James | 1/18/1967 | Kansas City, KS | Pleasant Valley | 1/21/1967 | W. R. Holt | 11/07/1883 | York Co. NE |
| Selgwick, Wanda E. (Mrs.) | 10/10/1965 | K. U. Med. Ctr. | Highland Park | 10/13/1965 | W. R. Holt | 1/6/1936 | |
| Service, Edna L. | 7/1/1967 | Kansas City, KS | Maple Hill | 7/5/1967 | W. R. Holt | | |
| Sharp, Eli (Mr.) | 7/19/1963 | Kansas City, KS | Mt. Hope | 7/22/1963 | W. R. Holt | 12/3/1869 | |
| Shaw, Emma (Mrs.) | 11/15/1967 | Bartlesville, OK | Memorial Park | 11/18/1967 | W. R. Holt | 05/24/1894 | |
| Shaw, Goma (?) Otis | 5/23/1966 | Kansas City, MO | Mt. Hope | 5/26/1966 | W. R. Holt | 5/5/1905 | |
| Smith, M. R. | 03/1957 | Vet. Hos. KCMO | | 03/1957 | W. R. Holt | | |
| Smith, Maurice Bee | 12/22/1966 | Kansas City, KS | Highland Park | 12/26/1966 | W. R. Holt | 02/17/1888 | |

| Last Name | Death Date | Place of Death | Burial | Date | Minister | Birthdate | Birthplace |
|-----------|-----------|----------------|--------|------|----------|-----------|------------|
| Smith, Orpha (Mrs. Sprout) | 9/20/1958 | Kansas City, KS | Memorial Park | 9/24/1958 | W. R. Holt | | |
| Snyder, Ethel P. | 4/19/1967 | Kansas City, MO | Mt. Hope | 4/22/1967 | W. R. Holt | 08/29/1890 | |
| Sowers, George Allman | 1/6/1969 | California | Tonganoxie, KS | 1/11/1969 | R. L. Rayson | 1/30/1907 | |
| Spencer, Ella (Mrs.) | 12/7/1969 | Kansas City, KS | MO | 12/10/1969 | Holt/Rayson | | |
| Spencer, Ernest N. | 4/10/1968 | Kansas City, KS | Gibbs, MO | 4/13/1968 | W. R. Holt | 11/19/1885 | Gibbs, MO |
| Stanley, Athur J. | 1/24/1967 | Kansas City, KS | Lincoln Ctr.KS | 1/28/1967 | W. R. Holt | 1875 | |
| Steele, Carol Sue | 2/16/1965 | Kansas City, KS | Quindaro Cem. | 2/18/1965 | W. R. Holt | 1937 | Ft. Scott, KS |
| Stemen, Harry (Mrs.) | 2/24/1958 | Kansas City, KS | Maple Hill | 2/26/1958 | W. R. Holt | | |
| Stevens, Frances (Mrs.) | 4/29/1962 | Kansas City, KS | Mt. Hope | 5/1/1961 | W. R. Holt | | |
| Stevick, Jessie Z. (Mrs.) | 6/5/1967 | Kansas City, KS | Mt. Hope | 6/7/1967 | W. R. Holt | 12/24/1906 | |
| Stott, Lulu M. | 2/17/1965 | Arizona | Highland Park | 2/20/1965 | W. R. Holt | 04/01/1885 | |
| Striekel, Bertha (Mrs.) | 10/14/1971 | Kansas City, KS | Kansas City, Ks | 10/18/1971 | Holt/Rayson | | |
| Sturgis, Janet | 12/1957 | Kansas City, KS | | | W. R. Holt | | |
| Swanson, Henry | 12/00/1970 | Kansas City, KS | Kansas City, Ks | Dec-70 | W. R. Holt | | |
| Taylor, Alonze J. | 11/6/1967 | Kansas City, KS | Memorial Park | 11/9/1967 | W. R. Holt | 5/14/1903 | |
| Taylor, Frank M. | 5/3/1966 | Kansas City, KS | Chapel Hills | 5/6/1966 | W. R. Holt | 02/16/1887 | |
| Teters, Jennifer Sue | 5/22/1969 | Kansas City, KS | Kansas City, Ks | 5/22/1969 | W. R. Holt | | |
| Thomas, Arthur | 4/17/1960 | Kansas City, KS | Memorial Park | 4/19/1960 | W. R. Holt | | |
| Thomas, Eliza Viola | 12/9/1966 | Kansas City, KS | Memorial Park | 12/12/1966 | W. R. Holt | 12/16/1883 | |
| Thompson, Hazel Bowling (M | 4/23/1966 | Kansas City, ? | DeSota, KS | 4/25/1966 | W. R. Holt | 12/17/1890 | Bennington, KS |

9 - DEATHS

| Last Name | Death Date | Place of Death | Burial | Date | Minister | Birthdate | Birthplace |
|---|---|---|---|---|---|---|---|
| Tombaugh, Clarence | 1962 | Kansas City, MO | | 1962 | W. R. Holt | | |
| Tomecal, Jewell (Mrs.) | 11/17/1963 | Kansas City, KS | Chapel Hills | 11/19/1963 | W. R. Holt | | |
| Truitt, Eva | 12/6/1960 | Kansas City, KS | Memorial Park | 12/8/1960 | W. R. Holt | | |
| Turney, William T. | 5/1/1966 | Kansas City, KS | Highland Park | 5/4/1966 | W. R. Holt | | |
| Tuttle, Goldie (Mrs.) | 12/19/1967 | Denver, CO | Mt. Hope | 12/22/1967 | W. R. Holt | 06/17/1892 | Plevin, AR |
| Vana, Josephine A. | 11/29/1966 | Kansas City, KS | Chapel Hills | 12/3/1966 | W. R. Holt | 8/17/1950 | |
| Warnick, L. Wayne | 9/3/1964 | Kansas City, KS | Highland Park | 9/8/1964 | W. R. Holt | 8/28/1904 | Kansas City, KS |
| Wheeler, H. D. (Mr.) | 12/2/1958 | Kansas City, KS | Memorial Park | 12/4/1958 | W. R. Holt | | |
| White, Ernest F. | 2/8/1965 | Kansas City, KS | Odessa, MO | 2/11/1965 | W. R. Holt | | |
| Wilcox, A. (Mrs.) | Sept. 1957 | Kansas City, KS | | Sept. 1957 | W. R. Holt | | |
| Williamson, Elgane (Miss) | 1/31/1965 | Kansas City, KS | Memorial Park | 2/3/1965 | W. R. Holt | 10/26/1889 | |
| Willoughby, Charles O. | 3/9/1968 | Kansas City, KS | Edwardsville | 3/12/1968 | W. R. Holt | 7/4/1911 | |
| Wilmoth, Frances (Mrs.) | 2/23/1971 | Kansas City, KS | Kansas City, Ks | 2/25/1970 | Baptist | | |
| Winchell, Hazel (Mrs.) | 9/18/1965 | Kansas City, KS | Maple Hill | 9/21/1965 | W. R. Holt | 02/10/1894 | |
| Wolch, Frank | 5/21/1965 | Kansas City, KS | Chapel Hills | 5/26/1965 | W. R. Holt | | |
| Woodring, Lydia B. | 5/8/1967 | Kansas City, KS | Highland Park | 5/10/1967 | W. R. Holt | 01/28/1890 | Enterprise, KS |
| Young, William R. | 1/16/1968 | Lansing, KS | Mt. Muncie | 1/18/1968 | W. R. Holt | 12/22/1884 | |

# RECORD OF MINISTERS

## 1919 - 2009

## Record of Ministers

| Start Date | End Date | Name | Title | Remarks |
|---|---|---|---|---|
| 1919 | 1920 | Reese, W. S. | Dean | |
| 1920 | 1921 | Fralick, C. R. | Dr. | |
| 1921 | 1923 | May, W. Frank | Dr. | |
| 1923 | 1923 | Testerman, -- | Dr. | Interim |
| 1923 | 1935 | Williams, Stanley B. | Dr. | Home Missions |
| 1935 | 1968 | Holt, W. R. | Dr. | Retired |
| 1968 | 1974 | Rayson, R. LeRoy | Rev. | |
| 1974 | 1980 | Harnden, Jerry | Rev. | |
| 1980 | 1984 | DeSpain, Ira | Rev. | |
| 1984 | 1986 | Stephenson, Ed | Rev. | |
| 1986 | 1988 | West, Roy | Rev. | |
| 1988 | 1994 | Gasau, Marie | Rev. | |
| 1994 | 1997 | Harper, Rob | Rev. | |
| 1997 | 2008 | Lamberty, Lynn | Rev. | |
| 2002 | 2004 | Smart, Cynthia | Rev. | |
| 2004 | 2008 | Thomas, Michael | Pastor | |
| 2008 | 2009 | Lee, Seong Keun | Rev. | |
| 2009 | | Roellchen, Gary | Rev. | Co-Minister, Central UMC |
| 2009 | | Miller, Marlene | Rev. | Co-Minister, Central UMC |
| 2009 | | Albert, Sharon | Rev. | Co-Minister, Central UMC |

2 - MINISTERS

## ABOUT THE AUTHOR

Lavone Johnson Anglen is a lifelong member of University United Methodist Church in Kansas City, Kansas. She was only six months old in 1934, when her parents, John and Ida Mae Johnson, and her older sister, Darlene, presented her for christening at University Church. Since then, Lavone has loved, laughed, grieved, and prayed alongside other University members. She was there in its heyday in the 1950's, and has been there through its long, courageous struggle to survive in a changing world.

Ms. Anglen is an experienced genealogist who was motivated to capture University's historical records for the benefit of other genealogists, as well as for the enjoyment of University members. Unable to find information on an ancestor, she realized that the records of University Church hold a wealth of genealogical information.

She is a member of National Society of the Colonial Dames XVII Century, Daughters of the American Colonists, Daughters of the American Revolution, Daughters of the War of 1812, National Society of the Dames of the Court of Honor, Huguenot Society of New Paltz, New York, Northland Genealogy Society (Missouri), and the Platte County (Missouri) Historical Society. She has compiled eighteen books of her family's surnames and served five years as editor of *The River's Bend*, a newsletter for the Northland Genealogy Society of North Kansas City, Missouri.

Ms. Anglen is married to Paul Gene Anglen. They live in Kansas City, Missouri, with Roscoe, their long-haired domestic tabby.